Mothers in the English Novel: From Stereotype to Archetype

Gender & Genre in Literature

VOLUME 1

Garland Reference Library of the Humanities
Volume 1302

Gender & in Genre Literature

Carol L. Snyder, General Editor

TITLES INCLUDE

Mothers in the English Novel: From Stereotype to Archetype
MARJORIE McCORMICK

Female Heroism in the Pastoral
GAIL DAVID

Redefining Autobiography in Twentieth-Century Women's Fiction: An Essay Collection
JANICE MORGAN AND COLLETTE T. HALL

Gender in the Theater of War: Shakespeare's Troilus and Cressida
BARBARA BOWEN

Library of Congress Cataloging-in-Publication Data

McCormick, Marjorie J., 1954–
Mothers in the English novel : from stereotype to archetype /
Marjorie J. McCormick.
p. cm. — (Gender & genre in literature ; v. 1) (Garland
reference library of the humanities ; v. 1302)
Includes bibliographical references.
ISBN 0-8240-7131-X
1. English fiction—History and criticism. 2. Mothers in
literature. I. Title. II. Series. III. Series: Garland reference
library of the humanities ; vol. 1302.
PR830.M69M37 1991
823'.009'3520431—dc20   91-24921
                                                             CIP

Printed on acid-free, 250-year-life paper
MANUFACTURED IN THE UNITED STATES OF AMERICA

Mothers in the English Novel: From Stereotype to Archetype

Marjorie McCormick

Garland Publishing, Inc.

New York & London 1991

Contents

Abbreviations

AB	*Adam Bede*
BH	*Bleak House*
BT	*Barchester Towers*
C	*Clarissa*
CW	*C. G. Jung, Collected Works*
DC	*David Copperfield*
DD	*Daniel Deronda*
DS	*Dombey and Son*
E	*Emma*
FGC	*Four-Gated City*
HE	*Henry Esmond*
HW	*Howards End*
JE	*Jane Eyre*
LS	*Lady Susan*
MF	*Mill on the Floss*
MP	*Mansfield Park*
NA	*Northanger Abbey*
NN	*Nicholas Nickleby*
NS	*North and South*
OMF	*Our Mutual Friend*
P	*Persuasion*
PI	*Passage to India*
PP	*Pride and Prejudice*
RN	*Return of the Native*
S	*Sanditon*
SBD	*Summer Before the Dark*
SL	*Sons and Lovers*
SP	*Spoils of Poynton*
SS	*Sense and Sensibility*
TL	*To the Lighthouse*
VF	*Vanity Fair*
WD	*Wives and Daughters*

Acknowledgments

During the long writing and rewriting of this book I was grateful for two things: a topic I never grew bored with, and the support and confidence of many people. Among the latter I wish to acknowledge in particular Carol Snyder, the series editor, who followed each of her judicious readings with equally judicious advice on how I might proceed; and Kennie Lyman, the general editor, who oversaw this process with enthusiasm, professionalism, and much patience.

I am also indebted to my former colleagues at Vanderbilt University, where this book began as a dissertation, especially Laurence Lerner, for his friendship as well as his instruction; Jack Prostko, whose humor and encouragement saved this project in its early hours; and Susan Gilroy, whose insights about women in literature have been as valuable to the content of this study as her support has been to its completion.

To the library staffs at Vanderbilt, Yale, Connecticut College, and my other *alma mater*, Bates, I wish to express my appreciation for the generous use of their facilities and collections.

Finally, I would like to thank my dear friend Paul Davis, my sister Jan, and above all my mother, Edith McCormick, whose archetypal qualities inspired this book in the first place.

Series Editor's Preface

If genre is a particularly suspect term in post-modernist criticism, that is in good part because feminist theorists have exposed some of the ways in which supposedly value-free literary classifications actually privilege male discourse. They have allowed us to see genre as the authorizing and valorizing instrument of the male canon, a grillwork barring women entrance, or a ladder on which women's writing occupies the lower rungs of the sub-genres. The literary types, we have seen, inscribe an economy of representation that profits male expression at the expense of women's experience; the "law" of genre imposes a regularity against which women's writing must, if it appears at all, appear deviant.

These broad attacks on genre as a sex-inflected system lay the groundwork for this series, an array of particular studies of the gender-genre linkage. There is much to be done. The past decade has given us explorations of such forms as the *Bildungsroman*, the *Kunstleroman*, the utopian and Gothic novel as women have written them; studies are even now emerging of the female-authored elegy, sonnet sequence and other pure and mixed poetic modes. Women's work in non-fiction prose and in the dramatic genres is being resurrected and reassessed. At the same time, feminist critics continue to deconstruct women as signs in patriarchal literary forms, explaining the effect of male gender on structures of signification, the narrative and stylistic codes of genre. This series welcomes such studies, encouraging as well accounts of sexuality and textual inheritance, the influence of female authorship on the evolution of a genre or the creation of a new genre, and challenges to genre theory from a gender perspective.

Such a project should reinvigorate a practical criticism which has for long proceeded questioningly along lines laid down by genre. A gain for literary theory can also be predicted, if not yet precisely delineated: as we accumulate a corpus of texts and submit them to analyses which include the variables of sex, race, and nationality, our premises about the patterns of literary construction, authority, and interpretation are bound to evolve. The ultimate aim of this series, however, as of all feminist endeavors, is not less than the revision of culture, a remaking of the reality we create and construe through symbolic action.

The current volume, *Mothers in the English Novel: From Stereotype to Archetype*, offers a long-overdue study of the depiction of mothers in the female and male-authored English novel, at once an analysis of a female type and of the fictional form that contains and eventually liberates her. The novel's view of her role, the author avers, issues originally from a powerful maternal archetype which by the eighteenth century had devolved into the negative stereotypes vested in the narrative patterns of folk and fairy tale and comic drama. Gauging the effect of this obstructive inheritance on the new form, McCormick nonetheless finds that the novel gradually recovers a serious and dramatically significant place for mothers. Her analyses of nineteenth- and turn-of-the-century works from Jane Austen to George Eliot and Henry James reveal no "precious specialty" for the mothers in novels written by women: gender, in this instance, does not transcend genre. By the twentieth century, however, both sexes can imagine mother protagonists who do overcome conventional limitations to suggest the unbounded power of the original Great Mother archetype. With its insights into our profound responses to mothers and its sensitive readings of the matriarchs of English fiction, McCormick's text enriches the ongoing inquiry into the maternal role in culture.

Carol Snyder
University of Houston–Clear Lake

Introduction

In order to understand the complex, contradictory representation of mothers in the English novel over the last three hundred years, one first has to acknowledge the fundamental paradox of motherhood in general. Motherhood is one of the most universal and reassuring of human institutions, yet at the same time it is one of the most exclusive, even mysterious. That tension has been at the heart of virtually every depiction of mothers in art or literature since long before the novel was even recognized as a genre, and it still determines the way the novel recreates the mother today.

There is no question mothers experience the world somewhat differently from any other group of society; as the reproductive agents for humankind, they must be granted a knowledge that is unique to them and only partially appreciated by the rest of society. Despite the seventeeth-century claim (probably made by a man) that maternity consists in nothing more awful than "the laying of a great Eg, by a Hen, or a Goose,"[1] humanity has always, in fact, recognized childbirth as a transformative experience. And in many respects, it is. The peculiar interdependency of child and mother, for instance, is not a mere sentimental fabrication but a documented psychological and even physical fact that reverberates well into adulthood.[2] The word itself—"mother"—attaches to a complex of images and emotions from the broadly political to the intensely personal.

Of course, to mothers who are still struggling to get fathers to participate equally in parenting, such talk may seem hazardous. For generations the favorite argument for keeping women out of the workplace has been that children need their mothers even more than they need their fathers and so mothers should stay home with the kids. It is a specious argument, of course: fathers have their own gifts, and a number of recent studies show that, other things being equal, children fare just as well under the care of one parent as the other.[3]

Yet that is not to say that no difference exists altogether. For clearly there *is* something different about mothers, whether in the context of the English novel or in the context of human history. Certain areas of the humanities and social sciences, especially mythology, psychology, and anthropology, have long acknowledged the unique implications of mothers and motherhood; and now, after centuries of relatively benign neglect by the literary establishment, the figure of the mother in the novel has finally become, especially in the last decade or so, the focus of an extraordinary amount of discussion. Whether this new focus in literature has been directly catalyzed by the studies done in those other fields is hard to say. What one can say with certainty is that these tangential studies furnish much of the necessary background for understanding the role of the mother in the English novel, because the mother in literature is inextricably bound to the mother in myth, in history, in the human mind, and even, finally, to our own actual mothers.

*   *   *

Ever since the English novel, early in its development, settled on the domestic stage as its principal setting and middle-class families as its principal actors, mothers were assured a prominent role in the genre, as ubiquitous in the landscape of the English novel as churchyards in the landscape of English poetry. Mothers have been remarkable for the broad range of roles they have been assigned, roles which over the centuries have ranged from comic sidekick to tragic lead. Probably no other single character type has provoked a greater variety of expression from English novelists; certainly few minor characters are remembered so enduringly as Austen's Mrs. Bennet or Dickens' Mrs. Nickleby.

Yet if mothers in fiction tend to be highly memorable, they are also highly problematic, the eccentricities which recur in individuals raising numerous questions about the validity of their characterization as a group. The nature of this "problem" is suggested by something as apparently innocuous as how they are labeled. Mothers are addressed almost always as "Mrs.," rarely by their first name. Taken at face value, this labeling may reveal nothing more meaningful than accepted forms of social address, just as fathers are usually "Mr.," spinsters "Miss," and clergy "Reverend." But more to the point, the absence of a personal name reinforces the fact that, especially in the novels of the eighteenth and nineteenth centuries, the identity of a mother as an individual tends to be subsumed by her identity as a mother. This is essentially true even in such a remarkable twentieth-century figure as Mrs. Ramsay in *To the*

Lighthouse, whose maternity, attractive as Woolf's portrayal of it is, is nonetheless the central fact of her existence. However, the difference between a woman like Mrs. Ramsay and her predecessors like Mrs. Nickleby is that her role as mother no longer automatically denies or depreciates her other selves. If anything, maternity in the modern mother makes her other selves more interesting, more complex, and more substantial. In novels written before the present century, on the other hand, mothers are almost always tedious, stupid, narrow, or self-involved—or else so selfless as to make them unpalatable in another way. Invariably it is the single women, or at best the married women with no visible children, whose lives seem varied, whose interests seem worthwhile, and whose discourse is not entirely self-reflective.

The "problem" with this unflattering portrait is not that it is altogether false but rather that it is far from true. While there assuredly were (and still are) mothers in "real life" whose lives fit this bleak model, as a blanket indictment of an entire class of women it is clearly distorted. And the distortion is the more noticeable, considering the direction the novel seemed otherwise to be taking. While other aspects of the genre moved steadily toward greater psychological and social realism, mothers remained in a state, more or less, of arrested development, caught in essentially the same farcical or idealized poses assigned them when the novel first emerged. When they played a part at all (that is, when they weren't dead or otherwise removed), they continued to play the bumbling incompetents, the insensitive autocrats, and the ridiculous flirts of the farce, or else, though less frequently, the ministering angels of the courtesy book. This is the obvious paradox about mothers in the formative years of "realistic" English fiction: in spite of the variety of surface detailing, their range of moral motion is unrealistically narrow. Taken collectively, mothers before the twentieth century are either much more flawed, or much more perfect, than any sampling of mothers, then or now, could possibly be in real life. The mother-as-monster-or-madonna is, of course, the two-sided stereotype referred to in my title, and the implication of such stereotyping is to dismiss or censure a role that was, by most contemporary accounts, neither trivial nor contemptible.

Thus, regardless of what she may have been in real life, the pre-twentieth-century mother is consistently portrayed as the most futile character type in fiction, in the sense that her wishes, lacking either moral endorsement, intellectual force, or sometimes merely physical stamina, are ultimately defeated. If she presents a threat, it is eventually undermined, and if she offers comfort, it is only temporary.

Yet for all that she is ultimately overthrown, "depotentiated," to borrow a term from Sylvia Brinton Perera, the mother clearly wields, albeit to no final purpose, an undeniable power. After all, it is the mother who, by her obstructive presence or her untimely absence, creates or aggravates the central conflict against which the hero/ine struggles. When Clarissa Harlowe is faced with a marriage that is hateful to her, her mother, to whom she looks for support, insists that she comply. When Elizabeth Bennet's future depends on coming to an understanding with Mr. Darcy, her mother repeatedly drives him away. Even the mother of Jane Eyre, though she can hardly be "blamed" for dying, consigned her daughter to a childhood of abuse by doing so. This capacity for disruption is so consistent and so pronounced in mothers in the early novels that it almost becomes a condition of motherhood. And though it must be labeled a negative power, it is a power nonetheless, and one that is clearly related to her maternal role.

And who is the original of the powerful mother, if not the mother goddess herself, the archetypal Great Mother? It doesn't require any great stretching of logic to make the connection: negative power is an essential component of the ancient mother goddess imago, expressed in such figures as the Indian Kali, the Gorgon of Greece, and Egyptian Isis on her bad days. According to Jungian scholar Erich Neumann, whose massive study of the mother archetype was suggested by Carl Jung himself, the Great Mother archetype is tripartite, a fusion of three forms: the good, the terrible, and the good-bad mother. Although both the Good Mother and the Terrible Mother can "emerge independently from the unity of the Great Mother," the unified Great Mother is the ultimately powerful form. "[T]he Great Mother . . . is good-bad and makes possible a union of positive and negative attributes," Neumann wrote. "Great Mother, Good Mother, and Terrible Mother form a cohesive archetypal group" (*The Great Mother* 21).

One of the purposes of this study is to show that even at her most absurd, her most vicious, or her most idealized, the stereotyped mother of the English novel has her origin in this archetypal complex. The reason she does not look especially goddess-like is that, for a number of reasons, largely psychological but also aesthetic, cultural, and political, she has been denied her Great Mother wholeness and forced to assume an extreme identity that, like a schizophrenic's, does not reflect a unified reality but only a fragment of reality, and therefore a distortion. If these extreme personalities reflect any truth at all, it is the material and psychological conditions that created the unnatural split in the first place.

The second purpose of this study is to show that, beginning with mothers in the late Victorian novels and continuing in some of the mothers of modern fiction, that ancient wholeness has begun to be reasserted. The new mother, like Neumann's Great Mother but also like our own flesh-and-blood mothers, is a complex combination of life-force and death-force, fulfillment and denial, sympathy and hostility, nurture and rejection, fecundity and barrenness. She is regarded, both as an individual and as a symbol, with a mixture of devotion and distrust, admiration and fear. Moreover, she herself often seems to wonder at the contradictions in her own soul.

Indeed, a number of mothers in the novels of this century so strongly evoke the archetypal paradox of creation and destruction that they seem to constitute a distinct type of their own. How this modern fertility goddess acts upon the sterility of the modern age constitutes such a dramatic change from the mothers of the previous two centuries that she may in fact be called a new archetype.

One can only speculate why, after so many centuries of denying the mother goddess, this change should be occurring now. Certainly there have been correspondingly profound changes in women's legal, social, and political status in western society, changes that are inevitably reflected in art. Presumably western readers today are more comfortable with the notion of a powerful mother than previously; if the earlier stereotypes were a subconscious means of circumscribing the mother's power, the new archetype seems to be a way of releasing it.

But though human response to the archetype has obviously changed in certain ways, the fundamental nature of the archetype itself has not. The mother archetype is still basically what it always was, the embodiment of what Jung calls the ambivalence of "the loving and terrible mother":

The qualities associated with it are maternal solicitude and sympathy; the magic authority of the female; the wisdom and spiritual exaltation that transcend reason; any helpful instinct or impulse; all that is benign, all that cherishes and sustains, that fosters growth and fertility. The place of magic transformation and rebirth, together with the underworld and its inhabitants, are presided over by the mother. On the negative side the mother archetype may connote anything secret, hidden, dark; the abyss, the world of the dead, anything that devours, seduces, and poisons, that is inescapable like fate. (*Collected Works* 9.1: 82; par. 158)

To Jung, the mythical nature of the mother, like that of all other archetypes (he also calls them "primordial images" and "preexistent forms") is unchanging, built into the subconscious of the human race much the way "the axial system of a crystal . . . preforms the crystalline structure in the mother liquid, although it has no material existence of its own" (*Memories, Dreams, Reflections* 381). Indeed, says Jung, the archetypes are the contents of that part of the psyche which is universal, and whose "contents and modes of behaviour . . . are more or less the same everywhere and in all individuals" (*CW* 9.1: 4; par. 3). This, of course, is Jung's notion of the collective unconscious, manifested in the recurring images with which people through time and space have expressed human experience—i.e., the archetypes. Though human history and even entire civilizations may undergo profound change, he says, the essential shape of the archetypes do not, because the "human brain . . . presumably still functions today much as it did of old" (*CW* 7: 135; par. 219). Though Jung cautioned repeatedly that many of his theories were in the testing stages and should not be taken as final, his definitions of the collective unconscious and of the archetypes have remained basically intact.

As evidence to support his theory, Jung cites those universal and recurring utterances of the human psyche—the myths, dreams, and fairy tales of all civilizations in all times. According to the autobiographical *Memories, Dreams, Reflections*, archetypes can be witnessed clearly through these unselfconscious portholes into the human mind. "The concept of the archetype," he says, is derived from the repeated observation that, for instance, the myths and fairytales of world literature contain definite motifs which crop up everywhere. We meet these same motifs in the fantasies, dreams, deliria, and delusions of individuals living today. These typical images and associations are what I call archetypal ideas. (382)

The only practical way to account for the recurrence of the same myths and folk legends across time and space is to assume that the patterns are preexistent in the human mind. Elsewhere, Jung defines archetypes as "myth-motifs" or "mythological motifs" and gives countless examples of such recurrent images; for instance, the motif of the dual birth, wherein a child has both mortal and divine parents, as in the case of Heracles, Pharoah, and Jesus Christ—even in the tradition of naming a set of godparents for newborn children. He cites, too, the dual mother motif, typified also by Christ, who was born first of Mary, then "reborn" via baptism in the Jordan River. In Jung's opinion, the universality of these images, the fact that they turn up in countless places isolated both physically and temporally from each other, proves that they reflect not personal, individual experience but something that is collective, impersonal, and ahistorical.

[I]t is absolutely out of the question that all the individuals who believe in a dual descent have in reality always had two mothers . . . . Rather, one cannot avoid the assumption that the universal occurrence of the dual-birth motif together with the fantasy of the two mothers answers an omnipresent human need which is reflected in these motifs. (*CW* 9.1: 45–46; par. 95)

There are hundreds if not thousands of examples of archetypal patterns in myth, fantasy, fairy tale, and so on. The next chapter examines several such tales as they demonstrate the archetypal origin of virtually all images of the mother. If the sample seems disproportionately weighted with negative images, it cannot be helped, for that is what has dominated western literature.

I realize that this theory—that an aboriginal prejudice against mothers accounts for much of their ongoing abuse in literature—runs counter to the feminist wisdom which says that negative portrayals of women in art are politically motivated and culturally enforced. But if Jung is right, and the mother archetype is at once "the solace for all the bitterness of life" *and* "the great illusionist, the seductress" (*CW* 9.2: 13; par. 26), then surely the human race cannot be blamed if it harbors some very mixed feelings toward her, feelings that will obtain regardless of personal experience or social conditioning. But Jung never implies that one or the other nature dominates; on the contrary, he seems to regard the dual nature of the archetypal mother as extraordinarily balanced, similar to the God of the Old Testament, whom he describes, in *Answer to Job*, as having "insight . . . along with obtuseness, loving-kindness along with cruelty, creative power along with destructiveness. Everything was there, and none of these qualities was an obstacle to the other" (*CW* 11: 365; par. 560). Not only does Jung often describe the mother archetype in god-like terms, he joins many other psychologists and anthropologists in believing that the earliest deities were probably mother goddesses.[4]

On the other hand, feminists are understandably wary of some of Jung's more reactionary claims, especially his prescriptive statements as to what constitutes the archetypal feminine. For instance, Jung believes that passion and emotion are female attributes, logic and reasoning traits of the male.[5] The anima, or male soul, he says, compensates men for their lack of earthy Eros, while the animus, or female soul, compensates women for their lack of spiritual Logos. Unfortunately, Erich Neumann follows Jung in making this distinction, and his reputation among feminists has suffered somewhat in consequence. James Hillman, for instance, scoffs at "the absurdities of Neumann" when the latter insists that consciousness always has a masculine character, even when it is found in women.[6]

Yet I would defend Jung against some critics who further reject what they understand to be his position that archetypes are absolute, inflexible entities, determining rather than determined by human experience. In their introduction to *Feminist Archetypal Theory*, for instance, Estella Lauter and Carol Schreier Rupprecht argue that if archetypes are to be viewed in terms that enable rather than restrict women, they must be understood as "explanations of reality experienced by females" instead of "categories to contain" them (7). Indeed, whatever grievances they may have with Erich Neumann on other scores, they approve of his definition of archetypes because of its built-in flexibility. In *Art and the Creative Unconscious*, Neumann defines the archetypes of the collective unconscious as

> intrinsically formless psychic structures which become visible in art. The archetypes are varied by the media through which they pass—that is, their form changes according to the time, the place, and the psychological constellation of the individual in whom they are manifested. Thus, for example, the mother archetype, as a dynamic entity in the psychic substratum, always retains its identity, but it takes on different *styles*— different aspects or emotional color—depending on whether it is manifested in Egypt, Mexico, or Spain, or in ancient, medieval, or modern times. The paradoxical multiplicity of its eternal presence, which makes possible an infinite variety of forms of expression, is crystallized in its realization by man in time; its archetypal eternity enters into a unique synthesis with a specific historical situation. (82)

Though Neumann's purpose here is to account for the shifting appearance of archetypes in general, this excerpt serves to explain how the stereotyped mothers in early fiction can be rooted in a far more ancient phenomenon. The "specific historical situation" of mothers in England until at least the late nineteenth century was that of a particularly rigid patriarchy. Like all women, mothers had few rights; as mothers, they had even fewer options. In order for the historical fact of powerlessness (the condition of contemporary mother-women) to coexist with the prehistorical image of power (the condition of the ancient mother-goddess), presumably the psyche would have to come up with an alternative image which would restrain that ancient power without actually denying it. This it did, via the stereotypes. As I have shown, even when she is most trivialized, the mother in the novel retains a certain undeniable power, though it is travestied into a caricature of either the Good Mother or the Terrible. Neumann's thesis would also explain how these earlier negative images could appear to change so dramatically around the turn of the century. That is, as the historical situation in England also changed (what with suffrage, birth control, World War I, and other equally cataclysmic events in women's history), the "emotional color" of the archetype would have been reshaped accordingly and so, in turn, would its expression in narrative and other forms of art, where these "formless psychic structures" become visible. If the mothers in the novels of this period begin to reflect the power of the unified archetype, rather than the two disjointed parts, it is at least partly because, according to Neumann and his endorsers, the new image accorded with the new reality.

As one should expect, it wasn't only in the realistic novel that the changes were manifested. Parallel changes occur in depictions of the mother in late Victorian fantasy fiction, and Estella Lauter notes that there were corresponding changes in the visual art of the period as well. Mary Cassatt (1844–1926), for instance, was one of the new breed of painters whose images "relate more to the painters' experiences or their observations of contemporary women than to the conventions of art." Such works as *Mother About to Wash Her Sleepy Child*, *Baby Reaching for an Apple*, and *Breakfast in Bed* express, without sentimentality and without the conventional idealism of the Pieta or the Madonna, "a turn-of-the-century preoccupation with feminine power in its maternal form" ("Visual Images" 52–53).

However, Lauter claims, the mothers depicted by modern women artists are not wholly powerful, in spite of their great strengths, because the negating, oppressing forces working against them are that much more powerful. As she reviews a number of art works spanning the last one hundred years, she finds that

> a pattern emerges—not the pattern of the good and terrible mother who either cares for or restrains her child, but of the vulnerable mother whose great capacities for sheltering, nurturing, protecting, supporting, caring, liberating, and reflecting the other (child or adult) cannot ensure her success. (59)

The modern mothers whom I look at in depth—Mrs. Moore from E. M. Forster's *A Passage to India*, Mrs. Ramsay from Woolf's *To the Lighthouse*, and Kate Brown from Doris Lessing's *The Summer Before the Dark*, all endure moments of futility, loneliness, doubt, and sorrow. They are periodically overwhelmed by a sense of powerlessness in the face of what they see as the disintegration and unmeaning in their worlds, even as they sometimes seem to embrace that chaos. Yet their

despair makes them more human, more accessible, than any big-bellied
Mesopotamian figurine, just as the Jesus of the New Testament made
the godhead more accessible to Christians; and Lauter is right to say
that this new attribute reflects the experiences and psychic needs of
today's women and men. Nonetheless, while there is an obvious and
intimate relationship between archetypes and individual experience, it
seems a bit presumptuous to insist that archetypes must "enable"
women in order to be valid. After all, an archetype isn't a piece of
legislation, drawn up for the people's benefit and subject to change at
their will. Much of the mythic power of the archetype owes to its
autonomy, its indifference to individual history, and I suspect we
inadvertently weaken it if we insist that it serve as a political voice on
our behalf. On the other hand, what could be more "enabling" for
women, more reassuring, than to know that one of the most indomitable
forces in human and psychic history is not only a woman but a Mother?

Thus the essential archetype has not changed, but perhaps what *has*
changed, urged along by the rapid changes in Western society, is our
point of view. Though the mother is as potent as ever, perhaps we have
finally gained (or regained) the courage to embrace that power rather
than deny or depreciate it. In the earlier works where the mother is a
ninny, a witch, or an angel, it is always from another's perspective that
she appears so. Mothers in those novels are invariably object, not
subject. Stories are told about them, rarely by them, so our view of the
truth is limited, if not distorted. When the information provided is so
implicative, the motives of the teller thus become as critical to
understand as the allegations themselves. And as Marianne Hirsch
suggests in *The Mother/Daughter Plot*, what is left out of the testimony
is as vital as what is included. Referring to the Oedipus legend, Hirsch
asks:

> What can we say about Jocasta? . . . We do not discover her
> feelings about handing her child over to die, except in
> Oedipus's own exclamation: "The child she bore!" (l. 1178).
> Beyond this Jocasta is represented by silence, negation,
> damnation, suicide. The story of her desire, the account of her
> guilt, the rationale for her complicity with a brutal husband,
> the materiality of the body which gave birth to a child she
> could not keep and which then conceived with that child other

children—*this* story cannot be filled in because we have no framework within which to do it *from her perspective.* (Hirsch's emphasis 4)

Hirsch sees the effacement of the mother to be a pattern that has continued unbroken through every age of history, one that does not stop even in the present, when "even feminist analyses fail to grant Jocasta as mother a voice and a plot" (3). Certainly the problem of stereotyping mothers does not magically disappear after 1900. Just as mothers continue to be typecast in the movies, in sitcoms, even in the funny papers, so does the pattern persist in some contemporary novels, where mothers are still cast as the stereotypical villains sabotaging their children's (usually daughters') lives. In such cases, the relationship of the son or daughter to the mother is still that of subject to object, self to other. Though novels today scrutinize the mother-child relationship far more intently than did most earlier novels—in fact, it is often the focus of modern narrative—the difficulties of that relationship have little chance of being resolved as long as the mother's story is told by someone else. Thus, when Hirsch asks, "[W]here [are] the stories of mothers . . . in the plots of sons and daughters[?]" (4) the question is largely rhetorical. If the stories of mothers are to be told, they must be allowed to tell them, and we must be prepared to listen. The English novel has come that far at least.

Notes

1. *The XV Comforts of Rash and Inconsiderate Marriage . . . Done Out of French* (London: n.p., 1682) 54. Quoted in Valerie Fildes, *Women as Mothers in Pre-Industrial England: Essays in Memory of Dorothy McLaren* 13.

2. Dorothy Dinnerstein in *The Mermaid and the Minotaur: Sexual Arrangements and Human Malaise* notes that one of the physical phenomena tying a child to its mother occurs in the central nervous system, in the bodily-based postpartum responses: the involuntary milk let-down and accompanying uterine contractions that can be triggered in a mother by the cry of a hungry infant. "Her future feelings for the child, when this close postpartum tie has been outgrown and it is a

rambunctious toddler (indeed even later, when it is a pimply adolescent, or a greying eccentric), will always be flavored on some level . . . with the memory of the passion which at this moment knots her belly and makes her nipples spurt" (78–79). She joins most psychologists, anthropologists, and child development professionals in acknowledging the early psychological basis for the complex maternal bond which follows most individuals through life. "The early mother . . . is a source . . . of ultimate distress as well as ultimate joy: . . . she is both nourishing and disappointing, both alluring and threatening, both comforting and unreliable. The infant loves her touch, warmth, shape, taste, sound, movement . . . . And it hates her because . . . she does not perfectly protect and provide for it" (95). Dinnerstein's theories are so mainstream now that it is almost superfluous to cite them; still, among the studies that enlarge upon the processes of infant attachment and separation are those of Freud, Karen Horney, Nancy Chodorow, Ann Dally, Charles Rycroft, Jean Baker Miller, and interdisciplinarians such as Adrienne Rich, Barbara Schapiro, and Paulo de Carvalho-Neto.

3. Among the many recent studies of the father's changing role are Arthur Colman and Libby Colman, *The Father: Mythology and Changing Roles*; Charlie Lewis and Margaret O'Brien, eds., *Reassessing Fatherhood: New Observations on Fathers and the Modern Family*; and Ross D. Parke, *Fathers.* Parke says that "the roles played by mothers and fathers are not biologically predetermined. Instead, the definition of sex roles can vary considerably depending on the social, ideological, and physical conditions in different cultures" (6).

4. The theory that in all cultures, a matriarchal phase precedes the patriarchal phase is widespread, although conclusive proof for it is limited, relying largely on the predominance of maternal icons found in cultures as early as Mesopotamia, where the matriarchy is thought to have disappeared around 3,000 B.C. In *Answer to Job*, Jung accepts the Greek idea of Sophia, a "pagan city-goddess" whose attributes are equal to or even superior to those of the Christian God or Hebrew Yahweh. Sophia is the "coeternal and more or less hypostatized pneuma of feminine nature that existed before the Creation." For other anthropogical and theoretical discussions of matriarchies, see Robert Briffault, *The Mothers: A Study of the Origins of Sentiments and Institutions*; J. J. Bachofen, *Myth, Religion, and Mother Right: Selected Writings*; Evelyn S. Kessler, *Women: An Anthropological View*; Monica Sjoo and Barbara Mor, *The Great Cosmic Mother: Rediscovering the Religion of the Earth*;

and Bruno Bettelheim, *Symbolic Wounds: Puberty Rites and the Envious Male.*

5. Jung makes this distinction frequently. For instance, in "The Syzygy: Anima and Animus," he refers to the "fact" that "woman's consciousness is characterized more by the connective quality of Eros than by the discrimination and cognition associated with Logos." In women, he says, "Logos is often only a regrettable accident" (*CW* 9.2: 14; par. 29).

6. *The Myth of Analysis: Three Essays in Archetypal Psychology* 289. The passage Hillman is referring to occurs in Neumann's *The Origins and History of Consciousness* 42.

Mothers in the English Novel:
From Stereotype to Archetype

Chapter One

Literary, Historical, and Psychological Backgrounds

No one can accuse the early English novel of having invented the negative maternal stereotype. From the avenging mothers of antiquity, to the mother-hags of post-Roman-empire Europe, to the stepmother-witches of medieval folklore, to the termagants of Elizabethan tragedy, to the manipulative matrons of farce and Restoration comedy, the mothers of the English novel merely continue a long and not particularly proud tradition of mother-bashing in Western literature. There is also, of course, an inverse stereotype, incarnate in the person of Mary, the Blessed Virgin Mother, loving, long-suffering, flawless. For reasons that should become apparent, idealizations are far less frequent than derogations in all genres, the novel included. But regardless which type they are cast in, the mothers in these early novels all do essentially the same thing. They are an obstruction to the hero or heroine's growth, welfare, and/or happiness. That is their primary role, handed down to them from generations of Good and Terrible Mothers.

The good mothers, that is, the idealized ones, are depicted as gentle angels, wellsprings of devotion, wisdom, and compassion, "contentedly submissive to men" and "queen in [their] own realm of the Home,"[1] but so rarefied that they cannot survive in the grosser atmosphere of everyday life.[2] Their one-dimensional passivity is as dangerous to their offspring as active aggression. The negative stereotype, on the other hand, includes a much greater variety of roles, from simpletons and buffoons to autocrats and libertines who, though they play more prominent roles than their idealized counterparts, are ultimately ineffectual also.

But at least the bad mothers are entertaining: idealized mothers are inherently boring, interesting primarily for their reticence: if they appear in the action at all, it is only fleetingly and for the most part inconsequentially. Most idealized mothers have already been dead for some time when the story opens; if not, they are sure to die in an early chapter. Occasionally the dead mother is remembered fondly by her child (usually, though not always, a girl): Jane Austen's Anne Elliot was fourteen when "her dear mother," the only member of the family with enough sense to appreciate her, passed away (*Persuasion* 47); Emma Woodhouse has an "indistinct remembrance" of her mother's caresses (*Emma* 5); and Molly Gibson, even though "she had been too young to be conscious of it at the time," learns to mourn heartily the loss of hers (Gaskell, *Wives and Daughters* 36). Alternatively the mother died while the heroine was still an infant, forcing the girl to get information about her second-hand: the circumstances of the death are usually romantic and tragic. Evelina's gentle mother, for instance, abused by her own mother, in desperation married a wealthy scoundrel who deserted her and denied the marriage; "the same moment that gave birth to her infant, put an end at once to the sorrows and life of its mother" (Burney, *Evelina* 5). Similarly, Jane Eyre learns that her mother had married a poor clergyman against the wishes of her family, who promptly cut her off without a shilling; both husband and wife contracted typhoid fever while ministering to the poor of a large industrial town. (The idealized mother is often a sort of Florence Nightingale to the oppressed.)

When idealized mothers *are* introduced, it is merely to amplify their formulaic virtues and so emphasize the loss to the child. For instance, in *The Mysteries of Udolpho*, Madame St. Aubert is Emily's companion in playing the lute, reading Thompson, rambling among the "vallies and plains of Gascony," and so on. She dies discussing "religious topics" (Radcliffe 19) and is followed to her grave by a long train of peasants, with whom she had been very popular. Indeed, a premature death tends to be the signature of idealization. David Copperfield's child-mother is a curious mixture of idealized and negative traits, her petulance and self-centeredness bespeaking the bad mother, her frailty, beauty, and tenderness the classic earmarks of idealization. Yet her maudlin death while Davy is still a schoolboy finally settles her as the latter. The last time he sees her, she is standing in the cold, still as a statue, staring intently at David and "holding up her baby in her arms" (Dickens, *David Copperfield* 129)—a sacrificial/sanctification icon if ever there was one. The death of Mary

Barton's mother in childbirth, when Mary is thirteen, is more typical, though no less pathetic; the girl, kneeling by the bedside, "almost crammed [the bedclothes] into her mouth to keep down the choking sobs. . . . 'Oh, mother! mother, are you really dead! Oh, mother, mother!'" (Gaskell, *Mary Barton* 56–57).

Including the mother's deathbed scene makes the most of an already lugubrious event, and therefore one can expect to find it in Dickens. When six-year-old Florence Dombey calls to her fast-declining mother, "[t]he little voice, familiar and dearly loved, awakened some show of consciousness, even at that ebb. . . . 'Mama!' cried the child sobbing aloud. 'Oh dear Mama! Oh dear Mama!'" (*Dombey and Son* 9). If the word "little" is the Victorian's favorite cue for pathos, then how doubly pathetic is the account of a friendless little child losing this most beloved parent. Yet such treatment may constitute other, albeit subtle, forms of derogation. For one thing, by publicizing the mother's weakness, her untimely desertion, and her absolute helplessness to comfort the grieving child, the author implicates her, in a rather perverse sort of way, as the cause of that grief. As Fanny Dombey lies dying, her sister-in-law's frantic admonitions that she "rouse herself," though intended, of course, to be poignant, suggest real blame: "Now, really, Fanny my dear, . . . I shall have to be quite cross with you, if you don't rouse yourself. It's necessary for you to make an effort, and perhaps a very great and painful effort which you are not disposed to make; but this is a world of effort you know, Fanny, and we must never yield, when so much depends upon us" (*DS* 8). So much, indeed: Florence Dombey's trials begin in the very next chapter, and much as she loves her mother, the reader feels no such affection.

Second, as John Kucich notes, such deathbed scenes are too predictable to be taken seriously. Even though "the ritual presence of the good society around the deathbed of a good character" might profess to do homage to the spirit of the deceased, he says, by calling upon prescribed emotions it may actually trivialize it. "Sentimentality seems to stop short of tragic knowledge, short of grief, short of terror; it assumes that fundamentally everything is all right, or that it will be all right." Thus "the communal context for sentimentality prevents us from seeing the element of loss in these scenes as anything but a formula" (53, 56–57).

Motherlessness is not always sentimentalized, however; very often, especially in eighteenth-century works, it is merely a condition imposed by the plot, with little or no mention being made of it.[3] The motherless character usually has a surrogate mother or guardian (for instance, Sophia's Aunt Western in *Tom Jones* and Liddy Melford's Aunt Tabitha in *The Adventures of Humphry Clinker*) whose irritating presence serves in fact as a tacit reminder of the absence of a good mother.[4] Occasionally a variation on the motherless theme occurs when a character presumed motherless turns out to have (or to have had) a mother after all. This happens, for instance, to Tom Jones, Caroline Helstone in *Shirley*, and *Bleak House*'s Esther Summerson. These eleventh-hour discoveries signify little, however, as the "point" of being motherless has already been fulfilled.

What this "point" is is suggested by Susan Peck MacDonald in her study of what she calls the "tradition of the absent mother."

> The nurturing that we usually associate with motherhood . . . seems to have been withdrawn or denied in order to goad the daughter into self-assertion and maturation. . . . Their mothers may be dead or weak or in need of help themselves, so that while the heroines sometimes receive help from other strong, supportive women, they rarely receive help from their own mothers.[5]

According to this theory, then, a mother may be perfectly robust and healthy but still be effectively "absent" to her child: the determinant is not whether she is sweet-natured or cruel but whether she provides adequate guidance, nurturance, and support for her offspring. Indeed, when I use the term "bad" mothers, I do not necessarily mean that these mothers are immoral; what I mean is that they do a consistently poor job of giving their children the proper spiritual, emotional, moral, intellectual, and practical guidance and support. Some of the bad mothers of eighteenth- and nineteenth-century fiction *do* appear to be genuinely wicked (Austen's Lady Susan, for example), but most mothers are merely exaggeratedly deficient in one or more areas ranging from sense, principle, judgment, compassion, and integrity, to discernment, liberality, good nature, good taste, or even just good manners. In fact, the worst fault of most mothers is simply a weak mind or a swollen ego or an easily compromised sense of honor. We cannot despise these women, but we certainly cannot like or approve of them.

Clarissa Harlowe's mother, though she professes to be acting in her daughter's best interests, is nonetheless insensitive, disloyal, and appallingly ignorant of Clarissa's character and personality—she could not be more "absent" to Clarissa in her anguish than if she really were dead. For instance, she reduces Clarissa's refusal to marry Solmes to a mere question of obedience which, once resolved, can be forgotten in the pleasure of selecting dress patterns. "Signify to us, now," she writes her daughter, imprisoned in an upstairs room, "your compliance with our wishes. And then there is an end of your confinement. You may, in this case, directly come down to your father and me in his study; where we will give you our opinion of the patterns, with our hearty forgiveness and blessings." She adds, as an extra incentive, "You don't know what I have suffered" (Richardson 95).

Mrs. Harlowe's chief fault—considering her own needs before her daughter's—is typical. Self-centeredness whether in large matters or small is at the root of most "bad" maternal behavior, from Lady Ashton's cruel domination of Lucy in Scott's *The Bride of Lammermoor* to the plaintiveness of Mrs. John Vernon in Mrs. Oliphant's *Hester*, who is fond of claiming, "I would not for the world say a word against my own child," but says it anyway (78). Rebecca Sharpe Crawley's neglect of little Rawdon makes her look even more heartless than when she merely neglects her lovers: hearing him sobbing for loneliness in his nursery, Becky keeps on chatting about the opera. "It's my cherub crying for his nurse," she calmly informs her guests, "but without moving toward the door. "He'll cry himself to sleep" (*VF* 447). That a mother cannot always be the soul of generosity is a fact we are encouraged to accept today—in fact, one of the prominent advancements in the depiction of mothers in the twentieth-century novel is that they are allowed to have interests different from their families'. But the eighteenth- and nineteenth-century novel does nothing to discourage this childish if common form of egotism that makes us all believe that our mothers' interests are identical with our own. "[T]he goodness or badness of the mother [is measured by] how far she really feels this identity of interests," says Nancy Chodorow (97). The stereotypes of a century or two ago demonstrate how fully this criteria was accepted by the age.[6]

But the antipathy expressed toward mothers in these novels is not limited only to patently opprobrious behavior; nor is it reserved exclusively for mothers of the protagonist (in one or two cases, such as Becky Sharpe's, the mother *is* the protagonist). Though it has been suggested that mothers are "bad" in order to force the heroine to exert herself, a theory which is certainly accurate, nevertheless the novel seems to demonstrate a more categorical disdain for mothers. Unless she is desperately poor, in which case she is merely patronized,[7] a mother is almost guaranteed to be censured, scorned, or at the very least mildly ridiculed. Her behavior may indeed be thoughtless or inappropriate, but the point is that, with few exceptions, there *are* no alternative characterizations. Apart from the paragons, whom it puts on a pedestal, and a handful of mixed portraits which I discuss below, the novel prior to the twentieth century puts practically all of its mothers in the pillory. Anna Howe's mother, whom Clarissa wishes to trust as a friend since her own mother has betrayed her, seems instead to take a certain spiteful pleasure in Clarissa's punishment; Isabella Knightly's overprotective mothering demands that everyone else be inconvenienced in *Emma*; Amelia Osborne debases and humiliates herself in *Vanity Fair*; Mrs. Micawber's household mismanagement is equalled only by her husband's in *David Copperfield*; both Mrs. Thornton and Mrs. Hale in *North and South* are unpleasant and irritable, the one because she is too rich and the other because she is too poor. Even proto-feminists like George Eliot do not extend their enlightened notions of women to the most oppressed woman of all: the wife/mother. Mrs. Bede is too cranky, Mrs. Transome is too imperious, Mrs. Vincy is too complacent, and Mrs. Davilow is too melancholic. Indeed it is nearly impossible to find a credible, positive, functioning mother in any English novel much before the 1870s.

There are, to be sure, a number of mothers who escape easy classification—mothers like Rachel Esmond, Mrs. Hamley, Eleanor Bold, and Mrs. Poyser. These are the "mixed" creations, a perplexing combination of strength and weakness. As such they come closer to the interesting portraits one sees later, in mothers like Mrs. Ramsay or Mrs. Morel. For that matter, they remind us of mothers we have seen in the past, such as Yrsa, the quasi-legendary queen of Sweden documented in the *Gesta Danorum* of Saxo Grammaticus.[8] But what is perplexing in these Victorian mothers is the sense one gets that their authors are not willing to accept their attractiveness without reservation: all are compromised somewhat by a suggestion of "female" inferiority. Mrs. Hamley, Molly Gibson's confidante in *Wives and Daughters*, is one such woman. Though the acknowledged spiritual head of her household, she is a figure of mixed respect and condescension: her status as an invalid is a metaphor for her ultimately powerless position in a family dominated by men.[9] As for Mrs. Poyser, she is highly principled, earnest, and energetic, but one suspects that Eliot is protesting too much the decency of the working class—particularly when Mrs. Poyser "has her say out" at Squire Donnithorne, full of honest indignation and homely domestic proverbs like, "If you could make a pudding wi' thinking o' the batter, it 'ud be easy getting dinner" (*Adam Bede* 331). Indeed, William J. Hyde has said that George Eliot "was in no sense ever a comrade of the peasant class," implying that even a portrait such as Mrs. Poyser's "suggests a generalized observation applied with a measure of stereotyped predisposition" (295). Eleanor Bold is intelligent, attractive, and conventionally devoted to her baby (she looks forward to the day when "its infant tongue will call her by the sweetest name a woman can hear" [*Barchester Towers* 15]), but as Merryn Williams points out, she is also passive, long-suffering, and intensely devoted to a man (125). Eleanor remembers her late husband John Bold with the sort of undiscriminating adoration Amelia feels for George Osborne, and Trollope takes very much the same tone of mixed condescension and contempt with her that Thackeray takes with Amelia, even using the word "parasite" to describe how she clings to her husband. "Poor Eleanor!" he says three times in rapid succession:

> Hers was one of those feminine hearts which cling to a husband, not with idolatry, for worship can admit of no defect in its idol, but with the perfect tenacity of ivy. As the parasite plant will follow even the defects of the trunk which it embraces, so did Eleanor cling to and love the very faults of her husband. She had once declared that whatever her father did should in her eyes be right. She then transferred her allegiance, and became ever ready to defend the worst failing of her lord and master. (*BT* 12–13)

Even Polly Toodle—the very name keeps us from taking her seriously—though obviously meant as a positive creation of the order of Peggotty, seems to me far less consequential than Peggotty because of her comic-grotesque presentation, the sort of woman Virginia Woolf would later accuse earlier novelists of trivializing as a "character," ignoring her human qualities and instead bringing out "her oddities and mannerisms; her buttons and wrinkles; her ribbons and warts."[10] Polly may not have ribbons and warts, but the point is the same: Dickens introduces her not as a person but a fruit-cart:

> a plump rosy-cheeked wholesome apple-faced young woman, with an infant in her arms; [accompanied by] a younger woman not so plump, but apple-faced also, who led a plump and apple-faced child in each hand; another plump and also apple-faced boy who walked by himself; and finally, a plump and apple-faced man, who carried in his arms another plump and apple-faced boy. (*DS* 11)

Although the "fruitful" imagery aligns Polly somewhat with Demeter or Gaia, goddesses of the fertile earth, the comic tone makes her look more like a nineteenth-century Aunt Jemima. It can be argued, of course, that comic treatment is Dickens' way of rescuing mothers from the angel stereotype; that may be true. Mrs. Boffin, for instance, in *Our Mutual Friend*, is a comic mother-figure. But she is a considerably more complex character than Polly: her symbolic maternalism does not restrict her; rather, it adds to her interesting, significant personality. It is therefore especially significant that Mrs. Boffin is childless. In contrast, by depicting Polly as a "character," an ample maternal lap, Dickens is in fact denying her plausibility as anything more.

It is worth noting here that, with the exception of Rachel Esmond's disastrous marriage, the "mixed" mothers are the only ones who achieve reasonably successful, loving marriages based on mutual esteem. (This statement does not count the reportedly successful marriages of some of the idealized mothers, nor does it count mothers like Mrs. Gardiner in *Pride and Prejudice*, whose role as mother is hardly acknowledged). For instance, the Squire's devotion to Mrs. Hamley is deeply yet convincingly poignant in *Wives and Daughters*, and Mr. Toodle's reply to Mr. Dombey's "You heard what I said to your wife just now?" is one of the most pro-feminist things Dickens ever wrote: "'Polly heerd it,' said Toodle, jerking his hat over his shoulder in the direction of the door, with an air of perfect confidence in his better half, 'It's all right'" (*DS* 15).

That there are as few happy marriages as good mothers in the novels seems to imply several things: one is that being a good mother is a natural extension of being a good wife, and vice-versa—a rather unreasonable though firmly entrenched precept throughout history but especially emphasized in the Victorian era.[11] Another is that, since one tends to encounter the happy marriage/good mother combination only in minor characters (Eleanor Bold is either single or widowed for most of *The Warden* or *Barchester Towers*, the only novels in which she figures prominently), the implication is that there is something negligible and/or improbable about marital harmony.

Not until the changing literary and cultural climates of the latter century brought with them a better opinion of women's abilities and a demand for greater psychological realism did the novel begin consistently to see mothers as viable subjects for "serious, problematic, and even tragic representation" which Erich Auerbach says constitutes the difference between comic and modern realism (554). In contrast to the predominant style of their predecessors, modern mothers *are* problematic and serious, even, as Mrs. Morel in *Sons and Lovers*, tragic. Their movements still tend to revolve around their families, may even be rather commonplace; but their psychic sphere is usually much wider. Indeed, says Herbert Marder, the domestic imagery often implies "the broadening, not the rejection, of the domestic wisdom traditionally cultivated by women" (35).

Mothers are finally being credited with the "capacities for significant work, intellectual growth, political action, creativity, emotional development, [and] sexual expression" that Annis Pratt claims a woman's authenticity depends on (6). If earlier generations feared that encouraging such qualities in mothers would mean the end of peace in the home (which they obviously did: witness Dickens' attitude toward ambitious or sexually active mothers[12]), they were right if one takes peace to consist in submissive silence or artificial harmony. The mothers of the twentieth century are often the source of tremendous psychological conflict, whether with their children, their husbands, their communities, or themselves (though some, like Brenda Last in *A Handful of Dust*, find the struggle less strenuous than others). These mental skirmishes are of the highest interest, and not simply because mothers in novels have never really experienced them before. They are compelling because they recognize the unique imperatives and the vast, even frightening implications of the mother's role. The resulting dialectic is infinitely more provocative and realistic than anything before credited to a mother in the novel.

For the earlier stereotypes are not, according to the definition usually applied in modern literature, inherently realistic.[13] Based on anticipated rather than actual behavior, on types rather than individuals, they recall the stock characters of farce or morality plays. Indeed, the obstructive mother is descended through, if not directly from, these genres: Belisa, the heroine's mother in *La discreta enamorada*, a seventeenth-century Spanish farce, is a distinct Mrs. Nickleby type. Not only does she try to lure suitors for her unmarried daughter's hand, at one point she mistakenly assumes one of them to be asking for her own. Similarly, Angela, the mother in *La casa del tahur*, prefigures Mrs. Gibson in her manipulations, feigning deafness so she can eavesdrop on her daughter's conversations with prospective husbands while pretending to read from non-existent passages in devotional books.[14] To be sure, the maternal stereotype in the novel (the negative type, that is; the same cannot be said for the idealized mother) is by no means as predictable nor as overt as, for instance, the villains and fops of Restoration comedy. Individual mothers tend to be distinct, highly particularized creations; there is also considerable variety within the stereotype itself.[15] It is only for the purposes of this study that I have grouped mothers into two extremes of characterization, bad and idealized, for certainly the single heading "bad mothers" could be further subdivided according to dominant personality traits, such as "garrulous, interfering female" (e.g., Mrs. Bennet, Mrs. Nickleby), "spiteful, domineering female" (e.g., Catherine de Bourgh, Mrs. Reed), "self-promoting female" (Mrs. Jellyby, Mrs. Proudie), and so on. Yet the very fact that these mothers can be classified in this way further establishes their relationship to earlier comic types, which are prone to similar labeling or motif-indexing: for instance, the "conniving old female" type in Spanish comedy.[16]

As Auerbach's *Mimesis* has shown, the boundaries of realism allowed by the purely comic are narrow.

> The individual characters, as well as the connecting narrative, are consciously and consistently kept on the lowest level of style both in diction and treatment. And this necessarily implies that everything problematic, everything psychologically or sociologically suggestive of serious, let alone tragic, complications must be excluded, for its excessive weight would break the style. (31)

At one time, everything that was commonly realistic, "pertaining to everyday life," was treated on the comic level only. Modern literature has changed that, Auerbach continues: "the technique of imitation can evolve a serious, problematic, and tragic conception of any character regardless of type and social standing, of any occurrence regardless of whether it be legendary, broadly political, or narrowly domestic." Thus it is that serious conceptions now fall within the proper sphere of the domestic novel. But the mixture of the high and low in art has not occurred equally on all levels; "traces of a comic and 'low mimetic' tradition remain visible even now," according to George Levine (6). The comic typing of mothers through most of the nineteenth century is one of those vestigial proofs that such a tradition continued to be active. Thus while it is not accurate to say that stereotyped mothers are unrealistic, their realism is usually of a low and limited order. Their concerns pertain almost exclusively to everyday life and as such possess a certain local authenticity—arguments with maids, plans for dinner, worries about marrying off dependent daughters. Certainly there is historical truth behind the comic understatement in Mrs. Bennet's claim that if she could see "but one of [her daughters] happily settled at Netherfield, . . . "and all the others equally well married, [she] shall have nothing to wish for" (*PP* 9). As a dependent mother in a society that did not approve of middle-class women working for a living, Mrs. Bennet has very practical reasons to wish husbands for her five girls. Nonetheless, her concerns are not treated "on any level but the comic, which admits no problematic probing" (Auerbach 31). Most novels give serious literary treatment to other characters or dramatic complications with which mothers are involved—*The Mill on the Floss* is a good example—but since the mothers themselves have remained primarily comic even while other features of the novel have evolved toward greater seriousness, Auerbach's rule of the separation of styles in this case "remains inviolate." Therefore, even when Mrs. Tulliver is treated most sympathetically by the narrator, she is still primarily a figure of low comedy: "I must put up wi' my children," she says sadly after Maggie's apparent ruin, "for my furnitur' went long ago" (*MF* 632).

One of the results of treating a mother comically is that the social issues peculiar to married women, complex and serious as they are, are overlooked or trivialized. Auerbach's comments about the sociology implicit (or not implicit) in the comic tradition of antiquity are applicable here.

> [T]he realists of antiquity do not make clear the social forces underlying the facts and conditions which they present. This could only be done in the realm of the serio-problematic. But since the characters do not leave the realm of the comic, their relation to the social whole is either a matter of clever adaptation or of grotesquely blameworthy isolation. (31)

Many bad mothers have *not* adapted to the social whole; one of their chief problems, as I will discuss in later chapters, is that they speak and behave in an idiom not generally understood by others. But why this isolation should exist for mothers, the novel does not seek to answer. It may explore other sociological questions relevant to other classes of the population, such as the difficult condition of the dependent unmarried woman which disturbs Emma Woodhouse and Elizabeth Bennet; but it rarely looks closely or seriously at the social forces which particularly oppress the mother. The early novel does not, for instance, sympathize with the effects of dependency on the mother, such as Mrs. Bennet's helpless anger over the entailment of the Bennet estate. Nor does it ever imply that the antisocial behavior of the mother may be at least partly the result of the antisocial behavior of the father. The fact that these very questions are addressed in *The Spoils of Poynton* and *Sons and Lovers* suggests the degree to which the mother had evolved by the end of the century as a figure for what Auerbach calls "serio-problematic consideration." For there is a link, suggests Judith Wilt, between women being treated as second-class citizens and women being treated as objects of comedy—even if women themselves are laughing. In spite of the popularity of contemporary women humorists such as Erma

Bombeck and Marilyn French, Wilt believes that comedy is ultimately an ineffectual, even destructive response to the inequities of being female. "If we must [do something], the first thing we must do is reject comedy—the myth and the mode" (173–74). A radical step, perhaps, but John Lauber's study of the fools in Jane Austen seems to justify it: "'[t]he delight that we take in literary fools no doubt can largely be accounted for by Hobbes' principle that we laugh when we feel a 'sudden glory' or sense of our own enormous superiority" (511). If generations of play-goers and readers have been accustomed to laugh at mothers as individuals, the danger Wilt fears is that this laughter encourages a belief in the inferiority of mothers as a class—a belief which we of the twentieth century, I assume, hold to be untrue.

Of course, anyone in the business of assessing the creations of earlier centuries must not insist on the beliefs and values of the present. We are cautioned these days against judging whether or not a novel is "true to life" or "realistic," since the act of judging implies, as Elizabeth Ermarth points out, the presence of a law which is "accessible to everyone and universally applicable."[17] In the interpretation of texts, such uniformity is impossible, since the subjective placement of the reader intrudes upon or even distorts what is perceived. What is needed to reconcile the various points of view, Ermarth says, is what she calls "management of distance." In other words, "one must step back from particulars in order to grasp them." In realism, points of view must intersect to create a uniform horizon, disagreement must be resolved so that the final picture of narrative achieves consistency in all its relationships. Realism forces its readers and viewers into a "middle distance" that makes possible the perception of a unified, single "set of meanings." (35–36)

Cecil Jenkins might be said to take Ermarth's theory a step further, declaring that the reader should be "less interested in 'reality' than in the alternative order which the artificiality of art provides . . . the story itself is a symbolic structure which is compelling in so far as it corresponds not to the immediate surface of life . . . but to the finality of life" (5). Ermarth's "particulars" are the bricks and mortar of Jenkins' "symbolic structure." As concrete facts they ground the story in place and time, but as symbols they defy empirical interpretation. The mother in literature must be regarded as a peculiarly accurate reflection of the attitudes and beliefs extant at the time the novel was written, not merely about mothers but in general. If this is so, the reader of eighteenth- and nineteenth-century fiction should be prepared to withhold any strictly twentieth-century attitudes and beliefs about the role of mothers. This does not mean an older text can never be illuminated by the values of the reader; it just means those values are as likely to constrict as enlarge the reader's point of view. Therefore one must look at her role in the context of the story and its style—only then can her development, consistency, and motivations as a character and as a player in the drama be judged as "realistic" or not.

Tested by these standards the mother in the eighteenth- and nineteenth-century novel is highly realistic in some respects, highly improbable in others. As I have said elsewhere, most bad mothers are fully detailed, act upon discernible (if questionable) motives, and have a certain amount of psychological credibility. The grotesques among them, such as Mrs. Skewton and Mrs. Nickleby, though they would strike one as unrealistic in other contexts, are no more so in the context of a Dickens novel than any other character. And Dickens, as we know, did not regard grotesquerie as in the least unfaithful to the truth— indeed he probably considers it closer to the "truth" of that finality of life that Jenkins refers to than moderation. In his preface to the first edition of *Bleak House* he insists that what looks like exaggeration is in fact a most strenuous respect for accuracy, from the Spontaneous Combustion of Mr. Krook to the preposterous litigations in the Court of Chancery:

> The case of Gridley is in no essential altered from one of actual occurrence, made public by a disinterested person who was professionally acquainted with the whole of the monstrous wrong from beginning to end. At the present moment there is a suit before the Court which was commenced nearly twenty years ago; in which from thirty to forty counsel have been known to appear at one time; in which costs have been incurred to the amount of seventy thousand pounds; which is a *friendly suit*; and which is (I am assured) no nearer to its termination now than when it was begun. (xxvi)

For Dickens (unlike Aristotle), reality is less a matter of what is *probable* than what is *possible*; extremes of behavior are to his mind more indicative of what the world is capable of than moderations. Certainly this applies to his mothers. As Vereen Bell says, "the bleak parent-child relationship [is] a kind of unifying metaphor for his total vision."[18] That vision, Bell continues, is one of moral and social chaos resulting from the generally irresponsible behavior of society. The nineteenth-century realist, says Levine, "far from apologizing for what is, deliberately subverts judgments based on dogma, convention, or limited perception and imagination. . . . What seems clear becomes cloudy as we see more and from different perspectives. Even as they articulate the social codes, these novels complicate them" (20).

Thus the extremes of behavior depicted in a mother are not only conceivable in literal terms but immanent in metaphorical ones: they represent reality on a certain level. Nonetheless, the exaggerated flaws of the mother tend to make certain aspects of her behavior look gratuitous, and her relations with her daughter in particular look contrived. These discrepancies may distract the reader, if not ultimately detract from the novel's overall realism. For instance, Susan MacDonald's theory of the absent mother, helpful though it is, nevertheless confronts one with a question of probability which by realistic standards is legitimate: how *does* the heroine acquire such a stock of virtues when she has no positive maternal model to learn them from? In spite of being deficient in strength of character, clarity of insight, and energy of moral spirit, these mothers produce daughters (and occasionally sons) who are remarkable for these very qualities. Other critics have noticed the inconsistency: Annis Pratt, describing the heroine in Fanny Fern's 1856 novel *Rose Clark*, notes that in spite of being mistreated first by the cruel mistress of an orphanage and then by an aunt who "forces her to work long hours, starves her, and locks her in dark rooms," Rose emerges a model heroine—that is, good hearted, well adjusted, and humble. "[O]ne would think the result of such treatment might be madness," Pratt comments drily (14). Some authors, Austen in particular, seem to have anticipated the inconsistency. Emma Woodhouse and Elizabeth Bennet, for instance, both have convincing mentors in the persons of Mrs. Weston and Mrs. Gardiner; but Jane Eyre, like Oliver Twist, is an orphan whose remarkable personality can only have sprung full blown from her own good soul and the sanguine influence of her long-dead parents; certainly she learns nothing of charity from her caustic aunt and insufferable cousins.[19] If, as Ian Watt says, it is true that "past experience is the cause of present action" in the novel and that "the novel in general has interested itself much more than any other literary form in the development of its characters in the course of time" (*Rise of the Novel* 22), then should not the experience of having a silly or mean mother—or no mother at all—result in silly, mean, or otherwise unspectacular children? Indeed, the equation does hold true elsewhere: this is the point of Dickens' parent-child metaphor, where even Caddy Jellyby's deaf and dumb baby, though a generation removed, has inherited the bad blood of her grandmother. And it holds true with, for instance, the incorrigible Lydia Bennet, the careless Cynthia Gibson, the "weazened and shrivelled" Pardiggle children, the haughty Harold Transome, even the thoughtless Tom Tulliver. All of these children have reaped what their mothers sowed, but somehow the protagonist seems to be immune to the effects of bad mothering. In contrast, the central conflict of many twentieth-century novels is the struggle of the offspring to overcome or at least define their problematic relationships with their mothers.

Another minor discrepancy may merely reflect a social double standard—the independence of thought and action that is invariably a virtue in the maiden is a defect in the matron. The heroine's wisdom in questioning, and courage in defying, the repressive dictates of society (including the one that says the chief business of a woman is to get married) no longer apply once she marries. Mothers who do not embrace these conventions, like Princess Halm-Eberstein in *Daniel Deronda* and Mrs. Jellyby in *Bleak House*, are treated with varying degrees of censure. "The powerful woman is . . . presented as an unnatural aberration, a monster, a witch," says Edith Honig. "She is not only an abnormal woman, but she is abnormal in a very negative way. The reader is not encouraged to sympathize with her . . . but to revile her."[20] Yet authors show no more respect for the women who *do* accept the hearth as their proper sphere—mothers like Mrs. Tulliver, Mrs. Musgrove, and Mrs. Quiverful. At one extreme they are made to look unnaturally harsh, at the other they look fatuous and trivial. When Mrs. Tulliver takes it upon herself to try to resolve the family's dispute with the lawyer Wakem, she is derided as if she were a particularly stupid animal trying to walk on its hind feet. Rarely do mothers before 1870 find an acceptable middle ground of intelligence and tenderness; those who attain it, like Lady Elliot (in *Persuasion*) and Molly Gibson's friend Mrs. Hamley, do so on pain of being eliminated from the story via an early death. Yet this creates a slight dilemma of characterization for heroines like *Middlemarch*'s Dorothea Brooke and Bronte's Jane Eyre. It is all right, even expected, for them to wish for broader horizons, but as Jean Sudrann asks of Jane Eyre, what is to be done with those yearnings after they marry?

> What of [Jane Eyre's] desire for freedom and wider knowledge that prompted her to leave the comforts of Lowood? What of the impulses that drove her to the windows and parapets of Thornfield to indulge in those "bright visions" of a wider world, "regions full of life" in which she might discover "a field for [her] efforts [other] than custom pronounced necessary for [her] sex"? [*JE* 112–13]. Surely to become, as she herself terms it, "prop and guide" [*JE* 451] for the blinded Rochester does not meet those expectations. (236–37)

Jane Eyre is a bit unusual in that the narrative follows the heroine further into her marriage than do most novels. "I have now been married ten years. I know what it is to live entirely for and with what I love best. I hold myself supremely blest . . . because I am my husband's life as fully as he is mine" (454). She has, of course, become a mother in the course of these ten years, and the ideal picture of the mother, Honig notes, "completely precludes the possibilities of independence, creative thought, and certainly rebellion" (11). Is this, then, a tacit denunciation of Jane's earlier intellectual and spiritual restlessness? Or is it a sort of socially-dictated form of amnesia? The pre-1870 novel does not, as a rule, allow mothers to play a central role, and therefore the narrative ordinarily ends before the heroine becomes one. However, this automatic cut-off point seems to create an awkward sort of split between the virginal heroine and her later, married self, a rather artificial separation between the generations represented in a novel. This is not necessarily a difficulty, but at any rate it is something we do not see in twentieth-century novels, where the continuum between generations is often emphasized.

One might say that these discrepancies are not difficulties at all, just relatively harmless manipulations of reality, justified on the grounds that they allow the author to accommodate, and the reader to enjoy, a good story. Nor does the lack of one-to-one correspondence between the portrait and the objects portrayed mean that the maternal stereotype is altogether inaccurate. On the contrary, like most stereotypes, it furnishes a peculiarly accurate account of the prevailing social values, prejudices, and traditions that give rise to it.[21] Yet these underlying values and prejudices may carry deeper, and more deeply disturbing, implications about attitudes toward mothers in the eighteenth and nineteenth centuries than are presented by the minor liberties taken with plot and character.

For though they may be believable as individuals, the mothers in the novel are somewhat less plausible as a class. Idealized mothers are obviously cardboard cut-outs whom not even their authors seem to have much interest in, inasmuch as they dispose of them so quickly; their significance is almost altogether psychological and so requires little historical analysis at this point.[22] What does bear more examination is the sheer volume of bad mothers in Victorian fiction. Although these mothers represent "reality" on some level—perhaps sociological, perhaps psychological—it is doubtful that their numbers correspond fairly with literal reality. It is only logical to doubt that there could have been such a dearth of competent mothers in the eighteenth and nineteenth centuries. Indeed, if bad mothers were the norm, what grounds would a child have to feel deprived if he did not get a good one? But judging by the novels, that was obviously not the case: society deplored bad mothers then at least as much as it does now. Thackeray's Beatrix Esmond tells Lady Castlewood, "I think I never can forgive you . . . . I always said I was alone; you never loved me, never—and were jealous of me from the time I sat on my father's knee" (*Henry Esmond* 376); Cynthia Kirkpatrick admits to Molly Gibson that her mother "isn't one to help a girl with much good advice" (*WD* 486); even the hardened Alice Marwood, after a life of crime, still feels bitterly the maternal wrongs she has suffered: "Nobody taught [me], nobody stepped forward, nobody cared for [me] . . . . The only care [I] knew . . . was to be beaten, and stinted, and abused" (*DS* 411). Despite the contrast in styles—the Thackeray character speaks in careful, almost theatrical prose, suggesting intense, smoldering feeling; Cynthia's syntax is colloquial and casual; and Alice Marwood is melodramatic in a very Dickensian way—obviously each character is responding to the same painful knowledge: that she *has* been deprived.

This more moderate view of mother-child relationships is supported by the closest thing we have to positive evidence: the diaries, correspondence, and other records of mothers and their children. Though not all classes of British society are equally represented in these records, certainly the middle and upper classes—the ones most characteristic in the novels—are. The actual feelings of nineteenth-century mothers and daughters cannot be read off from these records, using them as evidence the same way the economic historian might use trade figures as evidence. They are texts, and what we find in them is not only traces of actual experience but also the conventions and assumptions through which these experiences are perceived; nonetheless, their limited testimony seems to be that mothers in the late eighteenth and nineteenth centuries were reasonably well adjusted, reasonably well loved, and reasonably productive members of their homes and communities.

For one thing, in contrast to the stereotype of feeble-mindedness, mothers seem to have been capable managers and thinkers. "The exclusive keeping of accounts in diaries shows the scope of women's managerial functions and business acumen," writes Cynthia Huff in *British Women's Diaries*. "[T]hey were often responsible for recording variables such as weather changes, harvest yields, and the acquisition of animals."[23] Nor were mothers' concerns exclusively domestic. Diaries and letters indicate that women participated actively in the public life of Britain, though they did so less than men. Many followed political developments closely, "and virtually all noted particularly noteworthy events in the government": the condemnation of Napoleon was a common strain in many diaries.[24] Diaries even among the working classes frequently mention plays, exhibitions, lectures, public readings, religious services, and sports, and many include extensive reading lists, often responding to character delineation in fiction or drama.[25] The texts Huff examines also reveal the considerable charitable work performed by women when they were not tending to illness (a major occupation), including distributing coal and blankets to the poor, giving money to the needy, and teaching and supervising schools for destitute children (Huff xxxi–xxxiii).

Particularly interesting is a topic which surfaces again and again, as well among conservative women as more radical feminists: this is "a gnawing sense that men's superior status was largely a social construction. . . . Despite some acceptance of stereotypes of female purity and passivity and male worldliness and aggressiveness, the diarists saw men as considerably more flawed than the ideal of the omniscient, benevolent patriarch" (Huff xxvii-xxviii). A similar theme is the difficulties of marriage, for which their diaries and confidences served as a sort of pressure release valve: the Duchess of Devonshire, prototype of the modern-day "supermom," would get up early in order to have time with her small children, then stay up late, often until two or three in the morning, to spend time alone with her husband. The harried Duchess finally "admitted the unadmissable," reports Judith Lewis in *In the Family Way*: "*cette chienne de vie me tue* [this bitch of a life is killing me]"! (68).

As for their relationships with their husbands and children, Lewis finds that by the eighteenth century the traditional, non-emotive marriage had come to be replaced by the "companionate" marriage, marked by private emotions rather than public functions; it is also the period that saw the rise of domesticity. "The family should be a school of sympathy in equality, of living together in love, without power on one side or obedience on the other," wrote Mill.[26] Indeed, Lawrence Stone has said that the modern nuclear family grew out of the British aristocracy.[27]

Apparently this intimacy extended into the bedroom, despite the widespread belief that "[t]he best mothers, wives, and managers of households, know little or nothing of sexual indulgences. Love of home, children, and domestic duties are the only passions they feel."[28] It is clear that at least some women looked forward to marriage as a source of sexual satisfaction, says Judith Lewis. For instance, she cites the prolific Duchess of Leinster, who, widowed after having eighteen children, married her sons' tutor six months later and had three more (37). Indeed, the medical profession's obsession with masturbation in women and the proposed cures of clitoridectomy and ovariotomy, as well as the popularity of birth control (accepted as early as the 1820s) are a revealing source for attitudes to female sexuality as well as a recognition of its existence. An upper-class woman wrote to her fiancée in 1901 to remind him of her rather large order for contraceptive sheaths, colloquially known as "F.L." [French letters]: "Georgie has asked her masseuse about those F.L. . . . I told you about 6 dozen!! ought to be enough even for us I think. . . . You mustn't misunderstand me here. You know I love babies but I do so want to enjoy my married life" (Jalland and Hooper 278).

But most important for controverting the bad mother stereotype is the evidence of close and affectionate ties between mothers of this period and their children. Children, it is clear, were important emotional resources for both parents but especially for the mothers. Though some sociologists, Lawrence Stone and Ann Dally among them, believe that this represents a significant change from earlier centuries, when high infant mortality supposedly discouraged parents from getting too attached to their offspring, others argue that there is ample evidence "to contradict this impression of parental callousness."[29] Most mothers valued each of their children and took seriously their responsibilities in nurturing it:

> Mothers were the ones who, through affectionate bonding, inculcated the sense of self that their children would need to succeed. They nurtured children at the breast and in the schoolroom. . . . Motherhood became a moral, intellectual, and emotional pursuit. It became a woman's greatest source of dignity and emotional satisfaction. (Lewis 225)

Girl children came to be especially appreciated as companions. Lady Sarah Napier expressed the wish in 1790 to have another daughter "to comfort me in my old age," and Frances, Countess of Morley, lamented two miscarriages primarily because they deprived her of the chance of a girl (Lewis 65).

Thus it seems clear that, whatever else they may be symptomatic of, predominantly bad mothers in the novel are not symptoms of predominantly unhappy maternal relations in Victorian and pre-Victorian society. Therefore, if novelists are not precisely mirroring society in their derogatory portraits of mothers, what truths *are* they reflecting? I have noted already MacDonald's theory that the absent mother goads the daughter into selfhood and Honig's related theory that the absent mother allows the story to focus on the child, as well as to let him or her encounter maturing adventures, and I have no doubt these comprise the correct logical explanation. But I suspect there are several additional factors, all working more or less subconsciously, yet all expressing, if indirectly, certain realities about English society and the human mind.[30] One is that the hostility expressed toward mothers in novels (via their idealization as well as their derogation) may be a subconscious response to their depreciation in actual life, for married women were treated as vastly subordinate, denied economic, legal, political, and intellectual rights. Again, both sides of the stereotype arise from an impulse which trivializes and demeans the mother's role and the mother's rights. Laurence Lerner notes that idealizing women, "though it may represent a kind of emancipation, can also be a bulwark against further emancipation: the granting of something trivial in order to resist claims on what really matters" (*Love and Marriage* 139). A bullying article in the *Edinburgh Review* in 1841 reveals how much this denial was a matter of both male supremacy and male paranoia:

> In all modern civilized communities, and especially in the most refined and cultivated portions of those communities, women are treated by men with particular deference, tenderness, and courtesy. Do they owe this treatment to their strength or to their weakness? Undoubtedly to the latter. . . . But let women be made ostensibly powerful; let a sense of competition be introduced; let man be made to feel that he must stand on the defensive—and the spirit of chivalry . . . will speedily cease.[31]

The first half of this excerpt accounts for the idealization of women; the second for their derogation. Behave with proper submission (the male voice seems to say) and we will dress you in the most flattering raiments; but so much as voice an opinion contrary to ours and you will be stripped naked. The madonna is this close to the witch. A growing number of women, married women in particular, apparently would gladly have traded this brand of chivalry for more substantial proofs of respect, but in fact it took until well into the twentieth century to win the most important of them. For most of the period under study, married women had fewer rights than they did in Anglo-Saxon England, when they at least had some control over their property. In the eighteenth and nineteenth centuries, they had virtually none. In fact, upon her marriage, a woman ceased to have an individual legal identity; as William Blackstone, a fixture in eighteenth-century civil law, decreed, "By marriage, the husband and wife are one person in law: that is, the very being or legal existence of the woman is suspended during the marriage, or at least is incorporated and consolidated into that of the husband."[32] This doctrine had the effect of depriving women of any voice in managing or disposing of their property—including gifts and any property she had brought to the marriage. Though it was true that the well-to-do father of a prospective bride could establish a trust for her beyond the reach of either husband or state, only an estimated one in ten women married with a marriage settlement. If a couple divorced, the sole grounds for which was the adultery of the wife, she not only could reclaim no money or property from her husband—she could not even keep her children (until passage of the Infant Custody Bill in 1839, which granted temporary custody of children under seven years of age only). Until protective legislation was passed in 1857, a woman whose husband had deserted her also had no property rights, and until 1891 a woman was subject to physical confinement by her husband. Naturally, a woman who had no legal existence also had no voice in government; most men, and the more conservative women, believed that the franchise was unnecessary to married women who were already represented by their husbands; but "spinsters and widows" had just as much trouble as married women winning the right to vote, which, though the suffrage movement began in earnest by the 1850s, did not finally come until 1918 for women over 30, and 1928 on equal terms with men.[33]

Higher education was even less accessible to married women than to unmarried ones, even though Mary Wollstonecraft had recognized as early as 1792 that inferior education was women's principal oppressor. Before the 1860s women were ineligible for university degrees; many of the poorer classes did not attend school at all; and what education those of the middle and upper classes received was designed to prepare a woman for the only business she needed to know: marriage and mothering. But as Wollstonecraft and others after her pointed out, such superficial training as etiquette, dancing, drawing, deportment, and so on made women unfit for either vocation. "In the regulation of a family, in the education of children, understanding, in an unsophisticated sense, is particularly required: strength both of body and mind" (64–65).

Although some men championed the "Woman Question," including Mill who said, "We are perpetually told that women are better than men, by those who are totally opposed to treating them as if they were as good" (42), nearly all the activism which led to the passage of improved laws and the repeal of oppressive ones was carried out by women, among them Frances Power Cobbe, Emily Davies, Barbara Bodichon, Christabel and Sylvia Pankhurst, Emmeline Pankhurst, Bessie Rayner Parkes, Lydia Becker, and Harriet Taylor (who married Mill), many of them mothers themselves, and all of them intelligent, forceful, principled. Though the women's movement is mentioned infrequently in novels, and though we have no sure grounds for linking the improved treatment of mothers in fiction to the improved laws, nonetheless the strong women at the forefront of the liberation movement may have been a subconscious influence on the emergence of strong mothers in the novels.

Of course, there are some married women in the novels who prefigure the androgynous vision of Woolf and others: women who combine the *anima* of the woman and the *animus* of the male, who are remarkably strong, intelligent, spirited, and also intuitive and pleasant natured. These occur most notably in Jane Austen, in Mrs. Gardiner (*Pride and Prejudice*); but especially in Mrs. Croft, the admiral's wife in *Persuasion*:

> Mrs. Croft, though neither tall nor fat, had a squareness, uprightness, and vigour of form, which gave importance to her person. She had bright dark eyes, good teeth, and altogether an agreeable face; though her reddened and weather-beaten complexion, the consequence of her having been almost as much at sea as her husband, made her seem to have lived some years longer in the world than her real eight and thirty. Her manners were open, easy, and decided, like one who had no distrust of herself, and no doubts of what to do; without any approach to coarseness, however, or any want of good humour. (*P* 48)

Mrs. Croft has always been "blessed with excellent health, and no climate disagrees with [her]," as long as she can be with her naval husband; even on a man of war she claims "never to have met with the smallest inconvenience" (*P* 71). Though she loves and wishes to be with her husband, this is no sign of subservience in her. Mrs. Croft "look[s] as intelligent and keen as any of the officers around her" (*P* 168). And when she, "by coolly giving the reins a better direction herself," saves the Admiral from an upset in their carriage, Anne reflects that their style of driving must be "no bad representation of the general guidance of their affairs" (*P* 92). Anne takes to Mrs. Croft instinctively, likewise Elizabeth Bennet to Mrs. Gardiner. Their relations are friendly, confiding, concerned—in short, maternal. But one sees at once the important qualification. Mrs. Croft is *not* a mother, and though Mrs. Gardiner is, her children are mentioned only in passing. It is her relationship to Elizabeth that defines her for the purposes of the novel. In a similar fashion, Molly Gibson shares with Mrs. Hamley the closeness that is unimaginable with her stepmother. The fact that healthy, intimate relationships with strong maternal figures occur only with surrogate mothers seems to imply that while writers can conceive such relationships, nonetheless some obstacle, perhaps a suspicion of rivalry, perhaps some deeper prejudice, prevents them from envisioning intimacy between the child and her real (in Molly's case adoptive) mother. On the other hand, it happens with even more frequency that the role of the bad mother is transferred to a substitute—for instance an aunt, guardian, or stepmother such as Mrs. Reed in *Jane Eyre*, Mrs. Gibson in *Wives and Daughters*, Aunt Norris in *Mansfield Park*, Madame Duval in *Evelina*, Tabitha Bramble in *Humphry Clinker*, and Miss Havisham in *Great Expectations*. Obviously there are valid artistic reasons for shifting the mother's roles (both the ideal nurturing role and the negative obstructive role) to an aunt or other mature woman; in Tabitha Bramble's case, for instance, she is the more comic for being a blustering old maid with no real power.

Nonetheless, I believe that what we see in such cases is also the common psychological behavior called transference, similar to splitting, in which both good and bad mother appear in the same story.[34] In cases of positive transference, the child's subconscious fear or distrust of its mother is in conflict with its natural affection, and consequently that affection is transferred to a maternal substitute. In negative transference, it is the fear and distrust themselves that are reassigned. Of course I am not saying that this is consciously what Molly and Elizabeth are doing, nor even Gaskell and Austen; merely that transference is so universal and subconscious a behavior that it is sure to be reproduced in fiction from time to time.

If we can assume that unconscious motivations may underlie conscious literary acts, then the two extremes of mother characterization in the novel ("the monster and the madonna") very likely derive from a single though two-sided attitude toward mothers, primarily psychological in origin, but influenced also by literary, cultural, and social factors. In tracing the maternal stereotypes through the succeeding ages and literary forms leading up to the novel, I have assumed that virtually all representations of the mother throughout history, including the idealized and bad mother stereotypes, are at some level rooted in the subconscious as well as in anthropological and cultural history. To go back to Erich Neumann:

> When analytical psychology speaks of the primordial image or archetype of the Great Mother, it is referring, not to any concrete image existing in space and time; but to an inward image at work in the human psyche. The symbolic expression of this psychic phenomenon is to be found in the figure of the Great Goddess represented in the myths and artistic creations of mankind. (*The Great Mother* 3)

This does not deny that in many respects literary traditions, including stock characters or stereotypes, are discrete phenomena, signifying simply the tendency of an author to imitate the popular conceptions of his or her predecessors. It is also true that the figure of the troublesome or silly mother has been a commonplace, almost a topos, in Western literature and folklore, and that one would have to look no further than a comprehensive anthology of English literature to explain—if cursorily—the presence of the silly mother in the Victorian novel. Nonetheless I believe it is false economy to discuss the treatment of the mother in literature in purely literary terms. There are simply too many other potential determinants, from misogyny to mythology to material conditions. For instance, as Jung says, literary tradition alone cannot account for the striking parallels in mothers from geographically-segregated folk traditions.[35] Nor does it account for the fact that the typecast mother has all but disappeared from the English novel today. The way our literature has depicted mothers is an artifact which, if examined, reveals much more than simply literary history.

To provide a quantifiable system for plotting the maternal stereotypes through history, as well as to help explain their significance, I turn here to Vladimir Propp's *Morphology of the Folktale*. First published in 1927, the *Morphology* classifies an entire subgenre (the Russian folktale) according to its recurrent component parts, in order to demonstrate common elements not only in the tales' plots and ancestry but also in the cultural (and, though Propp does not say so directly, the psychic) milieu. Using folk and fairy tales as a unit of measure is especially apt for this study, as nowhere else are maternal stereotypes so easily accessible, so blatantly enacted, and the psychology behind them so readily transparent as they are in these archetypal genres. As Sibylle Birkhäuser-Oeri writes in *The Mother: Archetypal Image in Fairy Tales*,

> [o]bviously fairy tales express an inner psychological reality rather than an external one. The same is true of the mother figures, of course, and that is the reason for their oddity. They represent motherhood in its various aspects; not particular mothers, but symbols or archetypes of mothers. These peculiar figures point out that there is more to the concept and experience of mother than we might imagine. (13)

If many of the patterns of mother portrayal in English novels seem to have descended from fairy tales, it is presumably because, as Birkhäuser-Oeri says of fairy tales, they are "self-portraits of the human soul." Novels are much more self-conscious creations, of course; in fact, fairy tales are distinctly *non*-self-conscious. Nonetheless, throughout the range of the English novel one sees many of the same paradigms that occur in folklore, and hears echoes of the same specific tales.[35]

These distinct narrative patterns characterize all archetypal literature, including the hundreds of folktales examined by Propp. Russian folktales, he says, may be regarded as so many variations on a limited number of themes (or "functions," or "motifs," or "elements"). These narrative units are, in a sense, the standard genetic material from which countless permutations are made. "[T]he number of functions is startlingly small," Propp writes, "compared with the great number of dramatis personae. This explains the two-fold quality of a folktale: it is amazingly multiform, picturesque, and colorful, and, to no less a degree, remarkably uniform and recurrent" (19).

One can say the same of mothers in the pre-modern novel: while colorful and picturesque, they are also "remarkably uniform and recurrent." In fact, their role has not changed in essence from what it has been for hundreds of years, that is, to thwart or at least be helpless to advance the fortunes of the hero and/or heroine. And in fact, this is precisely what most mothers do in fairy tales. Here are the most common mothers' roles or functions as identified by Propp.

(1) She is one of the elders who leaves the child alone, thus exposing him or her to the misfortune which follows (e.g., she sends Little Red Riding Hood visiting through the forest, where a wolf, disguised as her grandmother, tries to eat her; this type corresponds to all the dead mothers in the novel, as well as to mothers like Mrs. Price and Lady Bertram in *Mansfield Park*).

(2) She is the tester or deceiver of the hero or heroine (e.g., she is the witch who lures Hansel and Gretel into her enchanted cottage, there to imprison them; compare this to mothers or mother types like Mrs. Norris, Lady Catherine, and Rachel Esmond, whose abusiveness puts to a severe test all the heroine's strength and integrity).

(3) She is the villain who is projected into the tale by means of the father's remarriage (e.g., she is Snow White's wicked stepmother who plots to have her killed; obviously this paradigm applies to Mrs. Gibson but also by transference to any bad mother surrogate who takes over after the death of the real mother, such as Mrs. Murdstone in *David Copperfield* and Mrs. Reed in *Jane Eyre*).

Mothers do not figure in all folk tales, and they are certainly not the only group to be allotted harmful functions; but it is crucial to note that when mothers *do* have a role, it is almost never (except in the occasional case when the mother is a magic helper) to be actively useful to the hero/heroine. Her part need not be aggressive to be negative. For instance, the mother who innocently sends her children into the forest does not do direct harm, but because the children are separated from her, she is unable to intervene in a crisis. More common, however, is the mother who *is* actively hostile or a hostile projection of the non-aggressive mother. The details differ from tale to tale (she may be a hag, a witch, or a cruel stepmother) but her function is the same: to machinate the ruin of the young and innocent protagonist, who may be a prince, a princess, a peasant girl, a handsome youth, or something similar.

Though the Terrible side of the Great Mother is much more common in fairy tales, sometimes the mother figure *is* helpful. Her supernatural powers enable her to rescue, reward, or otherwise abet the child hero/ine. Most often she is the spirit of the child's own dead mother, reborn as a magic tree or animal; sometimes, as in the story of "Woodminny," she even holds the power of regeneration and rebirth. As such, she is comparable at least in psychological origin to the idealized mothers in the novel, for she represents the qualities of the archetypal Good Mother. Birkhäuser-Oeri thus categorizes such figures as "life-giving nature mothers," "healing nature mothers," "self-renewing mothers," and "transforming mothers" (127–53). An example is the old woman in "The Sweet Porridge" who gives a magic pot to a poor girl whom she meets in the forest. The pot produces "good, sweet millet porridge" on command, so that the girl and her mother "had no further worry about poverty and hunger" (Grimm 358). Obviously the magic woman in the forest is the nurturing, protecting aspect of the archetype, a "life-giving nature mother." (The girl's own mother, on the other hand, is a lame-brain in the old tradition. When the little girl is out of the house the mother forgets the magic words to turn the pot off, and the little girl returns just in time to save the village from drowning in hot cereal.)

There are literally thousands of variants of these and other fairy tales, though as I have said, the predominant mode is that of the threatening mother/stepmother/witch/hag. "The Girl(s) in the Well" is the generic name for a tale type in which a cruel stepmother attempts to overthrow the obedient stepdaughter in favor of her own lazy child. This woman, having either tricked or commanded her stepdaughter to fall into a well, is outraged when the girl returns with gold coins. Smitten with greed, she then orders her own daughter down the well, who either drowns or finds only insects, toads, pitch, or the like. There are at least one thousand versions of this tale from all over the world, making this probably the most widely disseminated of all fairy tale types (Holbek 521). Alan Dundes in *Cinderella: A Folklore Casebook* identifies more than seven hundred variants of the Cinderella tale occurring in China, Africa, Indonesia, the Middle East, Japan, Russia, North America, and throughout Europe and Asia, some dating as far back as the third or fourth century. Likewise there are several hundred versions of Little Red Riding Hood (a.k.a. Little Red Cap), and nearly one hundred cognates of Hansel and Gretel.

A particularly gruesome and therefore particularly memorable motif is that of the mother who either bakes her child in a pie or stew, or who, alternatively, is made to eat such a pie unawares. The latter, of course, is how the vicious Tamora is punished in Shakespeare's *Titus Andronicus*; the tale is also told by the Grimms as "The Juniper Tree": After decapitating her stepson with the lid of a chest, "[t]he mother took the little boy and chopped him up and put the pieces into the pot and cooked him up into a stew" (164).

An interesting oral narrative recorded in *Folktales of England* combines the decapitation and human pie motifs with that of the good spirit who returns as a bird.

> Rosy were a little maid as had a stepmother and her were so wicked and good-for-nothing as twopennorth of God-help-us stuck on a stick. Rosy hadn'no love for she.
>
> One day she took 'n sended Rosy for to get some'at out of gurt chest up over in tallet. And the lid valled down on Rosy and killed 'n.
>
> There her was with her head cutted off by thic lid, and thic wicked toad took'n and cooked 'n and made she into pies vor her father and her two liddle sisters.
>
> [The father and sisters enjoy the pies unaware; the stepmother buries the bones; Rosy comes back "like a bird" and sings her story; the stepmother is abandoned.] "And no one wouldn' neighbor with the wicked toad, zo her died lonesome." (Briggs and Tongue 28)

Similar patterns of mother portrayal are found in Snow White, Sleeping Beauty, East o' the Sun and West o' the Moon, Rapunzel, Snow White and Rose Red, the Twelve Wild Ducks, The Peony Lantern, Bushy Bride, The Two Step Sisters, The Child and The Colt, and so on.[37]

The universal reach of these tales, the countless minor variations in them, the particularizations of place, persons, and culture, all serve to demonstrate the extent to which archetypal tales are "down-to-earth accounts of life in its universal physical and psychological aspects" (de

Witt 315–16). In a close echo of Jung, Holbek explains: "The same archetypes are expressed everywhere; their concrete appearances may be culturally or individually determined, symbols may lose their power to be substituted by others, but *the structure of the human mind which produces them does not change*" (emphasis mine 295).

That fairy tales are prone to psychoanalysis few scholars dispute, especially since the finding, attributed to the German folklorist Ludwig Laistner in 1889 and repeated by Jung, that the recurrent symbols of dreams are paralleled in fairy tales. Adriaan de Witt, a comparatist, agrees:

> All so-called archetypal tales, that is, tales arising directly out of [the] unconscious, and among which fairy tales and myths are the most prominent, have often also been experienced at first as "big dreams," dreams of such impact that when they occur in tribal societies, the individual feels compelled to tell his dreams in the tribal council or gathering in order to have it examined, discussed and evaluated for its deep-lying and important message to the group. (315)

In spite of the widespread belief, says Holbek, that fairy tales are naive, innocent fantasies for children, they should be seen more correctly as documenting the social, sexual, and psychological life of the culture as a whole (266). Whether or not they are factual records is largely irrelevant, he says; the feelings they convey are historical fact and must therefore be regarded as true. Yet he adds this cautionary note: "Psychoanalysis is, however, the analysis of a *psyche*, not of a text, for which reason [the analyst] has to stipulate a mind whose unconscious thoughts and feelings may be deduced from the text" (274).

Since the business of stipulating an unconscious mind is obviously an imprecise one, the only way psychoanalysis has of verifying its conclusions is to check them against a body of similar texts or similar symbols used in similar contexts. This is why the abundance of tales featuring mothers makes them particularly susceptible to interpretation. Though there is still considerable disagreement over details—for instance, psychoanalytical folklorists cannot agree whether Little Red Riding Hood's red hat symbolizes menstruation (e.g., Veszy-Wagner)—nonetheless certain general interpretations regarding the significance of mothers can be fairly confidently made. She is, above all, associated with the main stages in the development of the individual. Says Holbek: "The child is dependent upon his mother and is closely bound to her, but he must develop on his own, or she will turn from protector into devourer, from mother into witch: all symbols have a dark as well as fair aspect."[39] Thus the three women in Hansel and Gretel all represent stages of the individuation process: initially the child is in perfect union with its mother, the Cosmic Mother, the one who dies before or as the tale begins. She is replaced by the stepmother, the Evil Mother, representing materialistic life—"the hard life of illusion and disappointment, of delusion and shattered expectations . . . [the] child has to face Stepmother Earth and her many demands in order to survive."[40] Before Hansel and Gretel have fully matured, however, they attempt to return to the dependent stage (by entering the witch's house), but once inside they manage to achieve the separation completely, symbolized by shoving the witch—the devouring side of the mother—into her own oven. Their return to live and prosper with their father represents, says Arthur Ramos, "the conquest of virility by man and femininity by woman"—that is, the complete socialization of the libido (qtd. in de Carvalho-Neto 170).

The mother in the fairy tale may also represent the feminine principle or mother goddess, but again, she is usually associated not with the nurturing aspect but with the devouring side of the archetype. In *Sleeping Beauty* the mother-goddess malcontent is the fairy godmother who has inadvertently been left out of the christening festivities. She is also the old woman at the castle whose spindle has not been removed. According to Marie-Louise von Franz in *Problems of the Feminine in Fairy Tales*, she is the dark side of the feminine principle forgotten in our civilization, and also the dark, imperfect side of mother nature.

> . . . As our story is a collective and not a personal story, we
> have to find out where it is typical of our civilization, where
> some aspect of the mother-goddess, the archetype of feminine
> nature, has been artificially ignored. The answer is obvious:
> not only sexuality, but also some needs of feminine life have
> been ignored in Christianity. So the girl is cursed. (38–39)

As I point out elsewhere, all patriarchies (not just Christianity) tend to fear maternal omnipotence, and fairy tales often objectify this fear by casting the mother in the form of a hag or witch or, as here, a

malevolent fairy godmother. Dasent observes how, once the ancient
goddesses were identified as evil influences, "even before Christianity
came in," the step was easily made from the powerful goddesses of
Norse legend—the Valkyrie, Norn, priestess, and soothsayer—"into
that unholy deep where heathen hags and witches had their being" (57–
58). The ambivalence about the mother is always there: the child
wishes to remain with its mother, yet defines development in terms of
growing away from her. "In the face of this dependence, lack of
certainty of her emotional permanence, fear of merging, and
overwhelming love and attachment," says Nancy Chodorow, "a mother
looms large and powerful. [Thus she comes] to symbolize dependence,
regression, passivity, and the lack of adaptation to reality" (82). It was
never the intent of fairy tales to resolve these deep-lying feelings,
merely to give concreteness to them.

The mother archetype is apparently so pervasive, in fact, that it
transcends gender. Negative portraits are as likely to be written by
female as male authors, suggesting that, in this regard at least, the
"precious specialty" in women's handling of the novel does not apply.

Why this should be so is suggested by Dorothy Dinnerstein.
Women as well as men have anti-female feelings, she says, because
women, "like men, had female mothers" (90). In other words, the
biological and psychological imperative for clinging to, then rejecting
the mother is the same whether the baby is a girl or a boy, the adult a
man or a woman. But that does not explain why the artifacts of a given
culture should seem to emphasize the malevolence of mothers rather
than their equally impressive positive powers. The answer has to do,
believes Freudian psychoanalyst Karen Horney, with the predominance
of misogynist patriarchies and the fact that men have been primarily
responsible for the "creation of culture":

> Men have never tired of fashioning expressions for the
> violent force by which man feels himself drawn to the woman,
> and side by side with his longing, the dread that through her he
> might die and be undone. . . . The series of such instances is
> infinite; always, everywhere, the man strives to rid himself of
> his dread of women by objectifying it. "It is not," he says,
> "that I dread her; it is that she herself is malignant, capable of

any crime, a beast of prey, a vampire, a witch, insatiable in her desires. She is the very personification of what is sinister."[41]

As Neumann has shown, the specific appearance of the archetype is determined by the prevailing winds of the specific culture. In highly misogynist cultures, therefore, images of the Terrible Mother predominate, regardless whether the author is a man or a woman. In societies where women are valued, on the other hand, the "winds" are more favorable, and more likely to bring out the qualities of the Great Mother, again regardless of the sex of the artist.

Certainly there can be little doubt that mothers in fairy tales are manifestations of the psychological as well as physical conditions in the cultures that create them. However, it is still a long way from fairy tales to novels, and I am not sure that one can prove beyond a doubt that the same impulses that split mothers into extreme character types in folklore are the same ones responsible for the stereotypes in the early novel. After all, folktales are instinctive, collective, unselfconscious gestures of the psyche, not unlike dreams; whereas novels are deliberate, conscious efforts of the individual intellect and will. "The essence of folklore disappears with the development of contemplation," says folklorist Kaarle Krohn. "Folk poetry itself must be unaware of its creator" (25–26). Even assuming that the mother archetype is rooted permanently in every brain, a novelist is trained to process those psychic contents before ever committing them to paper. The raw material of mother-angst that is acceptable in "The Juniper Tree" would have trouble passing inspection in a realistic novel.

Nonetheless, by applying again to Propp's morphology of the folktale, and comparing certain structural and qualitative parallels, one can demonstrate that the images of mothers in folktale are closely related to the images of mothers in the novel, and that these parallels can be traced through intervening genres as well.

Propp catalogs and evaluates the numerous occurrences of the thwarting or deceptive mother formula to show that it is, in fact, a formula. As such his study is not merely a taxonomy. It also has to do with the presence and function of literary conventions, especially those which occur in so-called "realistic" narrative. The paradox that realistic narrative may be heavily laced with formulaic schema is acknowledged by Propp's colleague, A. N. Veselovskij, whose remarks conclude

Propp's study. Considering "the problem of typical schemes," Veselovskij asks:

Can these schemes, having been handed down for generations as ready made formulae capable of becoming animated with a new mood, give rise to new formations? . . . The complex and photographic reproduction on [sic] reality in modern narrative literature apparently eliminates even the possibility of such a question. But when this literature will appear to future generations as distant as antiquity from prehistoric to medieval times seems to us at present—when the synthesis of as great a simplifier as time reduces formerly complex events to the magnitude of points, then the lines of present-day literature will merge with those we are now uncovering in our examination of the poetic traditions of the distant past. The phenomena of schematism and repetition will then be extended across the total expanse of literature. (105)

In the English novel, defined as it is by realism, with its insistence on themes and conflicts from contemporary life, on the one hand, and by romanticism with its stress on originality on the other, we are perhaps not inclined to think of contemporary or even nineteenth- and eighteenth-century literature as part of a continuum of "schematism and repetition." The very word "novel" signifies a departure from, rather than a prolongation of, existing practice. However, perhaps we should begin to look, as Veselovskij does, at even the most contemporary literature as liable to "schemes . . . handed down for generations." What will then appear to be "novel" about the novel is how its realistic, romantic format assimilates the power of these schemes.

In the next chapter, it will be clear that many of Jane Austen's plots are schematic in this way, having reworked some of the most popular folkloric paradigms. Austen's fiction also adapts the other elements of mother portrayal to the realistic style that is her trademark and that was to become the predominant style of the nineteenth century. The recurrence of these traits through the latter part of the mid-nineteenth century, followed by a gradual decline toward the end of that period, suggests that mothers as a character group do indeed share a common heritage and do indeed undergo a significant change.

Notes

1. Elaine Showalter, *A Literature of Their Own* 14. This image sounds again and again throughout the eighteenth and especially in the nineteenth centuries; the best-known example is perhaps Coventry Patmore's poem, "The Angel in the House," but others promoted the Angel with no less zeal: John Ruskin, for instance, wrote in *Sesame and Lilies* (1865) that "[the woman] must be enduringly, incorruptibly good; instinctively, infallibly wise—wise, not for self-development, but for self-renunciation: wise, not that she may set herself above her husband, but that she may never fall from his side" (152); she should be educated "only so far as may enable her to sympathize in her husband's pleasures, and in those of his best friends" (160).

2. I tend to use the term "idealize" loosely throughout this paper, as referring to a literary convention, but I also understand it to have a consciously psychoanalytic interpretation. Psychiatrist Ann Dally, in *Inventing Motherhood: The Consequences of an Ideal*, defines idealization as "a feeling of love towards something or somebody towards whom one actually has feelings of both love and hate. The hate is ignored and so kept from consciousness. The love is unrealistic because it is separated from the hate with which it is actually inextricably connected" (93). Idealization of the mother is a potential consequence of that early ambivalence Dinnerstein refers to. Psychoanalyst Charles Rycroft describes the sequence of events as follows: the child needs the mother, invests much emotion in her, and needs her love. If she fails to satisfy this need, the child withdraws its love and feeling away from her as a real person and directs it inward, toward the image it has of her in its mind. The child splits this image into good and bad and directs its attention and love only onto what is good. What is bad the child ignores, denies, or projects elsewhere. ("On Idealization, Illusion and Catastrophic Disillusion," in *Imagination and Reality* 29–41.)

3. Richardson's Harriet (*Sir Charles Grandison*) and Fielding's Sophia Western (*Tom Jones*) are both motherless in this matter-of-fact way; so are Lydia Melford and the Methodist postillion himself in *Humphry Clinker*, Scott's Anne of Geierstein, Lizzie Hexam in *Our Mutual Friend*, as well as a host of other Dickens characters, including Estella and Pip in *Great Expectations*, the Gradgrind children in *Hard Times*, Miss Wade and the title character in *Little Dorrit*, and David Copperfield's friend Agnes Wickfield; Eliot's Hetty Sorrel, Esther Lyon, and Dorothea

Brooke, Thackeray's Becky Sharpe, Trollope's Eleanor Bold, James' Isabella Archer, and both Heathcliff and Catherine Earnshaw in *Wuthering Heights*. This is merely a representative sampling; there are many more.

4. Edith Lazaros Honig, *Breaking the Angelic Image: Woman Power in Victorian Children's Fantasy* 30. Honig's focus is children's fantasy fiction, not the novel, but as I show later, the archetype is reflected in both genres.

5. Jane Austen and the Tradition of the Absent Mother," in Davidson and Broner, *The Lost Tradition: Mothers and Daughters in Literature* 58–59. Honig offers a related explanation for motherless children: "carefully watchful mothers would keep their children away from rabbit holes, magic clocks, and such, preventing their adventurers from maturing through their adventurous confrontations. A Victorian child would also be expected to confide in his or her mother and tell her about all fantastic adventures that occurred. [L]eaving mothers out of these books was a way of freeing them for the fantastic and supporting the value of an adventure" (25). Honig also admits that the ideal mother "simply presented no narrative possibilities because she was too dull for words" (16).

6. Annis Pratt is no doubt correct in saying that the eighteenth- and nineteenth-century novels dealing with feminine conduct "became a highly popular way of inculcating the norms of womanhood into young readers" (*Archetypal Patterns in Women's Fiction* 14), including the ideal of self-denial. In this regard the novel of manners does what the courtesy books from which it evolved had done before it. See also Joyce Hemlow, "Fanny Burney and the Courtesy Books."

7. The best example of the "poor but dignified" mother may be Dickens' Betty Higden in *Our Mutual Friend*. Though all her own children are dead, she surrounds herself with other people's castoffs, and her attachment to her last dying grandson—"I love him, I love him, I love him"—is expressly maternal: "I love my children dead and gone, in him" (*OMF* 231).

8. Helen Damico describes Yrsa as "an ambivalent figure, potentially beneficent and injurious . . . . She is vengeful, avaricious, cunningly manipulative, and (according to Saxo) a thief. Contrarily, she is depicted as a beneficent treasure-giver—comely, generous, sexually enticing—a

yielding lover . . . and a doting mother" (*Beowulf's Wealhtheow and the Valkyrie Tradition* 108).

9. A popular sexist claim by Victorian physicians was that woman's "natural" state was invalidism; "[t]he stages of the female life cycle and the woman's reproductive destiny were identified by many doctors as special and peculiar sources of ill-health" (Pat Jalland and John Hooper, eds., *Women from Birth to Death: the Female Life Cycle in Britain 1830–1914* [6]). The characteristic infirmity (always patiently endured) of idealized mothers is thus a glamourization of the patriarchal insistence on mothers' pain; while the idly languishing female (Lady Bertram, Signora Neroni, et al.) is its negative inversion.

10. "Mr. Bennet and Mrs. Brown," *The Criterion* (July, 1924), rpt. in *Virginia Woolf: Selections from her Essays* 101.

11. Many of the social and moral guidebooks of the period were issued in sets which invariably included at least one relating to the proper role of mothers and one to the proper role of wives, and their themes were virtually identical. See, for instance, Sarah Ellis' series *The Wives of England, The Mothers of England,* and *The Daughters of England*: "To make [her] husband happy, to raise his character, to give dignity to his house, and to train up his children in the path of wisdom—these are the objects which a true wife will not rest satisfied without endeavoring to attain" (*The Wives of England, Their Relative Duties, Domestic Influence, and Social Obligations* 19).

12. Of course, there is very little sex anywhere in Dickens, but his attitude toward adultery is suggested by his original plan for Edith Dombey: having eloped with Carker, she was then to have died.

13. I realize how ambiguous the term realism is; Ian Watt's definition, with its emphasis on the rejection of universal in favor of individual experience, is the one I have in mind here (*The Rise of the Novel* passim).

14. Amy Williamsen-Ceron, "The Comic Function of Two Mothers: Belisa and Angela" 167–74. The obstructive mother is also a fixture in Elizabethan and Restoration comedy, including *The Maid's Revenge, Love's Cruelty, Rule a Wife and Have a Wife, The Wise Woman of Hogsdon,* Congreve's *The Double Dealer* and *The Way of the World,* John Webster's *The Devil's Law-Case,* and so on. The darker side of the stereotype also appears in mothers like Tamora in *Titus Andronicus,* Volumnia in *Coriolanus,* the faithless Queen in *Cymbeline,* and Margaret

in *Henry VI, Part III* and *Richard III* ("From forth the kennel of thy
womb hath crept / A hellhound," she says to the Duchess of York in
Richard III [IV.iv.47–48]). The tradition of obstructive, cruel, deceitful
mothers may, in fact, be traced throughout history, in for instance,
Clytemnestra, Eve, and Grendel's dam. Useful studies of mothers in
literature from antiquity onwards include Monica Sjoo and Barbara Mor,
The Great Cosmic Mother: Rediscovering the Religion of the Earth;
Phyllis Chesler, *Women and Madness* (good discussions of mothers in
Greek myth); Jane Chance, *Woman as Hero in Old English Literature*;
Martin Puhvel, "The Might of Grendel's Mother"; Jeffrey Helterman,
"*Beowulf*: The Archtype Enters History," (Helterman says Grendel's
mother symbolizes the evil latent in woman's function); Helen Damico,
Beowulf's Wealhtheow and the Valkyrie Tradition; Coppelia Kahn, "The
Absent Mother in King Lear"; and Davidson and Broner, *The Lost
Tradition: Mothers and Daughters in Literature*.

15. In "Jane Austen's Fools," John Lauber says that even though the life of
the fool appears to be a "set of variations on a theme," Austen "does not
repeat herself in her fools any more than in her heroes . . . [they] range
from broad caricature to meticulous realism" (511–512).

16. For examples and discussions of comic types in recent traditions, see J.
Wesley Childers, *Tales from Spanish Picaresque Novels—A Motif-Index*;
and Amy Williamsen-Ceron, "The Comic Function of Two Mothers."

17. *Realism and Consensus in the English Novel* 33. Ermarth's "consensus"
refers to her theory that realism exists only when there is agreement
between all points of view summoned by a text—similar to viewing a
painting. A work by M. C. Escher, for instance, poses contradictory
points of view and is therefore not realistic.

18. "Parents and Children in *Great Expectations*" 21. Also see Arthur A.
Adrian, *Dickens and the Parent-Child Relationship*.

19. See again "Jane Austen and the Absent Mother Tradition." Nancy
Armstrong makes a similar observation in *Desire and Domestic Fiction:
A Political History of the Novel*.

20. *Breaking the Angelic Image* 112. Honig's is a common complaint,
particularly among feminist critics. For a woman, especially an older
woman, to want a life of "significant action," say Sandra Gilbert and
Susan Gubar, "is so monstrous, so unnatural," that she is thought of as a
sort of witch (*The Madwoman in the Attic: The Woman Writer and the*

Nineteenth Century Literary Imagination 42). Mary Daly agrees that "the role of witch was often ascribed to social deviants whose role was feared" (*Beyond God the Father: Toward a Philosophy of Women's Liberation* 64). Merely being past childbearing was a form of deviancy, giving rise to the rather sinister, witch/procuress/midwife figures like Pamela's Mother Jewkes and Moll's Mother Midnight. See Robert A. Erickson, *Mother Midnight: Birth, Sex, and Fate in Eighteenth-Century Fiction (Defoe, Richardson, and Sterne).*

21. For instance, in *The Stereotype of the Single Woman in American Novels*, Dorothy Yost Deegan finds that novels written between 1850 and 1930 portray unmarried women over thirty as unattractive, dependent, and unambitious, even though they were often economically independent and professionally successful. The stereotype reflects, therefore, the common fear of and disgust for "old maids." John Berger's *Ways of Seeing* also considers the extent to which literature and other works of art may function as social/historical documents, as does F. R. Leavis' "Sociology and Literature" in *The Common Pursuit*; see also Morroe Berger's *Real and Imagined Worlds: The Novel and Social Science.*

22. It may be worth making again the distinction between idealization and non-idealization. When a mother is idealized, she is described or remembered in passionately sentimental terms: the most loving, the most wise, the most devout. However, what is unrealistic is not so much the presence of virtues as the implied absence of faults. Idealization thus implies a refusal to acknowledge imperfection. Yet many mothers *were* extremely loving, pious, nurturing: Laurence Lerner says that "there certainly were plenty of Victorian families where the wife was valued for moral influence"; however, rather than looking up to her "in a Dantesque cloud of unknowing," her family regarded her "as a responsible and intelligent guide" (*Love and Marriage* 133).

23. *British Women's Diaries: A Descriptive Bibliography of Selected Nineteenth-Century Women's Manuscript Diaries* xxi. This bibliographic survey excerpts over a hundred diaries representing all strata of British society except the poverty classes. Another intriguing book is Lewis' *In the Family Way*, a study of fifty women in the aristocracy who bore an average of 7.5 children apiece during what is called the century of greatest fertility in the entire history of the English aristocracy (5–6). For similar documentation of the real concerns of real mothers see Pat Jalland, *Women, Marriage, and Politics, 1860–191*, who records dozens of excerpts from contemporary sources; Erna Olafson Hellerstein, Leslie

Parker Hume, and Karen M. Offen, eds., *Victorian Women: A Documentary Account of Women's Lives in Nineteenth-Century England, France, and the United States*; and Helen Heineman, *Restless Angels: The Friendship of Six Victorian Women.*

24. Huff, xxxi–xxxii. Of course, Thackeray implies that Amelia's condemnation of Napoleon is evidence of her inability to think for herself: merely having opinions does not, of course, guarantee their thoughtfulness.

25. Mrs. S. M. Meirs, writing in the 1850s, read all the major writers of the period, including Carlyle, Tennyson, Thackeray, Poe, Byron, Goethe, Macaulay, etc. She also kept a diary for her mother, gave her children lessons, arranged for their entertainment, and took them visiting (Huff 63–64). Huff stresses that such a level of activity was not unusual or extraordinary.

26. John Stuart Mill, *The Subjection of Women* (1869) 45. Of course, the issue of equality was at best a controversial one: an amusing diary dated 1852 and belonging to a farmer's wife features a Punch cartoon titled "Progress of Bloomerism; or a complete change." The husband, holding the baby, asks his wife as she is heading out the door if she will dine at home that evening; she replies no, she will be eating at the club (Huff 65).

27. *The Family, Sex, and Marriage in England, 1500–1800* passim; see also Randolph E. Trumbach, *The Rise of the Egalitarian Family: Aristocratic Kinship and Domestic Relations.*

28. W. Acton, *The Functions and Disorders of the Reproductive Organs*, 4th ed., 1865, 112–13; quoted in Jalland and Hooper 234.

29. In *Inventing Motherhood*, Dally finds that as late as 1865–74, 14 to 16 out of every one hundred infants born alive died before they reached a year old; she echoes Stone in her belief that the low infant survival rate tended to discourage parents from forming strong attachments to their very young children (24–43). However, Valerie Fildes in *Women as Mothers in Pre-Industrial England* notes that "there are many examples of women suffering deep grief at the death of their babies," and quotes Mary Cary's description (in *The Little Horns Doom* [London, 1651], 290) of an ideal world in which "[parents] shall not be afflicted for the loss of their children" (23).

30. Barbara Schapiro, examining the almost pathological expressions of
     mother anxiety occasionally to be found in Romantic poetry, concludes
     that "a work of art, to a large extent, is the manifestation of the emotional
     dynamics and conflicts of the artist's internal world" (*The Romantic
     Mother: Narcissistic Patterns in Romantic Poetry* x).

31. "Rights and Conditions of Women" 204.

32. J. W. Ehrlich, *Ehrlich's Blackstone* 83. William Blackstone's
     commentaries on the laws regarding women are necessary background
     reading for understanding the misogyny behind the legal status of
     women.

33. For discussions of these and other historical factors, see, besides Bauer
     and Ritt and Lewis, Sheila Jeffreys, *The Spinster and Her Enemies:
     Feminism and Sexuality, 1880–1930*.

34. Bengt Holbek calls the phenomemon a "split" when the "conflicting
     aspects of a character are distributed upon two different figures" in the
     same tale. "The identity between them may be deduced from the facts
     that they occupy the same tale role and that they do not interact." Thus,
     the split "creates a distance between the heroine and the opponent which
     allows . . . the unchecked venting of aggressions" (435–36). In cases such
     as Fanny Price's, when there are no good mothers and three bad ones, the
     "split" has already occurred, more or less, in Fanny's head, in her
     awareness that she does not have a loving mother: her resentment is thus
     directed against the three bad ones.

35. Parallels exist not only in the negative portrayal of mothers in folktales
     from almost every continent: there are also parallel positive treatments in
     widely distant cultures. For discussions of several of these see especially
     Judith Ochshorn, "Mothers and Daughters in Ancient Near Eastern
     Literature"; and Helen M. Bannan, "Spider Woman's Web: Mothers and
     Daughters in Southwestern Native American Literature."

36. John Halperin in *Egoism and Self Discovery* notes that novelists are
     particularly fond of the Cinderella motif, including Austen, the Brontes,
     Eliot, Meredith, and James; Patsy Stoneman notes that the first two
     chapters of *Wives and Daughters* are full of references to fairy tales
     (172ff); Gilbert and Gubar point out the origins of the wicked stepmother
     figure (38–39); Honig sees clear parallels between children's fantasy and
     adult novels; and several critics see *Dombey and Son* as rich with fairy
     tale and folklore influence and allusion, especially William Axton

("*Dombey and Son*: From Stereotype to Archetype") and Harry Stone ("The Novel as Fairy Tale: Dickens' *Dombey and Son*").

37. Synopses of many of these are given in Sir George Webbe Dasent, *Popular Tales from the Norse*, but most of them may also be found in the numerous folktale surveys and studies available.

38. "Mothers and Stepmothers in Fairy Tales and Myths" 315–16. Alan Dundes calls fairy tales "time-tested facets of the human spirit" (xvii).

39. Holbek 298. This is of course the standard Freudian interpretation of infantile attachment followed (in healthy individuals) by separation and socialization. See Sigmund Freud, *New Introductory Lectures on Psychoanalysis*.

40. de Witt 317. The Hansel and Gretel interpretation is compiled from a number of sources making basically the same points. The ones I have referred to in particular include those of de Witt and of Emil Lorenz, quoted in Paulo de Carvalho-Neto, *Folklore and Psychoanalysis* 170; Lorenz says the tale expresses completely a fantasy about weaning.

41. *Feminine Psychology* 134–35. Susan Gubar notes also that women were exluded from the "creation of culture." The male is the primary author "and the female his passive creation" ("'The Blank Page' and Female Creativity" 77).

Chapter Two

"Occasionally Nervous and Invariably Silly": Mothers in Jane Austen

Considering what Jane Austen's novels are—mild domestic dramas—one would expect them to furnish a rich proving ground for a study of mothers in the early stages of the English novel. And so they do. After single young women, mothers are Austen's most ubiquitous character type. In the six mature novels there are at least eighteen mothers in supporting roles, besides another seven or eight in the two unfinished novels and *Lady Susan*; in addition to these, several deceased mothers, mother surrogates, and mothers known by reputation only (such as Mrs. Churchill in *Emma*) are also significant. Within this extensive family of mothers one sees virtually all the patterns which I have identified as characteristic of the treatment of mothers in fiction of the period: the comic types, the prominence of the bad mother, the parallels with archetypal and psychological models, the quest for individuation, the socio-economic milieu, and so on. What is so unusual about Jane Austen's treatment of mothers is that she is virtually the first to put them into the context of strict realism. Prior to Austen the predominant type of mother was the idealized or non-existent sort (that is, the mother whose absence is simply never mentioned); Austen is the first novelist consistently to portray mothers as active, individually realized members of their fictional families and communities. The fact that Austen creates such characters while at the same time conforming to the conventions of the maternal stereotypes is an index of her genius; the fact that she conforms to the stereotypes at all is an index not only of her place in literary history but of her share in the archetypal impulses of human history.

We know that Austen scorned to use at least one of the maternal stereotypes, that of the heavily Gothicized mother à la Ann Radcliffe or Fanny Burney. It is one of the improbabilities of the Gothic novel which *Northanger Abbey* makes fun of: "instead of dying in bringing [Catherine] into the world, as any body might expect, [Mrs. Morland] still lived on—lived to have six children more—to see them growing up around her, and to enjoy excellent health herself" (*NA* 13). Nonetheless, Austen's prejudice against convention does not extend so far as to abandon the other side of that practice, the mother as fool. Nearly all of her two dozen or so mothers are flawed, personally and/or morally (in Austen, the one usually presupposes the other). Lloyd W. Brown calls them "inept or worse as parents" and "associated with distorted or atrophied 'feelings' as mothers" (28, 40). LeRoy Smith observes that Austen's mothers "are missing, mean well but cannot act, or are fools" (29). As Margaret Lane says about Charles Dickens' gallery of "shrews, scolds, and near-idiots," so may we say of Austen's bad mothers that they "do seem to recur more frequently than one would expect from any law of averages" (170). Samuel Butler, whose own fictional parents in *The Way of All Flesh* would not win any congeniality contests, said of Austen's that they are "less like savage wild beasts than those of her predecessors, but she evidently looks upon them with suspicion" (52).

Of the whole maternal company, only a handful are unexceptionable, and at least two of these, the mothers of Anne Elliot and Emma Woodhouse, are dead/idealized. As I have noted in the preceding chapter, the pleasant and practical Mrs. Gardiner, embodying what we can take to be Jane Austen's maternal ideal, derives her maternal identity not from her relationship to her own small children (who are not so much as named to us), but to her nieces Elizabeth and Jane. As for the "normalcy" of Mrs. Morland's "useful plain sense" and "good temper," Austen stresses it only insofar as it enforces the anti-Gothic theme of *Northanger Abbey*: her lack of melodrama is a stage property no less than the laundry list Catherine discovers in the recesses of a locked cabinet. For as soon as Mrs. Morland has been introduced, she is, according to the requirements of the tradition, effectively put out of commission by being "so much occupied in lying-in and teaching the little ones, that her elder daughters were inevitably left to shift for themselves" (*NA* 15). Likewise, the only other mothers whose characters and judgment appear to be sound, such as Mrs. Blake in the unfinished novel *The Watsons* and Lady de Courcy in *Lady Susan*, have such minor parts that one hardly recalls them. In *Sanditon*, which the author barely had time to begin before illness made her put it aside, there is a glimpse of a mother who is not only agreeable *and* sensible but also quite vital; however, Mrs. Heywood was probably not destined to be a significant figure. It is unlikely that Austen planned any further elaboration of her beyond the second chapter, as she and the rest of her family remain behind while Charlotte goes to Sanditon with the Parkers. Mrs. Parker is more in the established Austen vein: though "evidently a gentle, amiable, sweet tempered Woman," she is "not of capacity to supply the cooler reflection which her own Husband sometimes needed, & so entirely waiting to be guided on every occasion, that whether he were risking his Fortune or spraining his Ancle, she remained equally useless" (*S* 372). And as for Lady Denham (a sort of stepmother to Clara Brereton), she has a "shrewd eye," a "self-satisfied air," and a manner that is "rather downright & abrupt" (*S* 391). However, in spite of these Lady Catherine-like faults, Lady Denham is really more like David Copperfield's Aunt Betsy: hers is "not an unagreable Countenance," and there is "a good humour & cordiality about her—a civility & readiness to be acquainted . . . & a heartiness of welcome towards her old friends" (*S* 391) that prompt one to wonder if perhaps Jane Austen was beginning to see more potential for complexity in her mother figures. On the other hand, Lady Denham is not a mother, and Austen invariably casts her positive maternal figures (those who are not dead) as surrogates. Since, therefore, her treatment of mothers is primarily and fundamentally derogatory (rather than primarily idealized), Austen may be seen as having rejected one convention only to emphasize another.

To say that Jane Austen relied on convention in creating a major portion of her characters is perhaps misleading, for Austen is a highly original artist. "[O]f all English and American novelists Jane Austen is perhaps the most secure in her reputation as a writer who delivers a compact and credible fictional world, orderly and sufficient within itself yet tangential at every point to our own disordered lives," says A. Walton Litz (64). Nonetheless, it is not unreasonable to ask whether her use of maternal stereotypes undermines or at least restricts her realism. The answer, I think, is: undermines, no; restricts, yes. One can hardly say that Austen's fiction suffers as a result of the limited way it portrays mothers. On the other hand, one *can* say that by limiting her mothers' dramatic complexity, Austen left a particularly rich field of characterization and interaction virtually unexplored. According to Margaret Kirkham, "the new species of writing, of its very nature, required, if it were to be a truth-telling form of literary art, . . . an examination of what was natural and probable in sexual and familial, as in other kinds of social relationships" (17). Certainly it is at least as probable that a girl would have a good mother as a bad one, but this rarely happens in Jane Austen. Similarly, Leroy Smith's comment in *Jane Austen and the Drama of Woman* that "[m]ore than any other novelist of her time she presents women who were potentially complete human beings" (28) also has to be reconsidered if one is to apply it to her mothers. Smith's is a thoughtful gender-oriented reading of Austen; he perceives, for instance, that the question of women's freedom in a world ruled by men is at the center of Austen's fiction: "What she found in the parlour was the drama of woman's subjugation and depersonalization in a patriarchal society"; nonetheless, he fails to draw a connection between Austen's theme of depersonalized women and the fact that Austen herself caricatured an entire segment of the parlour population. Thus, when he says that "Austen describes a potential in women that is substantially modern in character . . . a promise of individual happiness and fulfilment, social harmony and the full development of one's human possibilities" (29, 38), he clearly is not talking about married women with children.

Like most novelists of the period, Austen's focus is the young, single woman; with few exceptions, she alone is liable to grow. For the rest, their lots and personalities are fixed. The good (dead) mothers remain essentially perfect, just as the bad ones end with the same flaws they started with. "I wish I could say, for the sake of her family," says the narrator of *Pride and Prejudice*, that so much good fortune transformed Mrs. Bennet into a "sensible, amiable, well-informed woman" (*PP* 385); but no such miracle occurred. The only mother who shows evidence of improvement is Mrs. Dashwood, chastened into moderation by seeing one daughter nearly die, the other made intensely unhappy, by her own self-indulgence and immaturity: "She now found that she had erred" (*SS* 355). But since this scene comes at the end of the book, it suggests more an absolution of faults than a rehabilitation.

This either-or depiction of mothers thus represents a certain stagnancy in otherwise organic characterization which, according to Smith and others, is an Austen trademark. "In her view human personality is a *mixture* of virtues and faults," Smith says (my emphasis, 28). The response must be, again, that Austen did not see mothers as multidimensional personalities but types. Of course, neither did anybody else of her literary generation. Austen is thus hardly a reactionary in her negative depiction of mothers. In "Jane Austen and the Traditions of Comic Aggression," Ian Watt reminds us that

> when Jane Austen began to write there was no established narrative tradition that would serve her turn. More specifically, earlier writers of English comic novels, such as Fielding, Smollett, and Fanny Burney, had in different ways adopted the polar opposition between good and bad characters which is typical of stage comedy from the Greeks on. Through the finer and more detailed psychological calibration of her narrative, Jane Austen made the hero and heroine psychologically complex, and therefore capable of internal and external development. By this means the traditional conflict of "good" and "bad" characters in comedy was internalised as a conflict within and between the "good" characters. (191)

If Watt is right, then Austen's reputation as a realist need not be impugned. One must allow merely that her realism was selective, as indeed all character portrayal is, her principal concern being to develop one or two central characters in a psychologically credible fashion. This left her with a "problem," however: how to achieve the humor which, according to Watt, "stage comedy has traditionally allotted to other actors—to the witty helpers, blocking characters, and villains" (192). Austen gave some of these aggressive functions to the protagonists themselves (for example the verbal sparring between Darcy and Elizabeth), yet added to their dialogue a high degree of both psychological and moral acuity. Some of these comic functions, however, continue to be performed by the traditional roles, those which Austen apparently still regarded primarily as "humours"—above all the obstructive, vindictive, or bungling mothers.

Thus her mothers are stock characters inherited from traditions predating the novel and destined to endure for many years to come. The great step Jane Austen made over the mothers of farce or fairy tale, however, is that she would only use them if she could make a case for their psychological credibility: one might say that, in her treatment of mothers, she is a realistic conventionalist. For instance, *Northanger Abbey* rejects the more absurd conventions from the Gothic novel, such as the irresponsible chaperone:

> It is now expedient to give some description of Mrs. Allen, that the reader may be able to judge, in what manner her actions will hereafter tend to promote the general distress of the work, and how she will, probably, contribute to reduce poor Catherine to all the desperate wretchedness of which a last volume is capable—whether by her imprudence, vulgarity, or jealousy—whether by intercepting her letters, ruining her character, or turning her out of doors. (*NA* 19–20)

However, by using some of these very conventions in de-romanticized form (Catherine's physical separation from her own mother, Mrs. Allen's total lack of guidance), Austen implies that they have some validity, and *Northanger Abbey* is an attempt to define where that validity lies. Susan Peck MacDonald notes, for instance, that the absence of a mother *may* constitute a very real hazard to a child. Catherine may not be stalked by a wolf the moment she is out of sight of home, but she is made no less vulnerable by the fact that her mother is too busy having babies to pay attention to her. As for Mrs. Allen, who takes "more care for the safety of her new gown than for the comfort of her protegee" (*NA* 21), MacDonald says, "[T]he narrator's comments on the inadequate chaperone figure are directed only against its melodramatic trappings, not against its psychological substance, for Mrs. Allen's inadequacies do cause Catherine distress" (62).

It seems likely that, *because* they threatened to look too much like types, Austen saw a need to make her mothers ring true in other ways: in the variety of their personalities, in the nuances of their speech and manners, and especially in the effects of their behavior on their children. Thus they may nearly all be fools, but as John Lauber says they are fools such as only the most inventive author can create, "with nearly infinite authority," ranging "from broad caricature to meticulous realism" (512). Mrs. Bennet is one of those broad caricatures and so is the other memorable matriarch in *Pride and Prejudice*, Lady Catherine de Bourgh. Harding points out that Austen's caricatures work on two levels: one is the level of pure exaggeration and simplification; this is the level which makes us laugh, implying that "in some sense we see them as not seriously mattering"; the other level occurs when, though *we* continue to see them as ridiculous, they pose a very real threat to the heroine (89–90). This is certainly true of both of these women: their characters are reducible to a single, exaggerated dimension. Mrs. Bennet's monomania is that of getting her daughters married; Lady Catherine's that of presiding over the world. Each woman responds to events or people entirely as they do or do not interfere with that single controlling motive. Nonetheless, ridiculous though this makes her, each woman is capable of turning absurdity into what is very real danger to the heroine. Thus she recalls Susan MacDonald's thesis about the absent-though-present mother: "If the mother is to be present during her daughter's maturation, the mother must be flawed in some way, so that instead of preventing her daughter's trials, she contributes to them" (59).

Lady Catherine's ruling monomania is the need to dominate. Consequently she has great pleasure in toadies, but despises anyone who refuses to be impressed by her. As Mr. Collins hints to Elizabeth, Lady Catherine "likes to have the distinction of rank preserved" (*PP* 161). That she "will not think the worse of" Elizabeth for being "simply dressed" is true enough, though not in the way Mr. Collins means. It would be more accurate to say simply that, as Lady Catherine intends to be contemptuous of Elizabeth anyway, she will like her better for making herself contemptible. What Austen exaggerates, of course, is the fact that no amount of ostentation and intimidation can hide the fact that Lady Catherine is in fact exceedingly ill-bred and ignorant. Elizabeth wonders how she can bear the sycophantic manner with which "every dish was commended, first by [Mr. Collins], then by Sir William" throughout the dinner; but far from being annoyed, "Lady Catherine seemed gratified by their excessive admiration, and gave most gracious smiles" (*PP* 163). What this woman lacks, of course, is any "extraordinary talent or miraculous virtue" which could go toward explaining her self-importance, and therefore Elizabeth does not think she has anything to fear from her: "[she] suspected herself to be the first creature who had ever dared to trifle with so much dignified impertinence" (*PP* 166).

However, though we ourselves never cease to laugh at Lady Catherine, D. W. Harding points out that our view of her power is altogether different from Elizabeth's. When the dowager comes to Longbourne to demand Elizabeth's renunciation of her nephew, "[t]he handling of [Lady Catherine] as a caricature is a convention between author and readers; the other fictional figures are not party to it. . . . for Elizabeth she is a threat, a very real person" (89). Elizabeth feels no such security as the audience enjoys: "She knew not the exact degree of [Darcy's] affection for his aunt, or his dependence on her judgment, but it was natural to suppose that he thought much higher of her ladyship than *she* could do" (*PP* 360). On the one hand Lady Catherine must be assailable enough that she may eventually be overcome; on the other she must be sufficiently potent to make her overthrow a significant personal victory for Elizabeth. Therefore the scene in the garden when Elizabeth faces off with Darcy's aunt is an updated version of the witch being shoved into her own oven.

"What a fine thing for our girls!" exclaims Mrs. Bennet, in one of her characteristic enthymemes, of the news that a wealthy bachelor is moving in next door. And after twenty years of marriage, her husband knows exactly what she means, though he teases her into spelling it out: "You must know that I am thinking of his marrying one of them" (*PP* 4). She is driven by a single goal: "The business of her life was to get her daughters married" (*PP* 5). Thus the rumor of a new bachelor in the neighborhood is to Mrs. Bennet what the scent of blood is to a shark. Told that Mrs. Long has promised to introduce Mr. Bingley to the Bennets, she snaps, "I do not believe Mrs. Long will do any such thing. She has two nieces of her own. She is a selfish, hypocritical woman, and I have no opinion of her" (*PP* 6). She is prepared likewise to sever relations with her friends the Lucases when Charlotte accepts Mr. Collins: "a month passed away before she could speak to Sir William or Lady Lucas without being rude, and many months were gone before she could at all forgive their daughter" (*PP* 127). The opposite reaction occurs when Lydia, her utterly irresponsible teenager and the apple of her eye, "has to" get married (in the eighteenth-century sense of the phrase), and the family (so they think) must borrow from Mr. Gardiner the several thousand pounds necessary to buy Wickham's cooperation. Far from feeling any of the shame which oppresses the rest of the family, Mrs. Bennet cries, "[I]t is all very right; who should do it but her own uncle? . . . and it is the first time we have ever had any thing from him, except a few presents. Well! I am so happy. In a short time I will have a daughter married" (*PP* 306). The greedy, acquisitive quality of all this does indeed make one think Mrs. Bennet is in a particularly cutthroat sort of "business"—she reminds one of a commodities broker, weighing her options and lining up her sellers and buyers for when the market opens. This analogy has of course been applied to many of Austen's novels by critics like Mark Schorer and Lloyd Brown[1]; but only Mrs. Bennet so wholeheartedly embodies it. Such single-mindedness makes her ridiculous, but as Harding notes, it also makes her potentially dangerous: not only when she tries to force Elizabeth to accept Mrs. Collins but even more when she jeopardizes the futures of her two oldest (and most deserving) daughters by insulting Mr. Darcy, whose opinion she has not, thanks to her distorted reckoning, valued properly.

Mrs. Bennet and Lady Catherine are undoubtedly Austen's most memorable mothers, and yet I think they are not her most skillfully drawn. In Lady Middleton and Mrs. John Dashwood one sees much finer, subtler irony and, consequently, a much closer approach to realism. As John Lauber points out, perhaps facetiously but with some truth, Austen's "insipid fools" are necessarily realistic because "insipidity cannot be caricatured" (513). Instead Austen relies on indirection, satire, the veiled sarcasm, to convey how genuinely hateful and self-serving a mother can be. In fact, what Austen found so repugnant about insipid people is that their dullness is a blind behind which they indulge the most ungoverned impulses. When Laurence Lerner, looking at a scene in *Sense and Sensibility*, says that Jane Austen most admired the ability to "resist impulse" (*The Truthtellers* 187), he was speaking of Lady Middleton's children—but clearly the ungoverned child is an extension of the ungoverned parent, and Austen's satire falls more heavily on the latter.

The scene in which Mrs. John Dashwood racks her brain for arguments that will convince her husband to dishonor his death-bed promise to his father without reflecting ignobly on herself is a remarkable piece of sophistry:

To take three thousand pounds from the fortune of their dear little boy, would be impoverishing him to the most dreadful degree. She begged him to think again on the subject. How could he answer it to himself to rob his child, and his only child too, of so large a sum? And what possible claim could the Miss Dashwoods, who were related to him only by half blood, which she considered as no relationship at all, have on his generosity to so large an amount. It was very well known that no affection was ever supposed to exist between the children of any man by different marriages; and why was he to ruin himself, and their poor little Harry, by giving away all his money to his half-sisters?

"It was my father's last request to me," replied her husband, that I should assist his widow and daughters."

"He did not know what he was talking of, I dare say; ten to one but he was light-headed at the time." (*SS* 8–9)

One by one Fanny blocks and parries each of her husband's arguments, dropping the stakes steadily from three thousand pounds to fifteen hundred to a hundred a year to fifty, until in the end Fanny has reinterpreted their obligation to mean an occasional present of fish or game. Lady Middleton is cut from the same cloth: "There was a kind of cold hearted selfishness on both sides, which mutually attracted them; and they sympathised with each other in an insipid propriety of demeanor, and a general want of understanding" (*SS* 229). Austen demonstrates their common heritage in the scene where the mothers and grandmothers compare the heights of Fanny's Harry and Lady Middleton's William. "Had both the children been there, the affair might have been determined too easily," says the narrator, "but as Harry only was present, it was all conjectural assertion on both sides, and every body had a right to be equally positive in their opinion, and to repeat it over and over again as often as they liked" (*SS* 234). That ironic little word, *too*, assures us that, far from wishing to settle the conflict, they actually relish the dispute, implying that mothers are instinctively combative, no matter how trivial the issue, and are restrained from more open hostility only by decorum and pride:

The two mothers, though each really convinced that her own son was tallest, politely decided in favour of the other. The two grandmothers, with not less partiality, but more sincerity, were equally earnest in support of their own descendent. Lucy, who was hardly less anxious to please one parent than the other, thought the boys were both remarkably tall for their age, and could not conceive that there could be the smallest difference in the world between them; and Miss Steele, with yet greater address gave it, as fast as she could, in favour of each. Elinor, having once delivered her opinion on William's side, by which she offended Mrs. Ferrars and Fanny still more, did not see the necessity of enforcing it by any further assertion; and Marianne, when called on for her's, offended them all, by declaring she had no opinion to give, as she had never thought about it. (*SS* 234)

The main difference between Fanny and Lady Middleton is that Lady Middleton has a greater fortification of children and so demands proportionally more consequence and flattery, at proportionally less cost of consideration or exertion to herself. In scenes like these Austen very likely *does* see mothers with their children as representative of relations among adults.

She is assuredly no Dickens in this regard. Austen's only concern in bringing children into the action is to magnify the behavior of the adults. There are few models of appropriate childcare, the best perhaps being seen in Jane Bennet with her nieces and nephews, "teaching them, playing with them, and loving them" (*PP* 239). But Jane is far outnumbered. Mary Musgrove keeps her children "in tolerable order [only] by more cake than is good for them" (*P* 45); Lady Middleton's four brats "[pull] her about, [tear] her clothes, and put an end to every kind of discourse except what related to themselves" (*SS* 34); the adolescent Bertram girls are left to amuse themselves by "making artificial flowers or wasting gold paper" (*MP* 14); and while Isabella Knightly's maternal vigilance is neurotically hyperactive, Mrs. Price's is woefully moribund.

I think the reason Mrs. Price strikes the reader as perhaps the most realistic of all Austen's mothers is that there is essentially no comedy to lighten the serious implications of her poor parenting. Although Austen obviously can make her mothers wonderfully comic when she chooses, in the assessment of Mrs. Price there is neither humor nor irony. Although she seems briefly to recall Mrs. Dashwood in having, though not regulating, the "proper" maternal instincts, it soon becomes apparent that Mrs. Price has none of that impartial affection that Mrs. Dashwood feels for Elinor and Marianne. It is therefore the more poignant when Fanny, receiving a letter expressing "so natural and motherly a joy in the prospect of seeing her child again," begins to look forward to finding "a warm and affectionate friend in the 'Mamma' who had certainly shewn no remarkable fondness for her formerly" (*MP* 371); but where "she had hoped much," she finds, to her great disappointment, "almost nothing." Returning to Portsmouth for a family visit, she realizes that "her mother [is] a partial, ill-judging parent, a dawdle, a slattern, who neither [teaches] nor restrain[s] her children, whose house [is] the scene of mismanagement and discomfort from beginning to end, and who [has] no talent, no conversation, no affection towards herself" (*MP* 389–90). This, for Austen, is a strikingly explicit judgment; its impact depends at least partly on our never having heard such vehemence in her tone before.

In fact, when discussing parental sins, Austen is often at her least satiric. The reason, presumably, is that she wishes to convey the seriousness of the effects of bad parenting. The scene in which Elizabeth reflects on her parents' role in Lydia's behavior is one of the most sobering passages in *Pride and Prejudice*: "she had never felt so strongly as now, the disadvantages which must attend the children of so unsuitable a marriage" (*PP* 236). While Austen differentiates, both by tone and language, between venial and mortal failings—Mrs. Musgrove's sentimentalism hurts no one, for instance, and even Mrs. Bennet's hypochondria would be forgivable if she did not use it as an excuse to ignore her duties as a mother—she makes it clear that selfishness in a parent, whether by neglect or design, is paid for by the judgment, self-esteem, or character of the children, usually to the eventual sorrow of all parties. Lady Bertram's "hands-off" style of household management makes her as culpable as Mrs. Norris when that family's complacent existence is suddenly and violently uprooted. Lady

Susan's self-love precludes any hope of affection for her daughter, "who was born," she says, "to be the torment of [her] life" (*LS* 245), and even though she calls Frederica "the greatest simpleton on earth," still the girl has sense enough to know she is despised. "The poor girl looks so unhappy that my heart aches for her," her aunt writes, "perfectly timid, dejected and penitent" (*LS* 270). Lady Susan's selfishness is certainly monstrous, but Mrs. Dashwood's exaggerated emotionalism is just as much a form of self-gratification, the folly of which is felt by all of her children. Marianne suffers the most volubly, but that does not make Elinor any less a victim of her mother's misjudgment. Like most Austen heroines, Elinor must continually run interference for her parent, supplying the propriety and practicality that her mother lacks or, more accurately, that her mother refuses to cultivate. As the Dashwood women prepare to leave Norland for good, Marianne and her mother are pleased to prostrate themselves with sorrow, and yet

> Elinor, too, was deeply afflicted; but still she could struggle, she could exert herself. She could consult with her brother, could receive her sister-in-law on her arrival, and treat her with proper atttention; and could strive to rouse her mother to similar exertion, and encourage her to similar forbearance.
> (*SS* 7)

Having to answer for responsibilities and perform duties that should properly belong to her mother makes Elinor a strong and interesting person, of course; but the reader is meant to feel that there are more appropriate and fairer ways to develop resourcefulness in a young woman. Besides, Elinor is an exceptional woman (as are Elizabeth Bennet, Anne Elliot, Emma Woodhouse, Catherine Morland, and Fanny Price) whose resources have somehow proved equal to the challenges of parental mismanagement. Unfortunately, Austen implies, most cases of neglect result not in outstanding heroes and heroines but in maladjusted and unhappy adults.

Austen, in fact, might be seen as prefiguring such early modernists as Meredith in *The Ordeal of Richard Feverel* and Butler in *The Way of All Flesh* in her frequently-expressed conviction that bad children are invariably the product of bad guardians. Fanny Price questions whether

Mary Crawford's habitual impropriety "is a reflection itself upon Mrs. Crawford, as her niece has been entirely brought up by her. . . . She cannot have given her right notions" (*MP* 63–64). Mary Crawford herself, hearing a story about an ungoverned young girl, immediately charges the blame to the mother (possibly the author's foreshadowing of disasters to come, or perhaps an unconscious effort on Mary's part to exonerate her own behavior?): "Mothers certainly have not yet got the right way of managing their daughters. . . . it was entirely the mother's fault" (*MP* 50–51). In *Pride and Prejudice*, after Lydia has disgraced the family and nearly ruined herself, Mrs. Bennet is indicted as "the person to whose ill-judging indulgence the errors of her daughter must be principally owing" (*PP* 287). And when Marianne Dashwood ventures to blame her own misjudgment for the events which nearly cost her her reputation, not to mention her life, Mrs. Dashwood interrupts: "Rather say your mother's imprudence, my child. . . . *she* must be answerable" (*SS* 352).

At this point Elinor keeps silent, preferring to let both mother and daughter accept their proper share of responsibility and regret. Austen may subscribe to the theory that behavior is largely determined by environment but not to the extent that it nullifies individual freedom. Self-government, we are told, is not a knowledge which Marianne had been unable to learn but one which she "had resolved never to be taught" (*SS* 6). The ability (and desire) to make intelligent, ethically correct choices is what distinguishes the Austen heroine from her non-heroic associates and allows her to control her own destiny; to give the mother (or anyone else) absolute jurisdiction over her choices would be to write the most archetypal sort of fairy tale (which is what Richardson, by entirely subjugating the wishes of his heroine to those of her enemies, comes close to doing in *Clarissa*).

In Austen, the mother, whether by giving poor guidance or by removing good guidance, has only enough power to put obstacles in the heroine's way—and that only temporarily. Once she has matured, and earned her reward of house, husband, and happiness, she is free from her mother's damaging powers forever. In this regard Austen's plots conform fully to the individuation process outlined by the fairy tale. Because Austen makes her mothers so entertaining as individuals, the reader little notices that their bad influence is depicted as if it were a minefield which, once negotiated, the heroine need never encounter again; nonetheless, such portrayals vastly oversimplify and underestimate the dynamics of relationships and the complexity of the individual. By the twentieth century this trend shall have been utterly reversed.

One cannot dispute, then, that Jane Austen drew her mothers with infinitely more subtlety and attention to psychological detail than Burney or Radcliffe or any of her other predecessors; yet as I have just suggested, there is always a danger, when one is dealing in stereotypes, of overlooking, or trivializing, or becoming insensitive to, what is worthy and unique in the individual. Susan Morgan puts it this way:

> The forms of thought which often blind us begin as generalities. . . . To invoke universals is to live in a world of forms, to think with all the spaciousness and all the hollowness of preconceptions and thus withdraw from life in its demanding and inconclusive particularity. (10)

Morgan is referring here not to Austen's own perceptions but those of her characters, although her comments might apply in one sense to Austen herself. Although the ability to form conclusions based on a sampling of evidence is what separates intelligent from unintelligent life, it is also what creates prejudices. The fact that Austen draws virtually no good mothers and casts the few she does in powerless roles, suggests that she accepted, in literature at least, the prejudicial view that a mother's only real powers are negative. The explanation provided by Susan MacDonald, that "the good, supportive mother is potentially so powerful a figure as to prevent her daughter's trials from occurring, to shield her from the process of maturation, and thus to disrupt the focus and equilibrium of the novel" (58), goes far to explain why the mothers of Austen's heroines are flawed, but it does not account for the many other bad mothers who are hardly significant to the heroine's fate. If to be a mother in Jane Austen's fiction is to be somehow inadequate, then perhaps Jane Austen is not merely following tradition: perhaps this is how she viewed mothers in reality.

And in fact there are good reasons to think that Austen did *not* like motherhood—and extended that dislike, at least in the abstract, to mothers. One, though not the most telling, is that she objected to the physical demands of mothering, especially the difficult childbirths and the frequently unruly children. References to children, childbirth, and childrearing in both her fiction and her correspondence, when they are not cursory or conventionally polite, are negative. To her favorite niece Fanny Knight, a young woman who apparently shared her aunt's ironic eye and some of her literary talent, she wrote "by not beginning the business of Mothering quite so early in life, you will be young in Constitution, spirits, figure & countenance, while Mrs. William Hammond is growing old by confinements and nursing" (*Letters* 483; 13 Mar 1817). She had seen women die in or be months in recovering from labor, and this may be one reason, when she suspects her cousin Anna Lefroy to be pregnant with her third child, she remarks, "Anna has not a chance of escape. . . . Poor Animal, she will be worn out before she is thirty.—I am very sorry for her.—Mrs. Clement too is in that way again. I am quite tired of so many Children. Mrs. Benn has a thirteenth" (488; 23 Mar 1817). To the prolific Mr. and Mrs. Deedes she recommends the contraceptive of "the simple regimen of separate rooms" (480; 20 Feb 1817). And upon learning of another such acquaintance: "poor Woman! how can she be honestly breeding again?" (210; 1 Oct 1808). All of these comments, though expressing a sincere compassion for the plight of the "breeding" woman, seem also to blame them for allowing themselves to be so oppressed.

The pictures of young children in her letters correspond pretty well to those in the fiction. "The house seemed to have all the comforts of little Children, dirt & litter," she writes to Cassandra. "Mr. Dyson as usual looked wild, & Mrs. Dyson as usual looked big" (121; 1 Feb 1801). This visit might have been the inspiration for the memorable scenes of Fanny's homecoming in *Mansfield Park*: here the children are "ragged and dirty," with nothing to do but "run about and make a noise"; the boys, with "their hot faces and panting breaths," yell and tumble about and kick each other in the shins (*MP* 381, 383). When Lady Middleton's children pull on the Misses Steele's sashes or when Anne's nephew climbs onto her back like a little monkey, one is reminded of another letter to Cassandra telling how "[our little visitor] is now talking away at my side & examining the Treasures of my Writing-desk drawer. . . . What is become of all the Shyness in the World?" (178–79; 8 Feb 1807).

Yet Austen's resentment against mothers apparently went much deeper than that their children destroyed *their* health and disrupted *her* privacy. A second important letter to Fanny Knight suggests that a woman becomes a mother at the expense not merely of her health but of her very personhood. Increasingly anxious about Fanny's beaux, she writes, with more passion than usual,

> Oh! what a loss it will be when you are married. You are too agreable in your single state, too agreable as a Neice. I shall hate you when your delicious play of mind is all settled down into conjugal & maternal affections. (478–79; 20 Feb 1817).

Even if, as Lloyd Brown observes, Austen's earlier letter to Fanny may be dismissed as the childless woman's "envy of the maternal role," yet in the second,

> Austen seems to be more preoccupied . . . with the suspicion that motherhood as she knew it in her society seemed incompatible with the physical and intellectual vigor of the unmarried and childless woman. . . . Clearly, Austen is suggesting that marriage as an institution encourages a sense of roles, and that this role-consciousness subordinates even the complex personality of a Fanny Knight to the predetermined patterns of conjugal and maternal roles. (31–32)

Many critics consider Austen, particularly in light of her views on mothering and marriage, a feminist. Jane Austen was a woman's advocate, says Park Honan, "[a]s much as Aphra Behn or Mary Astell or gifted writers of her time such as Hannah More and Mary Hays" (40). Brown says that her "apparent preoccupation with unusually individualistic women" indicates her larger concern with the woman's experience as a whole (37). And Margaret Kirkham contends that "Jane Austen's heroines are not self-conscious feminists, yet they are all exemplary of the first claim of Enlightenment feminism: that women share the same moral nature as men, ought to share the same moral status, and exercise the same responsibility for their own conduct" (84).

Such ideas were not original to Austen. "The feminist tradition in the novel was well established when Jane Austen began writing," Bradbrook says (90). *The Female Quixote* by Charlotte Lenox, published in 1752 and ridiculing false taste and behavior, was apparently an important influence on *Northanger Abbey*, and *Sir*

Charles Grandison, one of Austen's favorite novels, includes a passage about the inequities of women's station; one assumes Austen accepted the philosophy. Bradbrook continues:

> The theme of education, the mistakes caused by self-deception encouraged by wrong standards and ideals, the attempt to live in accordance with principles that cannot be applied to the world of ordinary, normal personal relationships, lie behind much of Jane Austen's criticism of feminine triviality. (90)

Austen would have encountered such thinking not only in fiction but also, most likely, in a number of thinkers before and contemporary with her, particularly Catherine MacAuley and Mary Wollstonecraft. Although Austen's purpose was never didactic, nor her views ever so radical as Wollstonecraft's, nonetheless certain passages of *A Vindication of the Rights of Woman* (1792) echo distinctly in Austen's depictions of mothers. Compare, for instance, Mrs. Bennet's "I certainly *have* had my share of beauty, but I do not pretend to be any thing extraordinary now. When a woman has five grown up daughters, she ought to give over thinking of her own beauty" (*PP* 4), to Mary Wollstonecraft's argument that

> a being taught to please must still find her happiness in pleasing;—what an example of folly, not to say vice, will she be to her innocent daughters! The mother will be lost in the coquette, and, instead of making friends of her daughters, view them with eyes askance . . . because they invite a comparison, and drive her from the throne of beauty, who has never thought of a seat on the bench of reason. (49)

Next, consider Mrs. Dashwood's difficulties following the death of her husband. She, "a woman who never saved in her life," nevertheless makes sanguine plans for home improvements "from an income of five-hundred a-year" (*SS* 29). She is dependent on male relatives for housing and income and on her own daughter for guidance and practicality. Thus her predicament recalls *A Vindication* wherein the author describes what becomes of a woman whose husband dies, leaving her wholly unequal to the duties now devolved upon her. "[A]las! she has never thought, much less acted for herself. She has only learned to please men, to depend gracefully on them" (48).

Wollstonecraft's, and Austen's, principal complaint is that women's inability to manage their houses or their children stems from their lack of relevant education and denial of meaningful responsibilities. "[I]t would be as wise to expect corn from tares, or figs from thistles, as that a foolish ignorant woman should be a good mother," says the woman who would be herself the mother of Mary Shelley (191); while Austen, Lloyd Brown says, perceived "maternal failures as an extension of the inadequacies of the woman's education and individual development" (39). A woman like Lady Bertram, raised by marriage to the "comforts and consequences" of a baronet's lady (*MP* 3), is exempt from needing or applying any relevant knowledge; "she was a woman who spent her days in sitting nicely dressed on a sofa, doing some long piece of needlework, of little use and no beauty, thinking more of her pug than her children" (*MP* 19–20). Her daughters are being trained to follow the same course: "Only think," exclaim Julia and Maria, "my cousin cannot put the map of Europe together—or my cousin cannot tell the principal rivers in Russia—or she never heard of Asia Minor—or she does not know the difference between water-colours and crayons!" (*MP* 8). The uselessness of such superficial knowledge in the absence of solid moral training is clear when, by book's end, both Julia and Maria are in ruins.

Nonetheless, the fact that there were silly, self-centered mothers in Austen's experience and that she deplored the conditions that allowed them to be so does not, finally, explain why these are the only sort of mothers she draws. That she chose not to depict mothers as strong, capable women, or strong, capable women as mothers, says at least as much about the state of her mind as about the state of society. Again, here is her final word on Mrs. Bennet:

> I wish I could say, for the sake of her family, that the accomplishment of her earnest desire in the establishment of so many of her children, produced so happy an effect as to make her a sensible, amiable, well-informed woman for the rest of her life; [but] she was still occasionally nervous and invariably silly. (*PP* 385)

Because the narrator claims she *cannot* report any good news of Mrs. Bennet, Lloyd Brown concludes that Austen has an "essentially bleak vision of the individual and society. . . . By limiting individual maturity to women who are demonstrably unusual in their circle Austen implies a somewhat skeptical view of the possibilities of change in society at large" (37–38). Clearly, if Austen has little hope for humanity, she has even less—that is to say, none—for mothers. Almost every other class of society is allowed to have its occasional successes: young women have their Elizabeths and their Annes, married couples have their Gardiners and their Crofts, bachelors have their Mr. Darcys and their Mr. Knightlys, clergymen have their Edmund Bertrams and their Henry Tilneys. (Fathers perhaps alone are equally despaired of; but that is another study.) Mothers are an apostate race in her novels: those with intelligence, manners, and morals simply do not factor in her stories.

Thus it is important to stress that what is problematic about mothers in Jane Austen is not that there are bad ones but that she was apparently unwilling or unable to conceive good ones whom she could sustain through significant stretches of narrative. Even her good-hearted ones are lampooned. Although "good humoured [and] merry" (*SS* 34), Mrs. Jennings is also fat, garrulous, and vulgar, given to "hallooing [at] the window" (*SS* 106) and describing in detail the symptoms of her late husband's illness. Her "common-place raillery" and love of match-making give continual offense to the refined feelings of Elinor and Marianne: "Though I think very well of Mrs. Jennings' heart," Elinor says, "she is not a woman whose society can afford us pleasure, or whose protection will give us consequence" (*SS* 156). These imperfections, comparatively innocuous though they are, tend to dilute the reports of her benevolence during Marianne's illness, and one comes away with the impression that she is after all a clown. And although Austen credits Mrs. Dashwood's intense maternal loyalty and tenderness, she consistently condemns "that eagerness of mind . . . which must generally have led to imprudence" (*SS* 6). The potential harm posed by such an excess of emotion is as egregious, in its way, as the corresponding want of feeling in most of Austen's other mothers. Marianne has inherited all of her mother's sensibility and the wise Elinor sees it with concern; but "by Mrs. Dashwood it was valued and cherished" (*SS* 7). The result, of course, is that "[Marianne's] systems have all the unfortunate tendency of setting propriety at nought" (*SS*

56), as her sister says. This weakness leads her into a questionable relationship with Willoughby, and Mrs. Dashwood, rather than attempt to confirm or dispel the rumor that they are engaged, finds it more interesting to say nothing at all, and so to encourage it: "common sense, common care, common prudence, were all sunk in Mrs. Dashwood's romantic delicacy" (*SS* 85). Her eleventh-hour admission that she has been much to blame for Marianne's misfortune does her credit; but as with Mrs. Jennings' kindness, it is not enough to counteract our fundamental assessment of her as yet another of Jane Austen's incompetent mothers.

Nor is Austen's failure to conceive a thoroughly good mother owing to the fact that she had no definite ideas of what a strong, supportive mother could be. Emma Woodhouse, for instance, has shared with Mrs. Weston "equal footing and perfect unreserve" for the last seven years.

> [She] had been a friend and companion such as few possessed, intelligent, well-informed, useful, gentle, knowing all the ways of the family, interested in all its concerns, and peculiarly interested in herself, in every pleasure, every scheme of hers;—one to whom she could speak every thought as it arose, and who had such an affection for her as could never find fault. (*E* 6)

With the possible exception of the last detail, this is clearly Austen's vision of what intimacy and companionship should be between mother and daughter—this is what it means to be "little short of a mother in affection" (*E* 5). It may only be rather *too* indulgent, Austen implies; and for the needed corrective, we may turn to the portrait of Mrs. Gardiner. In a story about parental irresponsibility, Elizabeth's aunt embodies all that a mother should represent *including* discretion and impartial judgment. After observing her niece's apparent preference of Wickham with some uneasiness, Mrs. Gardiner takes Elizabeth aside with the utmost tact and goodwill:

> "You are too sensible a girl, Lizzy, to fall in love merely because you are warned against it; and, therefore, I am not afraid of speaking openly. Seriously, I would have you be on your guard. Do not involve yourself, or endeavour to involve

him in an affection which the want of fortune would make so
very imprudent. I have nothing to say against *him*; he is a most
interesting young man. . . . But as it is—you must not let your
fancy run away with you. You have sense, and we all expect
you to use it.". . .
. . . Elizabeth having thanked her for the kindness of her
hints, they parted; a wonderful instance of advice being given
on such a point, without being resented. (*PP* 144–45)

We arrive, via these various outlinings, at the sort of mother Jane
Austen approves of: prudent yet not prudish, intelligent yet good-
humored, practical yet affectionate, impartial yet loyal. Clearly Jane
Austen admired this sort of woman, and, what is more important, we
know that she knew several such women intimately. There was Anne
Lefroy, for instance, who, though twenty-six years her senior, became
Jane's special friend: "a dramatic, impassioned woman who had a
whirlwind effect on nearly everyone. She gave dances, rode donkeys,
flung open her doors to institute a 'daily school of poor children,'
and . . . innoculated 'upwards of 800' of the poor with her own hand"
(Honan 40). There was also her fascinating cousin Eliza, Comtesse de
Feuillide, a charming, generous, lively, clever, and beautiful woman
whom Jane admired and loved. Both women, incidentally, were
mothers.

As for her own mother, there is scant evidence for John Halperin's
contention, in his 1984 biography of Austen, that she disliked
Cassandra Austen nor that she modeled most of her bad mothers after
her. An irritable remark here, a sardonic dig there, form the basis for his
statement that Jane "perhaps felt something less than love for her
mother."[2] Of course, stated thus cautiously, one can hardly disagree.
Nonetheless, one is more inclined to accept the finding of Park Honan's
1987 biography that Jane Austen's relations with her mother were on
the whole favorable. The mother described by Honan is no Lady
Bertram, no Mrs. Musgrove, no Mrs. Price, certainly no Lady Susan,
and excepting the suggestions of hypochondria, no Mrs. Bennet:

[A]n indifference to appearances and an amused, ironic view
of life helped her to enjoy Steventon's simple, repaired
rectory. . . . Her pride was to be heavily pregnant and *also* the

mistress of a dairy and overseer of her home. . . . "I have got a nice dairy fitted up, and am now worth a bull and six cows, and you would laugh to see them. . . . In short you must come, and, like Hezekiah, I will shew you all my riches." George rejoiced in his foresight in marrying a lady who merely needed time to adjust to rural life before she loved it; his wife even became ironic about that "sad place" London. (16–17)

Apparently her mother appreciated and encouraged Jane's jokes and burlesques and was an intelligent, impartial critic of her fiction, calling Fanny Price "insipid" but in general considering her daughter's novels greatly entertaining, even more than Scott's *Waverly*. In short,

> Mrs. Austen was not an ogress who withered the wills of the disobedient but a mother who put family first. . . . There was an atmosphere of order in the household—strict, implicit, iron-bound and unchanging. But Jane warmly approved the domestic discipline, quiet strictness and natural order, and took delight in the family's talk, wit, and sense of well-being. (22, 28,37)

In fact, if Jane Austen is drawing her mothers from real life, there are others probably better qualified to be her models. According to Margaret Drabble's introduction to *Lady Susan*, "It has been suggested that Jane Austen drew on the character of the mother of her neighbour Mrs. Lloyd, a woman called Mrs. Craven, in this portrait. . . . Mrs. Craven, a beauty like Lady Susan, had treated her daughters shockingly, locking them up and starving them, until they ran away from home in desperation and married" (12). Another candidate is her imperious, aristocratic aunt Mrs. Leigh Perrot. Jane "perhaps had a foretaste of Elizabeth's experience with Lady Catherine," a dowager who "asked for assent without yielding an inch, and expected her nieces to admire her." However, as Honan continues, "the aunt took on gleams and colours the better one knew her. . . . In all she had been a factor in Jane Austen's education in human character and would remain interesting for her eccentricity, self-assurance, sheer nigglingness and courage" (148). This sounds much more like *Sanditon*'s Lady Denham than *Pride and Prejudice*'s Lady Catherine—and if Aunt Perrot is indeed the model for both characters, one wonders why Austen did not, until her final piece of fiction, attempt the more accurate portrait.

The answer must be that if Austen did draw from life, she did not feel compelled to make her portraits exact reproductions of the original. Instead, she cut and pasted as she chose, exaggerating some features—perhaps her mother's hypochondria—while ignoring or deemphasizing others—such as her mother's resourcefulness and ironic wit. So what determined her selection? Halperin suggests, apropos of Lady Susan, that Jane Austen came upon her malicious characterizations via some other means than first-hand experience.

> [S]he and her mother were not always congenial together . . .
> but this alone would not explain the character of Lady Susan,
> whose vulgarity and cruelty Mrs. Austen, from all
> contemporary accounts, certainly could not match. . . . [T]he
> novelist knows so much about the sort of personality described
> here that one must conclude some of that knowledge was
> instinctive rather than merely contextual—intrinsic rather than
> purely extrinsic. (48)

I propose that what Halperin terms "intrinsic" knowledge is in fact that preconscious, archetypal fear of the mother that Jane Austen was heir to and that Jung, Horney, et al have explored at such length. The anti-maternal prejudice that was implanted deep in the collective part of her psyche was further communicated to her via all the ways I have described in the preceding chapters—that is, in the derogation of women through their superficial education and political and economic subjugation as well as through all the monster/madonna imagery which she would have been exposed to as soon as she was old enough to listen to nursery rhymes.

It is clear that Austen was influenced by, and made use of, the conventionalized, stereotyped roles and depictions of mothers which would have been as much a part of her cultural heritage as folklore and Shakespeare. Austen's mothers have the advantage, at least, of moving widely across the canvas. But they are types nonetheless. Mrs. Jennings, for instance, like Juliet's Nurse and the Wife of Bath, is *Sense and Sensibility*'s Queen Mab, the matchmaker/midwife/procuress type—bawdy, comical, pandering but, underneath her apparent commonness, keenly perceptive. "He will have her at last," she declares about Colonel Brandon and Marianne, "aye, that he will" (*SS* 196). A similar type popular in farce but also in tragedy (*Romeo and Juliet*) and earlier novels (*Clarissa*) is the mother who tries to force her daughter (or son, or another young person in her sway) to marry against her will. For instance, when Frederica Vernon refuses the dissolute Sir James, Lady Susan pledges to make her daughter's life "thoroughly uncomfortable till she does accept him" (*LS* 254). Mrs. Norris is furious with Fanny Price for turning down Henry Crawford; and in the scene in which Mrs. Bennet tries to assure Mr. Collins that Elizabeth will eventually "be brought to reason" one hears echoes of Lady Capulet. "She is a very headstrong foolish girl, and does not know her own interest; but I will *make* her know it" (*PP* 110). Having applied without success to her husband, she directs her attack at the offending daughter: "I tell you what, Miss Lizzy, if you take it into your head to go on refusing every offer of marriage in this way, you will never get a husband at all . . . and so I warn you.—I have done with you from this very day" (*PP* 113).

The converse, whereby the mother despises the virtuous lover, is also popular, as when Mrs. Bennet repeatedly insults Mr. Darcy; when Lady Russell hinders Anne Elliot's early relationship with Captain Wentworth; when Lady Catherine descends upon Longbourne in fury after hearing rumors that Elizabeth is engaged to Darcy; and when Mrs. Ferrars makes it clear to Edward that not only will she cut him off if he makes a "low connection," but should he "enter into any profesion with a view of better support, she would do all in her power to prevent his advancing in it" (*SS* 267).

The figure of the imperious matriarch trying to control the lives of everyone around her recurs regularly, from the legends of the goddess Juno snapping her fingers at the mortals below, to the savagery of the wicked stepmother queen who demands the heart of Snow White, to the tyrannical hold which Volumnia asserts over Coriolanus, who finds himself powerless to prevent her:

> The gods look down, and this unnatural scene
> They laugh at. O my mother! mother! O!
> You have won a happy victory to Rome;
> But, for your son, believe it, O! believe it,
> Most dangerously you have with him prevail'd,
> If not most mortal to him. (V.v.184–89)

And when the overstepping mother is eventually undone by her own machinations, as when Lady Catherine, by attempting to scare Elizabeth away from Darcy, manages instead to seal their relationship, the audience feels the same rush of rather malicious satisfaction at the mother's expense that Lauber calls a "sudden glory," a sense of "infinite superiority."

Of course, the thing about conventions is that our responses to them are also meant to be conventionalized: predictably emotional, and primarily non-cerebral: if we are inclined to examine them too closely, they are not doing their job. And the emotions associated with mothers are so strong and deep-seated that it is no great challenge to tap into them. The expected response evoked by the convention of the disagreeable mother-daughter team such as appears in Cinderella, the Girls in the Well, and so on, is a sort of disgust combined with superiority at the spectacle of ugliness compounded; of loyal indignation at the unfairness and cowardice implicit in pitting two (or more) against one; but ultimately a gloating satisfaction in the knowledge that the more impossible the odds, the greater the glory in overcoming them. This convention dates back at least to Germanic and Celtic folk legends in which a demonic hag is assisted in fighting off the hero by one or more demonic offspring; however, the mother is always even more dangerous than her children, and the hero requires all his strength and wit to defeat her and, of course, is the more glorified for doing so.[3] Mother-daughter teams function in Austen's novels according to this paradigm, for instance when Mrs. Ferrars snubs Elinor (who represents the stepdaughter in this schema) by praising her intended daughter-in-law Miss Morton ("*she* does every thing well" [*SS* 235]); and when the Elliots meet their distant relations Lady Dalrymple and Miss Carteret. Sir Walter and Elizabeth fawn over them shamefully, but in Anne's opinion, "they were nothing. There was no superiority of manner, accomplishment, or understanding. [Miss Carteret] was so plain and so awkward, that she would never have been tolerated in Camden-place but for her birth" (*P* 149–50). The ugly mother-daughter pairing occurs most explicitly in the team of Lady Catherine de Bourgh and Miss De Bourgh, who is of course nowhere near so powerful as her mother but who has the advantage of position over Elizabeth. Rank and wealth are Miss De Bourgh's only advantages, however. Otherwise she is "pale and sickly; her features, though not plain, [are] insignificant; and she [speaks] very little, except in a low voice" (*PP* 162); while Elizabeth, of course, is vigorous, articulate, and though not a classic beauty, a provocative one. Lady Catherine's obvious partiality is consequently both rude and entirely misplaced. "[Miss Bennet's musical] taste is not equal to Anne's," she informs Darcy illogically, since Anne has never even learned how to play (*PP* 176). However, as in the fairy tales, their superior breeding comes to nothing, for as we knew would happen all along, it is Elizabeth, not Anne, whom Darcy brings home as mistress of Pemberley.

This is one of Jane Austen's favorite indexes to a character's sensibility and morality: whether or not he or she appreciates the right things and appreciates the deserving people. Mrs. Dashwood and Mrs. Jennings are approved of because they sincerely love Marianne and Elinor, and it is hard even to dislike Lady Bertram very strenuously, seeing that, in her indolent way, she values Fanny Price. Mrs. Norris, on the other hand, sees nothing but an irritant in Fanny and enjoys advertising her preference for Maria and Julia. In fact, *Mansfield Park* is one of the numerous Austen novels to employ the Cinderella motif.[4] Though Mrs. Norris is not, technically, Fanny's cruel stepmother, nonetheless that is clearly the role she fills: it is she who was first responsible for uprooting Fanny as a child from her home in Portsmouth and she who relentlessly torments her as an interloper after she arrives: "Remember, wherever you are, you must be the lowest and last" (*MP* 221). The parallel is further apparent in the treatment Fanny receives from almost everyone except Edmund (who becomes her rescuing prince in the end); the governess wonders at her ignorance, and even "the maid-servants sneered at her clothes" (*MP* 14). Fanny is soon installed as a virtual servant herself, waiting on Lady Bertram, and Julia and Maria complete the schema as the haughty stepsisters. "They could not but hold her cheap on finding that she had but two sashes, and had never learnt French. . . . They thought her prodigiously stupid, and for the first two or three weeks were continually bringing some fresh report of it into the drawing-room" (*MP* 14, 18). However, Fanny accepts all of this abuse meekly, and when winter arrives,

> Fanny had no share in the festivities of the season; but she enjoyed being avowedly useful as her aunt's companion, when

they called away the rest of the family. . . . . As to her cousins' gaities, she loved to hear an account of them, especially of the balls, and whom Edmund had danced with; but thought too lowly of her own situation to imagine she should ever be admitted to the same. (*MP* 35)

Later, Fanny/Cinderella *is* admitted to her share of the glamour at the Mansfield Park ball; resplendent in a borrowed gown and sought after by the neighborhood's most eligible bachelor, she discovers that "a ball [is] indeed delightful" (*MP* 281). But by the next morning, the visions have faded, "the ball was over . . . the last kiss was given," and Fanny grieves over "the melancholy change" (*MP* 282). Not until the end of the novel does her prince realize that he has been looking for his bride among the wrong ladies of the land.

It is important to keep in mind that all versions of the Cinderella story are about Cinderella's mother/stepmother as much as they are about Cinderella herself, for she is the force over which the child has to triumph in order to achieve selfhood. The archetypal conflict is not that Cinderella fails to leave the Prince's ball on time but that she is Cinderella—"Girl of the Ashes"—in the first place. Deprived of her nurturing mother, deprived of her rightful place in her father's home, she is now the scullery maid and object of her stepmother's and stepsisters' scorn. How may she overcome such odds? In the fairy tale, she relies to a great degree on magical intervention; in the realistic novel she triumphs merely by staying true to her own good instincts, which is difficult enough in the self-centered, self-serving world of Mansfield Park.

Obviously the conflicts in realistic novels are more subtle and psychologically complex than those in folk literature; the same is true of the maternal archetypes—either vindictive/monstrous or angelic/idealized. Mrs. Norris more obviously fits the terrible mother image than does Lady Bertram or Mrs. Price; but what is so admirable in Austen is her ability to make us believe in all three of these versions of the stereotype—indeed, to disguise the fact that they are stereotypes at all. In a sense, Victorian mothers will now have yet another tradition to follow, and that is the one established by Jane Austen.

Notes

1. See Schorer, "Pride Unprejudiced"; and Brown, "The Business of Marrying and Mothering."

2. *The Life of Jane Austen* 144. In light of all the evidence, Halperin's suggestion that the bad parents in Austen "may stand for her mother alone" (145) seems almost entirely conjectural.

3. Martin Puhvel, "The Might of Grendel's Mother" 85. Puhvel cites a number of such stories, including the Scottish tale of Feorn, who fights a monster and both the monster's parents. The female "Big Hag" is by far the most perilous. In an Irish variant on the Beowulf legend, the hero must fight a monstrous ugly hag who lives with her three foul daughters in an underwater castle. And in another Irish tale, "Wishing Gold," the son of Erin slays a trio of five-headed giants. When he is done, he says to himself, "As these three were in one place, their mother must be in it too." Sure enough, a "dreadful hag" soon appears, and the battle with her is the most ferocious, lasting three days and three nights.

4. Again, see John Halperin, "The Victorian Novel and Jane Austen" (3). Besides *Mansfield Park*, says Halperin, the motif is also present in *Emma* and *Pride and Prejudice*.

Chapter Three

"Rather Weak Withal":
Victorian Mothers

Jane Austen's mothers excepted, the most appreciable change in mothers in the novel from the eighteenth century to about the mid-nineteenth seems simply to be that they figure more prominently in the action. The tenor of those roles, however, continues to be negative, characterized principally by stupidity and selfishness. The discussion which follows compares these qualities as they appear in Victorian mothers, especially those of Charles Dickens (the mother of Nicholas and Kate in *Nicholas Nickleby*); George Eliot (Mrs. Tulliver in *The Mill on the Floss*), and Elizabeth Gaskell (Molly Gibson's stepmother in *Wives and Daughters*). Though in some ways Victorian novelists merely pick up the stereotype where those of the preceding years left it off, in most cases they begin to endow the maternal character with more significance and detail.

A quick inventory of the major eighteenth-century novels suggests that the mothers from this period who are dead or otherwise removed from the action outnumber the living, dramatically functioning ones; in contrast, a mother in nineteenth-century fiction is more likely not only to be alive but to have a fair share in the action. Thus, as authors begin to hold on to and find significant places for their characters' mothers, the challenge to the hero or heroine shifts from that of learning to live without a female parent, to learning to live *with* one—for the mother is still, almost without exception, a major liability. Since it is more believable that a heroine's problems should come from her own mother rather than from, say, a psychopathic monk, this change represents an important step in the movement toward fuller psychological realism. However, it is a half-step at best. For while the psychological dimensions of the mother-child conflict are growing in some respects, most Victorian authors still seem firmly entrenched in the old practice of placing all the error with the mother and all the virtue with the child. Thus the mother's fundamental purpose in the novel continues basically unchanged from her formulaic role in folklore and fairy tale: to "test" the virtue of the hero/heroine. Indeed, the influence of fairy tale and folklore continues to be as pervasive in the Victorian novel as it is in Austen. Florence Dombey, for instance, is a Cinderella type; in fact, says Harry Stone, *Dombey and Son* is a fusion of fairy tale with psychology and symbolism (1). Chapter 23 opens with strongly suggestive overtones: "Florence lived alone in the great dreary house, and day succeeded day, and still she lived alone. . . . No magic dwelling place in magic story, shut up in the heart of a thick wood, was ever more solitary and deserted" (*DS* 266). Likewise Patsy Stoneman notes in her book on Elizabeth Gaskell that the opening chapters of *Wives and Daughters* are full of references to folk legend, with Molly losing her "godmothers" at the Towers, falling asleep in a strange bed, and waking to find Lord Cumnor pretending to be Father Bear to her Goldilocks (*WD* 53). These formulae remind us that the Victorian novel continues to act out the individuation process of the child, and thus the dramatic focus continues to be on him or her, with the mother continuing to serve in her traditional role as "goading" agent. Stoneman continues:

> The ritual phrases of these first chapters suggest that adults perceive female adolescence not as an active phase of growth but as a period of unconscious waiting, marked by allusion to "the Sleeping Beauty, the Seven Sleepers, and any other famous sleepers" [*WD* 53]. Molly's own father is no fairy-tale ogre. . . . but he too conceives a sharp disjunction between the child and the woman, and instructs her governess not to "teach Molly too much . . . I want to keep her a child" [*WD* 65]. . . . [He is l]ike Sleeping Beauty's father, who tried to guard his daughter from the fairy's curse, the pricked finger, the ritual shedding of blood which signifies womanhood. (172–73)

As in fairy tales, most novels telescope the entire individuation process into the period covered by the tale. While the narrative occasionally begins with the protagonist already in the testing stage (for instance, Jane Eyre is already an orphan, already living with the Reeds when the book opens), very often the hero/heroine is first introduced while still in the egoistic, dependent stage—for instance, Florence Dombey. But this phase is by no means limited to childhood: both Emma Woodhouse and Gwendolyn Harleth in their twenties are still utterly self-centered. This secure, infantile stage, however, lasts only momentarily in the narrative, quickly preempted by the long period of testing and emotional and sexual maturation (Molly with Mrs. Gibson, Roger, and the Hamleys; Maggie Tulliver with her mother and Stephen and Philip); then, in the denouement, comes the accomplished separation from the ties and behaviors of childhood and dependence, which usually takes the form of a marriage but may also, less frequently, be a death (Maggie Tulliver) or a disillusionment (Gwendolyn Harleth). Lawrence Lerner seems to have these three stages in mind when he talks about "conversions" in George Eliot's characters: Hetty Sorrel, for instance, goes through "initial egoism, [then] the suffering that makes her accesssible to influence, and [finally] yielding and confession" (*Love and Marriage* 33). We may assume that, even though Eliot does not stress it, much of Hetty's tragedy comes from being an orphan: Mrs. Poyser tries to be Hetty's substitute parent, realizing that "she had no mother of her own to scold her, poor thing!" (*AB* 90). Thus, though Hetty's individuation does not conclude happily, it is still set in motion by the mother's absence.

Because most Victorian novels continue to use mothers mainly as obstructions, the result is a certain predictability of plot and characterization which only barely taps the psychological and dramatic potential of the mother-child relationship and of the mother figure herself. On the other hand, because the obstruction more often results from the mother's presence rather than her absence, the Victorians, following Austen, are concerned with the effects of poor mothering, and often, especially with children other than the hero/heroine, their dramatic treatment of these effects is psychologically quite accurate. Unlike Austen, however, Victorians tend to look rather more fully at children as individuals, not just as indexes to adult behavior. Angus Wilson has remarked that even though parental failure is an old theme in the novel, going back at least to *Moll Flanders*, the eighteenth-century novelists "felt no interest in this conflict where it affected those non-beings, children" (204). Moll, for instance, mentions her numerous children only to say how they were disposed of; the only time she expresses interest in their fates is when she encounters one of her sons, now fully grown, "in flourishing circumstances." Knowing Moll, we may assume that, had she found this son ragged and poor instead of handsome and successful, she would not have felt such "yearnings of soul . . . to embrace him, and weep over him" (*MF* 361).

If *Moll Flanders* represents one extreme of the eighteenth-century novel's interest in children, *Tristram Shandy* is the other. But in general it is true that there are not many significant pre-adolescents in eighteenth-century fiction. Wilson goes on to note that although "that proto-Victorian novel" *Mansfield Park* is probably the first to depict childhood suffering, Austen's ultimate concern is Fanny's struggle in an adult world against adult values. The Victorians, however, get considerably more didactic (not to say narrative) mileage out of dramatizing the dangers of entrusting defenseless children to incompetent mothers.[1] The results in terms of maladjusted children are much more psychologically believable than the "fiction," as Barbara Hardy calls it, "about the powerful human nature that could resist the environment" (40). Usually, of course, the fault consists in the mother's lack of love and care, and the victim is often deeply and sometimes angrily conscious that she or he has been wronged. These are the outspoken victims like Cynthia Kirkpatrick and Beatrix Esmond; even the Pardiggle boys, Esther Summerson thinks, "[look] absolutely ferocious with discontent" (*BH* 95). Sometimes the victim of withheld love never does publicly acknowledge (at least not in our hearing) that the mother is blameworthy: to an extreme degree this is how Maggie Tulliver deals with her rejection by Mrs. Tulliver; neither Kate nor Nicholas Nickleby ever grumbles about their mother (even though, as Margaret Lane very reasonably asks, "What home could really be tolerable with Mrs. Nickleby's inane inconsequential chatter going on, even though there was 'no evil and little real selfishness' in her nature?" (170). *Daniel Deronda*'s Gwendolyn Harleth, although aware she has been emotionally damaged and undoubtedly suspects her indulgent mother at least partly to blame, never accuses Mrs. Davilow outright. And sometimes the victim of overindulgence (usually a male, in these patriarchal homes, but sometimes a woman, like Lydia Bennet and for a while Gwendolyn Harleth and Bella Wilfer in *Our Mutual Friend*) is deliberately oblivious to the mother's error, but for opportunistic reasons, not generous ones. In these cases the mother's mistake has been in loving too much rather than too little, thereby endorsing her child's convenient belief in his or her importance and infallibility and making him/her obnoxious and occasionally cruel. Harry Warrington, James Steerforth, Tom Tulliver, Osborne Hamley, Georgy Osborne, and Arthur Pendennis, for example, all suffer not from their mothers' neglect or harshness, but rather, as Juliet McMaster says of the brood of brats in Thackeray, from "the kind of absorbing and clinging love that makes its object want to tear and rend at its entanglements" (*Thackeray* 98).

Psychoanalysis suggests that when someone is denied nurturance, acceptance, or love, the usual coping mechanisms are self-effacement, withdrawal, or aggression; thus, all of these responses to poor mothering are extraordinarily perceptive and psychologically realistic. There is, moreover, a great deal of psychological validity to the other side of the coin, that is, the premise that a mother's favoritism and excessive submissiveness produce not adoring little angels but malicious little tyrants. Georgy Osborne: "the boy grew up delicate, sensitive, imperious, woman-bred—domineering the gentle mother whom he loved with passionate affection [and ruling] all the rest of the world round about him" (*VF* 465); Tom Tulliver: "he was particularly clear and positive on one point, namely that he would punish everybody who deserved it" (*MF* 91); Gwendolyn Harleth: "Having always been the pet and pride of the household, . . . she naturally found it difficult to think her own pleasure less important than others made it" (*DD* 18); or Osborne Hamley: his mother had made "such an idol of [her] beautiful Osborne; and he turns out to have feet of clay, not strong enough to stand firm on the ground" (*WD* 230).

Clearly there is a good deal of acuity and sensitivity in the way Victorian novelists portray the damage a mother may do to her children. There is also psychological realism in the notion that the offspring may grow to adulthood resentfully nursing that hurt and the associated guilt: when Beatrix Esmond, now the old Baroness Bernstein in *The Virginians*, dies in America, she is still cursing her mother's rejection. Yet even this heightened psychological realism has a stereotypical slant, for its subject is not the mother but the daughter or son. Most of the psychological attention, and virtually all of the narrative sympathy, are focused on the child: the mother in all but a few cases is found guilty without a trial. To be sure, not all Victorian mothers are liable to such easy analysis, Thackeray's in particular, but also Eliot's Princess Halm-Eberstein, several of Hardy's, and some other of what I am calling transitional mothers. But the majority of Victorian mothers conform to a fairly predictable, fairly straightforward model of ignorance and selfishness.

One is not surprised to hear Dickens' characters accused of being predictable, as his characters are less individuals than personalities; strict one-to-one realism would be oppressive to his comic-cum-didactic purpose.[2] In the 1839 Preface to *Nicholas Nickleby* Dickens very readily acknowledges that "Mr. Squeers and his school are faint and feeble pictures of an existing reality"; after all, Squeers is "the representative of a class, and not of an individual," his stock character traits being "imposture, ignorance, and brutal cupidity"; indeed, Dickens claims to have drawn only two characters in the book from life, the brothers Cheeryble (*NN* 45–46). But the charge of predictability sits somewhat less familiarly on George Eliot, whose insights into character and motivation are generally thought to be among the most acute of any Victorian novelist. Eliot's mothers, especially the Princess Halm-Eberstein but even to an extent Bessy Tulliver, are not meant to be blatantly comic caricatures; they are drawn in nothing like the Dickens manner. Their behavior, if objectionable, usually has a discernible motive; and they have a conscience with which they wish to be at peace, though they lack either the moral or mental energy to achieve this. Given the central consciousness of a twentieth-century mother, either woman could easily be reworked into a tragic figure. Yet when everything such a mother says or does has significance mainly as it injures her son or daughter, her fictional personality seems unnaturally flat.

There are, however, even within the confines of this predominantly negative characterization, a range of personalities as well as varying degrees of conformity to the stereotype which assure that every Victorian mother is by no means merely a clone of all the others. In addition to Rachel Esmond, whom I discuss as a mixed figure, and Daniel Deronda's mother the Princess Halm-Eberstein, a.k.a. the

Alcharisi, whom I discuss as a transitional mother, this discussion focuses primarily on Mrs. Nickleby, Mrs. Tulliver, and Mrs. Gibson as representing a progression of sorts in the style of the mid-Victorian fictional mother. Mrs. Nickleby (1838–39), as the most blatantly comic, most directly recalls the stock character of farce; Bessy Tulliver (1860) is typical of the mother who, though given an emotional life of her own, nevertheless inspires rather more contempt than either pity or interest; and Hyacinth Clare Gibson (1864–66), whose close analysis by the narrator foretells the coming shift in the treatment of mothers, is still too foolish to be taken very seriously. Whether or not these mid-century mothers are "taken seriously," not only by their fellow characters but by the author and the reader alike, seems to me the chief measure of their evolution: the main reason the Alcharisi seems fundamentally different from Bessy Tulliver is not that she is any *better* a mother—in fact she is probably worse, if one can make such judgments—but that she demands more care and circumspection. For a number of reasons, we take her seriously.

Among the numerous character flaws ascribed to mothers through all the ages and all the forms predating the novel, stupidity—here interpreted broadly to mean anything from simple-mindedness and lack of imagination to sloppy reasoning and wilful ignorance—had never been so prominent as it comes to be in the nineteenth century. Mrs. Bennet may be merely one of the earliest in a tradition of silly or stupid mothers that comes to include, besides Mrs. Nickleby, Mrs. Tulliver, and Mrs. Gibson, Dickens' Mrs. Jellyby (*Bleak House*), Gaskell's Mrs. Hale (*North and South*), Charlotte Bronte's Mrs. Reed (*Jane Eyre*), Mrs. Oliphant's Mrs. John Vernon (*Hester*), Trollope's Mrs. Stanhope (*Barchester Towers*), Thackeray's Amelia Osborne (*Vanity Fair*), and numerous others. In earlier genres, bad mothers were noted more for their malice or cunning than for their ignorance: Hecuba, Clytemnestra, and Grendel's mother are all murderers; Tamora, Queen of the Goths, sets her sons to terrorize the Roman forces, even to raping and mutilating the daughter of Titus Andronicus; Volumnia taunts Coriolanus into ruthlessness; even the clownish mothers in Spanish farce craftily used their perceived foolishness to manipulate others. The nineteenth-century mother, in contrast, often has not got enough sense to be sly—although as Dickens says of Mrs. Nickleby, she "was commonly in the habit of giving herself credit for a pretty tolerable share of penetration and acuteness" (*NN* 426).

Why stupidity should have superseded viciousness as the dominant maternal quality, one can only speculate; an obvious assumption is that a Tamora-like figure would have been too offensive to the famous Victorian sensibility—after all, the same public that delighted in Mrs. Nickleby also put great stock in images of the Angel in the House. But it isn't simply that Victorians were squeamish. They were also maturing as readers. As Kaarle Krohn, Jack Zipes, and other folklorists point out, the more closely a society examines its literature, the less it can be satisfied by the raw, undigested stuff of folklore. The nineteenth-century psyche was still attuned to archetypal images, of course, but its increasing intellectual sophistication perhaps demanded that the archetypes (or stereotypes, in this case) stand up to closer scrutiny.

Presumably such a mind is less likely to choke on the image of a mother as merely irresponsible than that of a mother as blatantly immoral, a wanton or a murderer, for instance. (Such characters can be created, of course, and very effectively, too; but they require more attention to psychological development than Victorians were in the habit of allotting to mother characters). It is interesting to note that mothers who are portrayed as both intelligent *and* immoral (with a strong emphasis on the sexual component of their immorality)—Becky Sharpe and Trollope's Lizzie Eustace come immediately to mind—are de-emphasized in their role as mothers: their careless mothering is only one of many defining flaws in their character, not the chief one. And returning for a moment to Jane Austen's early novella *Lady Susan*: this story of a mother who is at once malicious, coarse, licentious—as well as witty, intelligent, and charming—was not published until 1871, about the time fictional stereotypes were losing their hold on the reading public. *Lady Susan* was never especially popular, but it would probably have been even less so with earlier Victorian readers—even though, as Margaret Drabble observes in her introduction to *Lady Susan*, this would not necessarily have been the case a century earlier, when frivolity and immorality were more frankly acknowledged than in the "prudish and discreet" nineteenth century (12). Yet if the nineteenth century, with its selective notions of propriety, refused to see its mothers depicted as patently monstrous, at least it eventually rejected the feeble-minded stereotype as well.

One way to gauge the ignorance of a Victorian mother is to ask how well she understands, and how effectively she functions in, the prevailing idiom (both literal and figurative) of her environment. In other words, to what extent does she speak, act, and think so as to understand and be intelligible to most other people? In a culture which places a high premium on intelligent and appropriate social discourse, it is a significant issue; yet most of the mothers in this period seem afflicted with a sort of chronic dissociation of ideas, language, and perception. Mrs. Nickleby's case is the worst: in fact, the vagaries of her thought and conversation are her most remarkable feature. Her daughter Kate generously calls them "curious" (*NN* 616), and they are admittedly entertaining, but Mrs. Nickleby's fantastic associations of ideas are also rather bizarre. "I don't know how it is," she muses, "but a fine warm summer day like this, with the birds singing in every direction, always puts me in mind of roast pig." It is not, as one might think, and as indeed Mrs. Nickleby herself first thinks, that she had served pork on such a day many years before; but rather, after piecing together an erratic trail of hazy memories, she finally recalls that a parrot had been squawking obscenities in the dining room where she had been a guest at a dinner featuring roast pig.

> Roast pig—let me see. On the day five weeks after you were christened, we had a roast—no that couldn't have been a pig, either, because I recollect there were a pair of them to carve, and your poor papa and I could never have thought of sitting down to two pigs—they must have been partridges. Roast pig! I hardly think we ever could have had one, now I come to remember, for your papa could never bear the sight of them in the shops, and used to say that they always put him in mind of very little babies, only the pigs had much fairer complexions; and he had a horror of little babies, too, because he couldn't very well afford any increase to his family. (*NN* 616–17)

While Kate diplomatically tries to get her mother to drop the subject, Mrs. Nickleby pursues it "with as much gravity as if it were a question of the most thrilling and imminent interest."

Indeed, the things that hold the greatest interest for Mrs. Nickleby usually have the least practical relation to fact or reality. She lives in a world of her own creating, interpreting events to suit her needs. Michael Slater notes that she "is quite as versatile an actress as her wicked brother-in-law," but with the difference that she is unaware of how much she is acting: "she casts not only herself but everyone with whom she comes into contact in a bewildering variety of roles and constructs whole scenarios, complete with appropriate scenery" (intro. to *NN* 20–21). When Kate recoils at her Uncle Ralph's request to "keep house" for him during a "little party of gentlemen," at which, of course, he intends to offer Kate to one of his scurrilous associates, Mrs. Nickleby scoffs at her fears: "if some extraordinary good fortune doesn't come to you after all this, I shall be surprised":

> With this she launched out into sundry anecdotes of young ladies, who had had thousand pound notes given them in reticules, by eccentric uncles; and of young ladies who had accidentally met amiable gentlemen of enormous wealth at their uncles' houses, and married them, after short but ardent courtships. (*NN* 302)

Obviously, the peculiar relationship to reality which distorts this woman's judgment—what others see as foul, she sees as fair; what others consider virtue she judges to be vice—puts her children, especially Kate, at considerable risk; I will address this aspect of her mothering later. But it is essential to remember that Mrs. Nickleby is intended above all as a comic figure: she is meant to appear ridiculous, not dangerous; and however this trivializes her role and her impact on her children, the scenes which emphasize her silliness are by far her most characteristic ones. The foremost example is her "affair" with her lunatic neighbor, the one who courts her by throwing produce from his garden into hers and whose attentions she simperingly pretends to discourage. When Kate—whose mode of discourse with the world is altogether normal, if self-effacing—urges her mother to go inside to escape the "shower of onions, turnip-radishes, and other small vegetables, which fell rolling and scattering and bumping about in all directions" (*NN* 620), Mrs. Nickleby has no such thought: to a woman whose own semiotic system is so eccentric, the idea that a flung cucumber may be taken as a compliment is not so inconceivable. Indeed, when the gentleman's keeper arrives and explains that the fellow has been out of his mind for many years, we are tempted, hearing Mrs. Nickleby's response, to think she must be a little mad herself. "[H]e is nothing of the kind," she protests decisively.

> He may be a little odd and flighty, perhaps, many of us are that; but downright mad! and express himself as he does, respectfully, and in quite poetical language, and making offers with so much thought and care, and prudence. . . . No, no, . . . there's a great deal too much method in *his* madness.
> (*NN* 629)

Dickens alone of all the writers of the period creates his mothers with this sort of extravagance (though it is instructive to note the comic parallels between the "aerial architecture" with which Mrs. Nickleby builds her fantasy-scapes, and the "aerial castle-building" with which Mrs. Davilow plans for Gwendolyn's future magnificence in Eliot's much later, and generally much more sober *Daniel Deronda*). Most of Dickens' mothers—the ones who are not idealised, that is—are drawn in a heavy-handed style that often verges on the grotesque. "Cleopatra" Skewton, one of the mother grotesques of *Dombey and Son*, with her "false curls and false eyebrows [and] false teeth, set off by her false complexion" (*DS* 241), is, like Mrs. Nickleby, determined to deny the unpleasant truths about her age and position. Furthermore, though she schemes more ruthlessly than Mrs. Nickleby, she is fully as imperceptive: just as Mrs. Nickleby is pleased and impressed by Sir Mulberry Hawk, the man who would ruin Kate, so does Mrs. Skewton approve of Carker, pronouncing "very agreeable" (*DS* 334) the Machiavel who is plotting to ruin her daughter Edith and his employer Dombey. The fundamental difference between Mrs. Skewton and Mrs. Nickleby is that Cleopatra is meant to be dangerous as well as ridiculous, having caused the perversion of Edith's soul. She is among Dickens' most brutal female grotesques, like Quilp a spiritual if not altogether physical deformity. The obscenely mercenary quality of her relationship with Edith makes her probably the most disturbing of Dickens' maternal portraits (not even the old hag Mrs. Brown, whose daughter has become a criminal, and whom Dickens explicitly casts as Cleopatra's counterpart, seems as depraved); but for whatever reason, whether he himself was uncomfortable with them or whether he feared his audience was, he does not paint quite as chilling a relationship between mothers and children anywhere else. More typical are mothers whose faults, though foolish, do not, however, seem quite so fatal. Perhaps this impression stems from their children being yet young and so presumably more likely to escape, although Dickens was firmly convinced that such children carry emotional scars for life. An example of the mother whose malignancy is made to seem limited is Mrs. Squeers, wife of the schoolmaster of Dotheboys Hall. She is the type of the cruel (but stupid) stepmother whose doting fondness for her own horrid offspring contrasts with her sadistic hatred of her pitiable "stepchildren"—the scholars to whom she is, by Squeers' account, "more than a mother . . . , ten times more" (*NN* 150). If her heartless treatment of the boys is formulaic according to the fairy tale model—"Mrs. Squeers stood at one of the desks, presiding over an immense basin of brimstone and treacle, of which delicious compound she administered a large installment to each boy in succession, using for the purpose a common wooden spoon" (*NN* 152)—so is her punishment when Nicholas arrives to "break up" the hall. Like the witch who burns in her own oven, Mrs. Squeers is likewise hoist with her own petard: "[One] boy seized the cane, and confronting Mrs. Squeers with a stern countenance, snatched off her cap and beaver-bonnet, put it on his own head, armed himself with the wooden spoon, and bade her, on pain of death, go down upon her knees, and take a dose directly" (*NN* 928).

Also typical are the two do-gooders in *Bleak House*, Mrs. Jellyby and Mrs. Pardiggle: the former, enrapt as she is in the philanthropic salvation of Barrioboola-Gha, can spare no time either to pick her bruised toddlers up off the floor or her soggy African correspondence out of the gravy pitcher. The latter, "a formidable style of lady" who has dedicated herself to such causes as the Tockahoopo Indians and the Great National Smithers Testimonial while her own six sons physically and emotionally waste away, "had the effect of wanting a great deal of room," sweeping over chairs and small tables wherever she walked (*BH* 94). This sort of excess clearly was what most appealed to Dickens: it allowed him to be comic while at the same time to express the violence which, says John Kucich, was generally his attitude toward his writing (36–37). At any rate he clearly had violently mixed feelings about mothers, which is suggested in his predominantly hostile maternal portraits.[3] Although Dickens also painted idealized images of the cozy hearth, for instance the Cratchit family's Christmas Eve and the Toodles' simple but clean home, these are among the few times when he conceived such settings with a mother in them. Mrs. Peerybingle in *The Cricket on the Hearth* is typical of the newlywed child-wife (as opposed to a mature matron) who oversees such a home. Margaret Lane believes that the small and childlike wife was Dickens' ideal (156–57); indeed, almost all of Dickens' good mothers are described as tiny, the bad ones as physically large or formidable. Even as late as *Our Mutual Friend* (1864–65), one of his most complex novels which J. B. Priestly called "a dark mixture of anger and despair," the heroine's mother has only changed in details, not in essence. Mrs. Wilfer is "*of course*, a tall woman, and an angular" (my emphasis); she is "heroically attired" and accustomed to talk in an "Act-of-Parliament manner" (*OMF* 50, 55). She is so pompous, posturing, and small minded that when the Boffins come to "adopt" Bella, Mrs. Wilfer goes into her prima-donna routine:

> [O]pening the door a little way, simultaneously with a sound of scuttling outside it, the good lady made the proclamation, "Send Miss Bella to me!" Which proclamation, though grandly formal, and one might almost say heraldic, to hear, was in fact enunciated with her maternal eyes reproachfully glaring on the young lady in the flesh—and in so much of it that she was retiring with difficulty into the small closet under the stairs. (*OMF* 130)

In fact, with the possible exception of Mrs. Steerforth, whose adulation of James in *David Copperfield* is pathological but not wilfully stupid (in contrast to Mrs. Heep with her Uriah), all Dickens' mothers are remarkable for their ignorance.

The stupidity of Bessy Tulliver is of a slightly different order—for one thing, unlike most of Dickens' stupid mothers, she does not pride herself on her perspicuity. "I could never see into men's business as sister Glegg does," she says (*MF* 158). Consequently, far from being absurdly self-satisfied, as Mrs. Nickleby is, she is chronically *dis*satisfied, for she cannot make out the logic on which the rest of the world turns. Thus her ignorance is of a slightly subtler nature than Mrs. Nickleby's. Another difference is that the narrator of *The Mill on the*

Floss frankly acknowledges and frequently comments on Bessy's simple-mindedness—implying that this weakness plays more than a diversionary role in the story. We are warned as early as the second chapter of Mrs. Tulliver's weak understanding and the peevishness that comes from too mild a temper. "[M]ilk and mildness are not the best things for keeping, and when they turn only a little sour they may disagree with young stomachs seriously" (*MF* 62). Later she is called "an amiable fish" who, no matter how many times she has bumped her head into the glass wall of her fish-bowl looking for an exit, "would go at it again today with undulled alacrity" (*MF* 134). Eliot is not only foreshadowing the character traits that will later prove disastrous; she is openly belittling her character.

Dickens, on the other hand, is never quite so blunt a critic, preferring to make his judgments via oblique sarcasm or even feigned sympathy rather than direct analysis. Typical is the scene in which Nicholas is accused of thievery:

> "It is impossible," said Kate. "Nicholas!—and a thief, too! Mama, how can you sit and hear such statements?"
>
> Poor Mrs. Nickleby, who had at no time been remarkable for the possession of a very clear understanding, and who had been reduced by the late changes in her affairs to a most complicated state of perplexity, made no other reply to this earnest remonstrance than exclaiming from behind a mass of pocket-handkerchief, that she never could have believed it— thereby most ingeniously leading her hearers to supppose that she did believe it. (*NN* 321–22)

While this is amusing, it is also heavily sardonic: pretending to excuse Mrs. Nickleby, in fact it indirectly accuses her of disloyalty toward her own son—and disloyalty, according to Dickens' code of ethics, is one of the cardinal sins. His tone, of course, deliberately undermines the severity of his reproach. These narrative dissemblings, for all that we are never seriously misled by them, nonetheless are yet another of the reasons we do not take his mothers seriously, since Dickens himself makes a game of uncovering their motives.

In Bessy Tulliver we see the slightest shift toward a more realistic accountability. While she is still very much a one-dimensional character, George Eliot makes sure that we understand the implications of that single dimension—namely, her inability to understand subtle or conceptual thought, revealed in an early conversation with Mr. Tulliver:

> "That's the fault I have to find wi' you, Bessy: if you see a stick i' the road, you're allays thinkin' you can't step over it. You'd want me not to hire a good waggoner, 'cause he'd got a mole on his face."
>
> "Dear heart!" said Mrs. Tulliver, in mild surprise, "when did I iver make objections to a man, because he'd got a mole on his face? I'm sure I'm rether fond o' the moles, for my brother, as is dead an' gone, had a mole on his brow." (*MF* 57)

She goes on to cite other proof of her tolerance of moles, until at last Mr. Tulliver says, "No, no, Bessy; I didn't mean justly the mole; I meant it to stand for summat else; but niver mind—it's puzzling work, talking is."

In fact, not talking only but life itself are puzzling to Bessy Tulliver, and her inability to understand them conceptually is at the root of all her frustration and blunders. When it begins to be apparent that the family is heading for a crisis, she protests in a *non sequitur* worthy of Mrs. Nickleby that she cannot be to blame, for "I'm sure at scouring time this Ladyday as I've had all the bedhangings taken down" (*MF* 158). Similarly, when Mr. Tulliver and Sister Glegg argue over his intention of sending Tom away to school, Bessy desperately tries to calm the waters with an offer of almonds and raisins, to which the sharp-tongued older sister retorts, "It's poor work talking o' almonds and raisins" (*MF* 131). In her nasty way, of course, Sister Glegg is right—few conflicts can be resolved in the limited and literal vocabulary of domestic economy, but unfortunately for poor Bessy, that is all she knows. Moreover, that is all she has ever been expected to know, so it is hard to tell whether to blame or to pity her. On one hand Bessy is a product of a culture that devalues an intelligent woman as "no better nor a long-tailed sheep—she'll fetch none the bigger price for that" (*MF* 60). Indeed, Mr. Tulliver admits that he married Bessy for her ignorance: "I picked [Bessy] from her sisters o' purpose 'cause she was a bit weak, like; for I wasn't a-goin' to be told the rights o' things by my own fireside" (*MF* 68).

On the other hand, we see with building resentment and scorn the results of her ignorance—her obvious preference for Tom over Maggie, her frequent disloyalty to her husband, and especially her disastrous "business" call on the lawyer Wakem which precipitates Mr. Tulliver's full and final ruin. So it is unlikely that George Eliot meant Bessy Tulliver to represent in ideological terms the oppression of the middle-class housewife. The issue seems more present in *Daniel Deronda*, but in this earlier work, if there is any real doubt as to how the author would have us view Bessy, the answer lies in the derisive metaphor describing her resolution to approach Wakem:

> Imagine a truly respectable and amiable hen, by some portentous anomaly, taking to reflection and inventing combinations by which she might prevail on Hodge not to wring her neck or send her and her chicks to market: the result could hardly be other than much cackling and fluttering. (*MF* 332)

First she was an "amiable fish"—now she is an "amiable hen" plotting strategy. That Eliot chooses to deprecate and dehumanize Bessy in this way suggests that the author in no way identifies with her character or with mothers in general: the "portentous anomaly" is that a mother in a small country town should act and think independently; the mock heroic language underscores the author's amused contempt. What she expresses, at best, is what one might feel for the severely retarded—a degree of interest, even a humane compassion, but hardly respect.

Yet there is a subtle change, not so much in Bessy as in the tone the narrator takes with her, as the novel nears its end. In a poignant scene following the "downfall," most of the family's property having been removed to satisfy creditors, Eliot is at her most compassionate:

> Poor Mrs. Tulliver, it seemed, would never recover her old self—her placid household activity: how could she? The objects among which her mind had moved complacently were all gone: all the little hopes, and schemes, and speculations, all the pleasant little cares about her treasures which had made this world quite comprehensible to her for a quarter of a century, since she had made her first purchase of the sugar-

tongs, had been suddenly snatched away from her, and she remained bewildered in this empty life. (*MF* 368)

As the misfortunes fall thickest around her and her family, we see pathos replacing condescension: that patronizing little word "little" appears twice in this passage, cueing the reader that pity is now to be joined with contempt. When Tom brutally turns Maggie from his door, "the poor frightened mother's love leaped out . . . stronger than all dread. 'My child! I'll go with you. You've got a mother'" (*MF* 614). But this is as pathetic as Eliot allows Bessy to get. However much genuine sorrow may have galvanized her proper maternal instincts, it has no such effect on her brain. To Maggie's gesture of pity and compunction—"you might have been happy, if it hadn't been for me"—Mrs. Tulliver wanly agrees. "I must put up wi' my children. . . . [I]f they bring me bad luck, I must be fond on it—there's nothing else much to be fond on, for my furnitur' went long ago" (*MF* 632). The final word on Mrs. Tulliver must be that she is after all a profoundly stupid woman—arguably the stupidest mother in any serious novel. But the fact that Eliot tried to explain and even a little to sympathize with her behavior suggests that she had some misgivings about casting Bessy as thoroughly foolish.

This ambivalent sympathy is even more apparent in *Wives and Daughters*, for the stupidity of Mrs. Gibson is even more complex. In some ways, especially in her conversations with Mr. Gibson, it sounds like conventional foolishness, a perfect echo of Mrs. Bennet nagging Mr. Bennet in *Pride and Prejudice*. For instance, in a passage late in the novel she is complaining about her daughter Cynthia's fashionable marriage to a London barrister. She is clearly jealous, and looks for some response—preferably sympathy or guilt—from her husband. "I have to live in a little country town with three servants, and no carriage," she gripes, "and she with her inferior good looks will live in Sussex Place, and keep a man and a brougham." It is with difficulty that she keeps from blaming Mr. Gibson outright. "I always think if you had gone to the bar you might have succeeded better." Failing still to get an answer, she finally assumes a noble indifference. "I only hope all this indulgence won't develop the faults in Cynthia's character. It's a week since we heard from her, and I did write so particularly to ask her for the autumn fashions before I bought my new bonnet. But riches," she sighs philosophically, "are a great snare." To which Mr. Gibson makes a rejoinder at last: "Be thankful you are spared temptation, my dear" (*WD* 703–704). Like Mr. Bennet, Mr. Gibson finds that since he cannot communicate rationally with his wife, the peaceful alternative is to ignore her. And if vanity and shallowness were the extent of Mrs. Gibson's ignorance, we could more easily ignore her, too. However, underlying those artificial smiles and false terms of endearment is the complex, alien mentality of the professional mercenary. We are not meant to like Mrs. Gibson, or even to forgive her, but we *are* meant, I believe, to pay attention to her. She may be considered, in fact, the first mother anti-heroine in the novel. Her inner life, hollow of real substance though it is, is revealed to us fascinatingly, extensively, and above all convincingly. Only Molly Gibson herself receives more narrative time, and no one else, not even Cynthia, gets more psychological exposition.

In fact, because of what we know about her psychology, it is probably wise to redefine "stupidity" if we are to apply it to Hyacinth Gibson. Far from being slow-witted, she is a genius at dissembling, extremely shrewd in figuring out which people are likely to be the most useful to her goal of self-advancement and then adapting her behavior accordingly. When she realizes that Osborne, the attractive heir to the Hamley estate, is dying, she immediately begins to curry favor with his brother Roger who, though clumsy, is nonetheless next in line to the inheritance. Mrs. Gibson's stupidity is thus not so much a case of confused intellect as of distorted values. Unlike Bessy Tulliver, a bonnet interests her not precisely because it is a tangible reality but because it is a tangible reality with certain precious intangibles behind it: namely wealth, refinement, and—on a deeper level—security. Granted that Mrs. Nickleby likes fine clothes and fancy carriages for basically the same reasons—the prestige they confer—; still the important difference is that whereas Dickens barely glances into Mrs. Nickleby's psyche, Gaskell spends a great deal of time inside Mrs. Gibson's, carefully establishing and attempting to explain (though not necessarily to excuse) her personality. What we see is a woman who is convinced that she was born into the wrong economic and social class and is bent on escaping it. Judging from the significant fact that *her* mother named her something as pretentious as Hyacinth Clare, and

Clare in turn "perpetuated her own affected name by having her daughter called after her" (*WD* 156), she has been bred from the cradle to fancy herself destined for greatness. Nearly every thought she has, nearly every culpable act and every deficit in her heavily deficient character, is traceable to this single overwhelming motive in Mrs. Gibson's personality.

> It was a very pleasant change to a poor unsuccessful schoolmistress to leave her own house, full of battered and shabby furniture . . . and to come bowling through the Towers Park in the luxurious carriage sent to meet her; to alight, and feel secure that the well-trained servants would see after her bags, and umbrella, and parasol, and cloak, without her loading herself with all these portable articles, as she had had to do while following the wheelbarrow containing her luggage . . . that morning; to pass up the deep piled carpets of the broad shallow stairs into my lady's own room, cool and deliciously fresh, even on this sultry day.

To Clare, even certain cuts of meat have relative status:

> Then there was the contrast between the dinners which she had to share with her scholars at Ashcombe—rounds of beef, legs of mutton, great dishes of potatoes, and large batter-puddings—with the tiny meal of exquisitely cooked delicacies, sent up on old Chelsea china, that was served every day to the earl and countess and herself at the Towers. (*WD* 130)

The language of Clare's reflections—"well-trained servants, deep piled carpets, broad shallow stairs, old Chelsea china"—suggests the profound, almost hallucinogenic joy she derives from images of physical comfort and plenty. What Mrs. Gaskell wishes the reader to perceive, I think, through this and countless similar passages, is that the dominant feature of Hyacinth Clare's psychology is an almost obsessive abhorrence of poverty and everything that she, in her imperfect experience of wealth, associates with it. "Bread and cheese!" she exclaims upon learning one of her husband's favorite lunches. "Does Mr. Gibson eat cheese? . . . we must change all that" (*WD* 162). Such exaggerated delicacy makes her ridiculous, and such self-importance makes her obnoxious, but there is more to her behavior than these outward manifestations of it. Her pretensions stem greatly from her fear of being poor, and that fear stems at least in part from having experienced want firsthand—"Money had been so much needed, so hardly earned in Mrs. Kirkpatrick's life" (*WD* 174). It shows up in peculiar, otherwise unaccountable behavior: from her gobbling down Molly's dinner at the Towers ("as if she was afraid of someone coming to surprise her in the act" [*WD* 48]) to her dislike of owing money to strangers. "Whatever other faults might arise from her superficial and flimsy character, she was always uneasy till she was out of debt. Yet she had no scruple in appropriating her future husband's money to her own use" (*WD* 175). Being rich means to Mrs. Gibson never having to ask "how much the washing costs, or what pink ribbon is a yard" (*WD* 131); but above all, being rich means the right of self-determination.

> She recollected how, one time during this very summer at the Towers, after she was engaged to Mr. Gibson, when she had taken above an hour to arrange her hair in some new mode carefully studied from Mrs. Bradley's fashion-book—after all, when she came down looking her very best, as she thought, and ready for her lover, Lady Cumnor had sent her back again to her room, just as if she had been a little child, to do her hair over again, and not make such a figure of fun of herself! ... These were little things; but they were late samples of what in different shapes she had had to endure for many years; and her liking for Mr. Gibson grew in proportion to her sense of the evils from which he was going to serve as a means of escape. (*WD* 175–76)

Having been lorded over herself, Mrs. Gibson is now determined to lord it over others. For instance, having accepted (no doubt with smug satisfaction) the resignation of an old servant who objected to the new regime, Mrs. Gibson takes additional pleasure in watching the repentent old woman eat humble pie: "She might have stayed for ever for me, if she had only attended to all my wishes; ... [but] it is quite against my principles ever to take an apology from a servant who has given warning" (*WD* 212). The author's ironic use of the word "principles" here as a verbal sleight-of-hand for "pride" is meant to deflect any sympathy the reader might be inclined to feel: Clare is so adept at manipulating the meaning and application of words, and does it with so little apparent burden of compunction, that one can hardly feel sorry for a woman with such semantic resources, no matter how desperate her finances. "I wonder if I am to go on all my life toiling and moiling for money?" she muses, while still a widow running an unsuccessful girls' school. "It's not natural. Marriage is the natural thing; then the husband has all that kind of dirty work to do, and his wife sits in the drawing room like a lady" (*WD* 131). "Natural" is of course Clare's word for "convenient."

Thus we see, as Coral Lansbury claims, that although Clare "functions like a slightly inefficient calculating machine," dealing in trifles rather than ethical or moral problems (206), yet she is not stupid in the usual sense. Indeed, the narrator tells us that Clare has a great "boldness of invention to eke out her facts" as well as "skill in the choice and arrangement of her words" (*WD* 217) which allow her to be an agreeable companion when it is in her interest to make the effort. She can listen "with tolerable intelligence" to the conversations of distinguished people, so long as

> the subjects spoken about did not refer to serious solid literature, or science, or politics, or social economy. About novels and poetry, travels and gossip, personal details, or anecdotes of any kind, she always made exactly the remarks which are expected from an agreeable listener; and she had sense enough to confine herself to those short expressions of wonder, admiration, and astonishment, which may mean anything, when more recondite things were talked about. (*WD* 130)

This is the sort of frivolous knowledge which the more progressive Victorians blamed a patriarchal education system for encouraging in women, and presumably Elizabeth Gaskell was one of those who condemned it. As a Unitarian she believed that equal education was the right of every child,[4] and no doubt in some ways Clare's portrait serves as a condemnation of the system. However, I cannot agree with critics like Enid Duthie who insist on seeing Gaskell's mothers as evidence of her liberated views about women. When Duthie praises Mrs. Thornton of *North and South* as "a sensible as well as devoted mother" who is more affectionate to her daughter than to her son "because she realises that the weaker Fanny is in more need of support and reassurance" (96), she is clearly reading Mrs. Thornton's portrait more generously than the text warrants. "Sensible" is hardly the term for a woman "not . . . much given to reasoning" (*NS* 355); "devoted mother" hardly describes her jealous hatred of the woman whom her son loves; and as for Fanny, Mrs. Thornton has "an unconscious contempt" for her weak character, seeking to hide with shame "the poverty of her child in all the grand qualities which she herself possessed" (*NS* 109). The scene in which Margaret Hale first meets mother and daughter presents an inescapable comparison with the scene in *Pride and Prejudice* in which Elizabeth visits Lady Catherine de Bourgh and her daughter at Rosings. Mrs. Thornton is "more than usually stern and forbidding"; the first thing her insipid daughter says is "I suppose you are not musical . . . as I see no piano" (*NS* 112). Mrs. Gaskell does indeed picture women as resourceful, intelligent, and spirited in defiance of the social norm but (with the exception of *Cranford*) only insofar as her fellow novelists do: that is, in young, single women. The central character in *Ruth* may demonstrate deep maternal love for her illegitimate child, but Ruth is young, and to all intents single. Mrs. Hale is querulous, hypochondriacal, and envious, offering to share more intimacy with her maid than with her daughter. And as for the strong-minded spinsters of *Cranford*, I agree with Stoneman that this work embodies not triumph over patriarchy but the doctrine of separate spheres. As I have pointed out elsewhere, even Mrs. Hamley, kind as she is, is stereotypically weak and blinded by love of her eldest son. Gaskell's mothers are certainly not all stupid, but they conform to the stereotypes in other ways.

Like the other silly mothers, Mrs. Gibson speaks in an entirely self-centered idiom which renders her either ridiculous or unintelligible— except indeed to the folks at the Towers, with whom, ironically, she *can* communicate. Nobody with real sense can penetrate Mrs. Gibson's veil of ignorance, not her husband—"You either can't or won't see what I mean," he says (*WD* 429)—and least of all poor sensible Molly, who gets the brunt of her stepmother's pettiness and illogic. "[O]ften she had to get up and leave the room to calm herself down after listening to a long series of words . . . which at the end conveyed no distinct impression of either the speaker's thought or feeling" (*WD*

495). For her father's sake Molly tries to talk reasonably with her stepmother, but it is pointless. When the new bride pouts over being left alone while Mr. Gibson attends a sick patient, Molly observes that the sick man cannot put off his dying. Mrs. Gibson, however, is not moved by such an humane rationale. "[I]f this Mr. Smith is dying, as you say, what's the use of your father's going off to him in such a hurry? Does he expect any legacy, or anything of that kind?" (*WD* 209). It is no use trying to reason with a woman for whom words like "loyalty" or "compassion" are flexible concepts, defined according to the circumstances of the speaker. Such deliberate indifference, whether in speech or in actions, to the needs, rights, and values of others goes beyond mere stupidity—it is sheer selfishness; and even allowing much for the emotional hang-ups of a disadvantaged childhood, it is altogether condemnable in Mrs. Gibson. To varying degrees this quality exists in nearly all "bad" mothers in fiction: if stupidity is their most pervasive foible, selfishness is their most prolific vice.

Inasmuch as the principal victims of their selfishness are their innocent daughters and sons, this is where nineteenth-century mothers most closely resemble their wicked-witch forebears. In outward appearance, of course, few of them look like villains: they manage their homes, mix in society, discuss fashions and do needlework; most of them even believe they love their children. Such a mother would never have her child poisoned, or trick it into drowning in a well; we have become too civilized, at least in our literature, to admit such unambiguous evil. Yet the ancient, ambiguous, subconscious fear of mothers that underlies the bad mother tradition in archetypal literature has never gone away, it has simply taken less primitive forms. Mrs. Gibson cannot send a woodsman into the forest to cut out Cynthia's heart, so she punishes her perceived rival instead by years of emotional injury and neglect. She leaves Cynthia with a series of schoolmistresses over holidays, taking no pains to disguise the fact that her daughter is a burden. Cynthia sums up the results of such abuse with characteristic indifference: "[I]t's no use talking; I am not good, and I never shall be" (*WD* 258).

Of course, because Cynthia is "not good," because she has been too deeply tainted by her mother, she can hardly be a nineteenth-century heroine. Even though novelists may stress that the child is flawed through no fault of its own, nonetheless that tolerance is often undercut by a distinct, if subtle, air of censure, as if to say, "Others have overcome worse; you could too." The same is true of Edith Dombey, for instance, and, going back to Jane Austen, of Mary Crawford. Mary, Edith, and Cynthia are acutely interesting characters—more so, in most readers' opinions, than Fanny or Florence or Molly. Yet a Victorian novel would as soon make them its heroine as the Girls in the Well would award the gold coins to the lazy, arrogant natural daughter. Just as Roger Hamley is reserved as a sort of prize for the long-suffering Molly, and Edmund Bertram is awarded to Fanny Price, so the gold coins in the Girls in the Well folktale are reserved for the pure-hearted stepdaughter. Although as I have noted earlier, it is compellingly realistic to confront the ravages of bad mothering, and Victorian novelists do so with convincing insight, still the novel had not yet evolved so far as to put the truly ravaged child, with all of its faults and complexities, at its center. More comforting, I suppose, though far more improbable, was the possibility that prolonged exposure to irresponsible or selfish parenting could bounce off a child's natural incorruptibility as off a shield—as it does off Florence Dombey, Little Dorrit, Maggie Tulliver, and so many others. Such an assumption seems to parallel the emblematic, black-and-white nature of the struggle between mother and child in fairy tales—the threatening mother is always vanquished, the child prospers—thus satisfying, as fairy tales presumably do, the preconscious need of the child not only for a total separation from the mother but also a total vindication of any guilt the child might feel for desiring that separation.

The archetypal nature of these relationships is further suggested by the innocence and virtual impotence of the hero/heroine. Like Rapunzel, like Cinderella, like Snow White, like Hansel and Gretel, the children of fiction's bad mothers, despite their superior intelligence and sounder judgment, must submit wordlessly and dutifully to their mothers' defective authority. It is often as true of these novels as it is of fairy tales that, as Adriaan de Witt notes, "the fathers . . . seem to play no more than tag-along roles, if any at all" (316); the child is thus deprived of a potential advocate. The eventual victory belongs entirely to the child, but so does the struggle. This is true even of Mr. Gibson: in fact, one wonders how Molly can continue to idolize him so, since it was he who brought this awful woman home and now will have little to do with her himself, though he has no compunctions about inflicting her on Molly. This beloved daughter of his endures a great deal in stoic silence, but when she finally appeals to him to veto an unusually oppressive ruling of Mrs. Gibson's, he gets angry not with his wife but with her: "Come, Molly! sit down and be quiet. . . . One comes home wanting peace and quietness—and food too" (WD 236). The tradition assures us that Molly will eventually "overcome" this mother and resume her rightful place, both sexually and socially, in the world of men represented by her father, but first she must endure this period of testing by herself.

Kate Nickleby is even more vulnerable. Her father dead, her brother usually absent, and herself uncommonly timid, Kate has only her mother to protect her from various wolves, the most dangerous being her uncle and Sir Mulberry Hawk; yet far from protecting her, Mrs. Nickleby throws her daughter, with compliments, to her enemies. She does not do so maliciously or even quite knowingly. Yet inasmuch as she ignores Kate's needs largely to gratify her own fantasies, she does so selfishly. With typical sardonic understatement, Dickens allows that Mrs. Nickleby is "a well-meaning woman enough, but rather weak withal" (NN 85). Ignoring the fact that Kate is shrinking from her uncle's "cold glistening eye," her mother eagerly makes plans to put her in Ralph's way: "Kate, my dear, you're to dine with your uncle at half-past six" (NN 300). Though her instincts revolt, Kate cannot protest directly—she never does; she merely hangs her head in chagrined acquiescence. Later, following the arranged encounter between Kate and Sir Mulberry at the play, Mrs. Nickleby is too much dazzled by her titled escorts and the prospect of seeing her only daughter married to a peer to pay attention to Kate's distress: on the contrary, she takes "particular care not so much as to look at her daughter during the whole evening" (NN 431). Ironically, Dickens is not explicitly questioning the code of parental obedience under which Kate must defer to her mother's wishes; he himself was a strict disciplinarian before whom his children "dared not express their displeasure openly," but whose resentment, as his son Harry would later recall in Memories of My Father, "took the more insidious form of deeply whispered mutterings among [themselves] on the subject of 'slavery,' 'degradation,' and so forth" (26). What he does blame are parents who selfishly or self-servingly misuse or ignore their proper role as authority and advisor. For all that he calls her a "good" or "worthy" lady, and for all that he trivializes her self-absorption, as when she assumes Frank Cheeryble's frequent visits are in compliment to *her*, not Kate (*NN* 734), Dickens really does hold Mrs. Nickleby responsible for many of the hazards Kate must negotiate. That she manages to negotiate them successfully owes purely to the fact that *Nicholas Nickleby* is a comedy.

Maggie Tulliver's fate, on the other hand, is tragic, and therefore her mother's faults appear more serious. In some ways Maggie's relationship with Mrs. Tulliver conforms to the Victorian model: though Bessy's authority in the house is marginal and though the mother's intellect is no match for the daughter's, still Maggie comes almost entirely under her jurisdiction, which is usually ill-natured and preferential. Yet Maggie's is an unusual case in other respects. She has a champion in her father, who, unlike Mr. Gibson, is happy to intercede for her. Furthermore, Maggie is not naturally submissive, occasionally even ignoring her mother's peevish orders. Nonetheless, Mrs. Tulliver's incessant scolding, her undisguised regret that she got such a "wild thing" for a daughter instead of the docile Lucy Deane, the way she exposes Maggie to—indeed invites—Mrs. Glegg's and the other aunts' attacks, and her evident favoritism for her vastly inferior son, all serve to inhibit Maggie's natural buoyancy and weaken her self-esteem. Her life becomes, in consequence, a quest for acceptance, love, equality, and respect.

The fuss made over Maggie's hair is typical of what Elizabeth Ermarth calls the Dodson sisters' "peculiar view of human priorities [which] puts a premium on physical manifestations and leaves little room for deviation" ("Maggie Tulliver's Long Suicide" 588). Maggie's straight black locks are a constant thorn in Mrs. Tulliver's side ("there's her cousin Lucy's got a row o' curls round her head, an' not a hair out o' place" [*MF* 60–61]) and a constant source of contention between them (Maggie "vindictively" dips her head in a bucket of water so as to foil her mother's attempts to make it curl). So on a day when all the aunts and uncles have come for dinner and Maggie has again endured their critical inspection ("I think the gell has too much hair"; "it isn't good for her health"; etc. [*WD* 118]), and even her beloved father and brother have commented on it, she sneaks upstairs and chops it off. The "chorus of reproach and derision" which follows is destined to take its place, Eliot assures us, as "one of those keen moments [of remembered suffering that] has left its trace and lives in us still" (*MF* 125, 122). Yet despite such alarming outbursts of behavior it never occurs to Mrs. Tulliver to soften her touch with Maggie; her concern is eternally with herself: "Folks 'ull think it's a judgment on me as I've got such a child—they'll think I've done summat wicked" (*MF* 78). This is primarily where her selfishness lies—in her inability or refusal to look beyond her own feelings and concerns. She has no idea, for instance, that Maggie keeps a fetish, "entirely defaced by a long career of vicarious suffering," whose mutilation she effected by driving three nails into its skull, then "alternately grinding and beating the wooden head against the rough brick of the great chimneys" (*MF* 79). This behavior is by no means psychopathic or even abnormal; on the contrary, Bernard Paris finds that Maggie's method of dealing with her mother's rejection incorporates all three of the normal coping mechanisms: Maggie is alternately insecure, vengeful, and intellectually and emotionally withdrawn. My point is simply that Maggie represses a great deal of frustration and resentment that her mother ought to be aware of and attempting to heal—rather than exacerbate.

On this issue of selfishness and parental neglect we may look again at the manner and idiom of mothers' speech, for one may be selfish with conversation no less than with things. Through it one may share not only ideas and information but also concern, affection, confidence, advice, and support. Molly Gibson, for instance, thrives on her long talks with Mrs. Hamley ("to find her, was to find love and sympathy" [*WD* 285]), and Maggie Tulliver gets counsel and support from her kind Aunt Moss. The heroines (more so than the few heroes) in these novels, in fact, clearly put great value in a reliable confidante. Thus the fact that we rarely, perhaps never, see a really good, substantive, mutually satisfying conversation between them and their mothers is yet another index of the deficiency of their relationships. Their talks tend to be chronically one sided, with all the opinions coming from, and nearly all the attention focusing on, the mother. The daughter thus lives in a noisy yet paradoxically uncommunicative household. It is true of Kate and Mrs. Nickleby: the former tends to speak in conciliatory monosyllables ("Yes, mamma"; "No, mamma"; "I was only thinking, mamma") while Mrs. Nickleby typically runs "through a dozen or so of complicated sentences addressed to nobody in particular" (*NN* 198). It is true of Maggie and Mrs. Tulliver: the latter's conversations with Maggie, if they can be called that, consist of complaints, admonitions, or accusations, while Maggie's responses tend to be either rebellious silences or guilty apologies. And it is true above all of Molly and Mrs. Gibson. Mrs. Gibson claims from the first to wish to be intimate with her step-daughter: "Oh! We shall have a great deal to say to each other, I foresee!" (*WD* 163); but what she really means is that she, Hyacinth, will have a new audience to boast to, complain to, and lecture to. She has absolutely no interest in the things that concern Molly—in fact she is downright hostile to them. When Molly returns sadly home from Hamley Hall, knowing that Mrs. Hamley cannot live much longer, "Mrs. Gibson received her kindly enough. . . . but she did not care to hear any particulars about the friends whom Molly had just left," and the comments she does make are calculated to hurt rather than comfort: "What a time she lingers! Your papa never expected she would last half so long." Molly, to her credit, tries to be diplomatic, but to any observation of hers, no matter how correct, Mrs. Gibson is ready with a contradiction. "You don't know how the Squire values every minute," Molly says, to which Mrs. Gibson replies, "Why, you say she sleeps a great deal, and doesn't talk much when she's awake, and there's not the slightest hope for her" (*WD* 235). To so sensitive and loving a girl as Molly, the abolition of easy, happy, interested conversation at home, such as she shared for years with her father, is a severe deprivation.

Of course, one of the primary reasons Mrs. Gibson does not wish to talk about Mrs. Hamley is that she is jealous of her: "a parvenue, I've heard them say at the Towers" (*WD* 218). Sexual jealousy, for all that it is never alluded to directly, is in fact the motive of much of Mrs. Gibson's antagonism toward Molly, and even more so toward her own daughter. The reason she keeps Cynthia away from her wedding is that "she had felt how disagreeable it would be to her to have her young daughter flashing out her beauty by the side of the faded bride" (*WD* 156). Of course, such rivalries, especially when the mother is faded and ridiculous, are traditionally highly comic. Mothers in competition with their daughters' youth and good looks have always been a popular satiric device especially in earlier, openly bawdy genres such as Restoration comedy. For instance, in Congreve's *The Double-Dealer*, Lady Plyant protests to Mellefort, her stepdaughter's fiancé, that it would be impossible for them to run off together: "I must not love you,—therefore don't hope,—but don't despair neither—" (II.i.).

This theme of a mother's sexual vanity often gets light-hearted treatment in the more comic novels. For instance, when Roger Hamley takes leave of Molly from the garden before going overseas one last time, Mrs. Gibson takes his blown kisses as a personal compliment: "I call this so attentive of him . . . Really, it is quite romantic. It reminds me of former days. . ." (*WD* 702). Mrs. Bennet is similarly flattered by her husband's comment that she might send her five girls alone to Netherfield lest "Mr. Bingley . . . like you the best of the party" (*PP* 4). But the issue of sexual jealousy between mother and daughter can have rather darker implications. Mrs. Gibson's one-time rivalry with Cynthia for Mr. Preston has created an uneasy consciousness that makes it impossible that the two should ever trust each other. And the thing that is so disturbing about Cleopatra Skewton, I think, is that her sexual frustration in the face of Edith's potent sexuality has contented itself by turning her own daughter into little more than a prostitute.

> "There is no slave in a market: there is no horse in a fair: so shown and offered and examined and paraded, Mother, as I have been, for ten shameful years," cried Edith, with a burning brow. . . . "Is it not so? Have I been made the byword of all kinds of men? Have fools, have profligates, have boys, have dotards, dangled after me, and one by one rejected me, and fallen off, because you were too plain with all your cunning . . . ? Have I been hawked and vended here and there, until the last grain of self-respect is dead within me, and I loathe myself?" (*DS* 333)

I have noted elsewhere that the midwife/hag/procuress is among the series of degradations through which the dethroned mother goddess passes; this image is especially threatening because it is intimately connected with woman's fearful sexuality.[5] The fact that Mrs. Skewton is both a procuress for Edith *and* a sort of decaying whore herself brings uncomfortably close to the surface the illicit core of her nature, one guaranteed to upset what Robert Clark calls the "Victorian myth of middle-class women being without sexual desire" (70). The "woman past her prime"—i.e., past childbearing age—was regarded with a mixture of pity and contempt by much of patriarchal England, because the primary meaning of the woman's life was, so they believed, to bear children.[6] That the post-menopausal woman should continue to be interested in sex was generally denied, or else ascribed to some medical anomaly, "such as a tumour in connection with the internal genitals."[7] But even more disgusting was the post-menopausal woman who refused to "act her age."

> [O]lder women are not graceful if they disregard the warnings of their gradually failing powers, and cling with pathetic but futile tenacity to the dress, the amusements, aye, and even to the duties, of former years. Old age may be beautiful, venerable, and much beloved, upon condition that the woman herself thoroughly accepts the new role assigned to her in life's drama. Gradually she must learn that diaphanous materials and bright colours do not suit her altered figure and her fading complexion. She must also learn that although artificial teeth are a great blessing, . . . yet she is committing a sin against her personal appearance as well as against her self-respect if she dyes her hair.[8]

Cleopatra Skewton not only continues to assert her own decrepit sexuality, flirting with Major Bagstock—"you aggravating monster," she calls him, "rude man," "insupportable creature," and "mercenary wretch," all the time playfully hitting him with her fan (*DS* 308ff)— even worse, she is willing to sell her daughter's sexuality in exchange for a meal ticket and presumably, in some malicious way, for the gratification of seeing this beautiful daughter suffer.

However, as in everything about Mrs. Skewton, the excesses of the grotesque are a sort of barrier against our believing in her. It is a different case altogether with Rachel Esmond, Lady Castlewood in Thackeray's ambiguous novel *Henry Esmond* (1852). Harriet Martineau said of Thackeray that "he never can have known a good and sensible woman."[9] Thackeray's women may be good, or they may be sensible, but rarely both at once, and this includes his mothers. His attitude toward Amelia in *Vanity Fair* is typical: the narrator seems to be sincerely sorry for her when he describes her decision to entrust her son to his paternal grandparents because she cannot afford to keep him with her.

> The combat . . . lasted for many weeks in poor Amelia's heart: during which she had no confidante; indeed, she could

never have one: as she would not allow to herself the possibility of yielding; though she was giving way daily before the enemy with whom she had to battle. One truth after another was marshalling itself silently against her, and keeping its ground. Poverty and misery for all, want and degradation for her parents, injustice to the boy—one by one the outworks of the little citadel were taken, in which the poor soul passionately guarded her only love and treasure. (*VF* 576)

Once again, however, the cue words "little" and "poor" should alert the reader that Thackeray's sympathy for Amelia is heavily tinged with condescension, even contempt. "Poor simple lady, tender and weak," he says, "how are you to battle with the struggling violent world?" (*VF* 575). As for the effects of her "timorous debasement and self-humiliation" (*VF* 581) on little Georgy, I have already said that they produce a miniature version of his self-centered, callous father. Amelia, of course, worships them both, taking "all the faults on her side [and courting] punishment for the wrongs which she has not committed" (*VF* 581).

Yet there are several disturbing hints of another side to Amelia's nature: her "parasitic" treatment of the faithful Dobbin; her jealousy of their daughter Janey, mentioned momentarily but revealingly in the penultimate paragraph of the novel; and her reaction when she finds her mother giving Daffy's Elixir to the infant George.

Amelia, the gentlest and sweetest of every-day mortals, when she found this meddling with her maternal authority, thrilled and trembled all over with anger. Her cheeks, ordinarily pale, now flushed up, until they were as red as they used to be when she was a child of twelve years old. She seized the baby out of her mother's arms and then grasped at the bottle, leaving the old lady gaping at her, furious, and holding the guilty tea-spoon.

Amelia flung the bottle crashing into the fire-place. "I will *not* have baby poisoned, Mamma." (*VF* 455)

What is particularly interesting about this scene is that it prefigures similar scenes in *The History of Henry Esmond*. Rachel Esmond is normally the most angelic of women: "It was this lady's disposition to think kindnesses, and devise silent bounties and to scheme benevolence, for those about her" (*HE* 78). Henry, narrating his own story, describes her as a Mary, an angel, a goddess. Devoted to her husband, "[she] clung to his arm as he paced the terrace, her two fair little hands clasped round his great one. . . . Her little son was his son. . . . Her daughter Beatrix was his daughter. . . . Not regarding her dress, she would wear a gown to rags, because he had once liked it" (*HE* 53–54). And Henry, to whom she showed kindness when he first arrived at Castlewood, soon becomes her "little pigmy adorer" (*HE* 53). However, when Henry realizes that he has been exposed to smallpox and unwittingly may have infected the little boy, Rachel sends Frank and Beatrix out of the room, then astounds Henry and her husband with her fury:

> "My lord," she said, "this young man—your dependant—told me just now in French—he was ashamed to speak in his own language—that he had been at the alehouse all day, where he has had that little wretch who is now ill of the smallpox on his knee. And he comes home reeking from that place—yes, reeking from it—and takes my boy into his lap without shame, and sits down by me, yes, by *me*. He may have killed Frank for what I know—killed our child. Why was he brought in to disgrace our house? Why is he here? Let him go—let him go, I say, to-night, and pollute the place no more." (*HE* 63)

A similar outburst occurs when Lady Castlewood visits Henry in prison where he has been sent for taking part in a duel in which Lord Castlewood has been killed. For reasons which I will discuss shortly, Rachel holds Henry responsible for her husband's death. "Give me back my husband, Henry! Why did you stand by at midnight and see him murdered? Why did the traitor escape who did it? You, the champion of our house. . . . Why did you come among us? You have only brought us grief and sorrow: and repentance, bitter, bitter repentance" (*HE* 138–39).

Contrasted with the idealized descriptions of Rachel, these scenes may be taken merely to indicate that Thackeray rejects the Angel in the House and wants to show that Rachel has human flaws, one of them being a very bad temper. But the facts are much more complex and much more damning of Rachel, for she is in love with Henry and he with her. What looks like savage defense of her children and her husband is in fact a confused denial of her passion for the boy who came to live with them when he was twelve years old, she twenty. As Juliet McMaster notes in her study of Thackeray's novels, Henry's narrative as regards either her feelings or his own is unreliable. "He describes the deterioration of the marriage with an authority which his limited knowledge does not warrant; and according to his analysis the main fault lies with the husband. . . . There is much that is penetrating about his analysis of the situation; but he still does not tell us the whole truth" (112).

The truth can be arrived at only by considering all the evidence and dismissing a good deal of what Henry writes. Rachel's growing absorption in Henry and her rejection of her husband and her daughter do not escape the eyes of the latter two. Lord Castlewood has momentary suspicions of Henry which, generous-hearted man that he is, pain him deeply; and Beatrix says bluntly to Henry, "[S]he loves you, sir, a great deal too much, and I hate you for it" (*HE* 306). Thus we begin to determine whose accounts of Rachel Esmond are the accurate ones. Castlewood confides in Henry that "the very notion of a woman drives her mad" (*HE* 64); it was the thought of Henry courting the sister of the boy with smallpox rather than the smallpox itself that infuriated her. "She neither sins nor forgives," he says sadly. "I am not good like her—I know it. Who is—by Heaven, who is?" (*HE* 124). Beatrix says very much the same: "Oh, what a saint she is! Her goodness frightens me. I'm not fit to live with her. I should be better, I think, if she were not so perfect" (*HE* 306). As McMaster notes, much of the source of Rachel's power over these two is, in fact, sexual. After the accident of the smallpox, when she betrays to herself her love for Henry, she begins to deny her husband sexually. And as for poor Beatrix, although Henry claims she disdains his love for her, McMaster believes that "Beatrix is by no means as unattainable as he likes to suggest": "[i]t is not for his poverty or his bar-sinister that she rejects him, but for his lack of resolution" (115). And of course that lack of resolution comes from having given his primary allegiance to the mother—Beatrix can see this even if Henry cannot. Beatrix, in her hurt and anger, frequently makes a malicious joke of their self-deception. Tauntingly fondling her mother, Beatrix turns archly to Henry: "There, sir; would not *you* like to play the very same pleasant game?" "Indeed, madam, I would," he replies, meaning, ostensibly, that he would like to play thus with Beatrix. But Beatrix is insistent. Running up to Lady Castlewood and giving her another kiss, she laughs, "Oh, you silly kind mamma, . . . that's what Harry would like," and Lady Castlewood "blushed as bashful as a maid of sixteen" (*HE* 305).

All this is disturbing enough, though remarkably acute psychologically; but what makes Rachel so difficult a character to resolve, and Thackeray's attitude toward her so ambiguous, is the way the two sides of the stereotype clash in her. She is not stupid like most bad mothers, nor is she selfish in the small-minded way they are. Nonetheless, it is not that Rachel is the Victorian's answer to the Great Mother composite, combining the archetypally good and terrible aspects; for Rachel Esmond does not combine them. Rather, she is alternately one or the other. Her idealized aspect, as Henry describes it, is inviolate; likewise her terrible aspect, including the devouring sexuality, is softened, as her husband says, by no mark of sympathy or love. She is, I believe, the most problematic mother of the period.

Thackeray's mothers *are* harder to classify than most; nonetheless, most of them still submit to being judged, though certainly not easily dismissed, by the qualities of stupidity and above all selfishness. The mothers of Pendennis and Barry Lyndon, for instance, are, like Mrs. Thornton, extremely strong, but their values and priorities are clearly censured as inhumane. Helen Pendennis worships her son in a way that recalls Gertrude Morel, and her sexual jealousy makes her vicious, especially to her adopted daughter Laura. As for the misogynist Barry Lyndon, his cruelty to women may be traced to his childhood experiences with his mother, whose fits of anger he recalls vividly, as well as the reconciliations which, says Micael Clarke, were "still more violent and painful" (115).

Stupidity and/or selfishness continue to be the leading indicators of bad mothers throughout the century; and as the transitional period for mothers begins, these are valid measures for calibrating change. By these standards one can see immediately how Daniel Deronda's mother both differs from and hearkens back to her predecessors. Because she is so infinitely superior intellectually, it is hard at first even to compare Leonora Charisi to most of the others. Yet she is indisputably selfish, in which she conforms to the model. However, the moral complexity of both these qualities as revealed in her two conversations with her son must finally prove that the Princess Halm-Eberstein represents a shift in the characterization of mothers and the valuation of motherhood. She still bears recognizable marks of the monster-mother stereotype, but these are mitigated somewhat by the sympathy and strength that will later be seen as characterizing the treatment of mothers in the twentieth century.

The Alcharisi's intellectual force is striking. She says herself that she has "a man's force of genius"; and even though her hatred of Judaism is almost a mania with her, still it reflects her powers of independent thought and critical judgment.

> I was to be what [my father] called "the Jewish woman" under pain of his curse. I was to feel everything I did not feel, and believe everything I did not believe, I was to feel awe for the bit of parchment in the *mezuza* over the door; to dread lest a bit of butter should touch a bit of meat; to think it beautiful that men should bind the *tephillin* on them, and women not,— to adore the wisdom of such laws, however silly they might seem to me. (*DD* 540)

What the Princess' intelligence lacks, of course, is a spiritual dimension, and therefore she does not have Eliot's full sympathy. Yet the author clearly wishes us to see the Princess as tragic rather than demonic or even merely hyperbolic. Hers is the pitiable position of the nature that from the first was malformed for the life it had been born to. "I was to care for ever about what Israel had been; and I did not care at all. I cared for the wide world, and all I could represent in it" (*DD* 540). Though she explicitly blames Judaism for her status, nonetheless the repression of women which she deplores is universal, and one can detect the sentiments of George Eliot behind her words: "To have a pattern cut out—'this is the Jewish woman; this is what you must be; this is what you are wanted for; a woman's heart must be of such a size and no larger, else it must be pressed small, like Chinese feet; her happiness is to be made as cakes are, by a fixed receipt'" (*DD* 541). One needs to know very little about Jewish culture in particular or patriarchies in general to know that, full of invective though she is, there are undeniable elements of truth and reason in what she says.[10]

Unlike so many other mothers before her, the Princess sees no need to create her crises nor to feign or exaggerate her responses to them. Yet she does have feelings, even though she instinctively dramatises them: her nature is one "in which all feeling—and all the more when it was tragic as well as real—immediately became matter of conscious representation: experience immediately passed into drama, and she acted her own emotions" (*DD* 539). The narrator implies that acting her emotions out is a sort of anesthesia for the Princess—"each nucleus of pain or pleasure had a deep atmosphere of the excitement or spiritual intoxication which at once exalts and deadens" (*DD* 539). Yet, perhaps paradoxically, there is nothing maudlin or melodramatic about her: she perceives the truth about herself and others acutely and unflinchingly. "I am your mother," she greets Deronda. "But you can have no love for me. . . . I have not the foolish notion that you can love me merely because I am your mother, when you have never seen or heard of me all your life. . . . I will not deny anything I have done. I will not pretend to love where I have no love" (*DD* 536, 539). How different this is from the vanity of Mrs. Gibson, the inconsequential chatter of Mrs. Nickleby, or the self-pity of Mrs. Tulliver. And yet her maternal error is in a way more extreme than any of theirs, because she deliberately had a child she did not want and deliberately gave him up. "I was a great singer, and I acted as well as I sang. All the rest were poor beside me. Men followed me from one country to another. I was living a myriad of lives in one. I did not want a child." Even in the twentieth century, when mothers as well as fathers may have careers, there is something rather appalling about such open-eyed selfishness—she denies Daniel his birthright in order to gratify her own anti-semitism; she addresses virtually all her energies to self-glorification.

The selfishness of the Princess is so deeply entangled with her spiritual ideology that it is impossible to condemn one without implicating the other. Yet when she tries to explain her actions it is clear that judging either must be intensely difficult.

> Every woman is supposed to have the same set of motives, or else to be a monster. I am not a monster, but I have not felt exactly what other women feel—or say they feel, for fear of being thought unlike others. When you reproach me in your heart for sending you away from me, you mean that I ought to

say I felt about you as other women say they feel about their children. I did *not* feel that. I was glad to be freed from you. (*DD* 539)

Many mothers in literature have given their children up for selfish reasons, such as Bridget Allworthy and Becky Sharpe, but the critique of such behavior, invariably censorious, has been made either implicitly or by the narrator or another character.[11] The Princess' self-defense is surely the first time the mother herself has been allowed to try to justify her actions, and once the matter has been put on so personal a level, it is far easier to renounce the Princess' actions than it is to renounce the Princess herself. This complication—that mothers may deserve sympathy even if their actions do not—is one of the main factors distinguishing the transitional mothers in the following chapter.

Notes

1. Bad fathers are dangerous, too, of course, but it is not my purpose to discuss fathers here. I will merely note an interesting correspondence between fathers in fairy tales and fathers in novels: the return to or reconciliation with the father (i.e., the orderly patriarchal universe) which traditionally concludes fairy tales seems to be paralleled in novels as well, usually in the form of the heroine's marriage.

2. On Dickens' use of types, see, for instance, Earle Davis, *The Flint and the Flame* 17–36; and John Holloway, "Dickens and the Symbol." According to Holloway, nearly all of Dickens' characters may be labeled by types, i.e., Dotard, Rake, Innocent Child, Lively Old Man, and so on (64).

3. In *Dickens and the Parent-Child Relationship*, Arthur A. Adrian suggests that Dickens' mother's willingness to keep him working at the blacking warehouse "may have permanently soured her son's love for her. The fictional character he partially modeled on her, Mrs. Nickleby, is certainly portrayed as fatuous in the extreme" (24). Adrian goes on to list other unsatisfactory mothers, some of whom, like Mrs. Dickens, inflict grave emotional damage, including Mrs. Varden (*Barnaby Rudge*) and Mrs. Clennam (*Little Dorrit*).

4. See Coral Lansbury, *Elizabeth Gaskell: The Novel of Social Crisis*, especially "The Woman, the Writer, and the Unitarian" 11–21; and Enid Duthie, *The Themes of Elizabeth Gaskell.*

5. See, for instance, Robert Erickson's *Mother Midnight*; Frank Donovan, *Never on a Broomstick*; and Adrienne Rich, *Of Woman Born.* "Childbearing was, of course, intimately associated with sexuality," says Rich, "and the Puritan midwife was believed to administer aphrodisiacs, to empower women to get control of their men's sexuality" (136). Erickson notes that a crucial characteristic of midwives is that they are past childbearing. "Old, wise, experienced, they have entered the 'change of life,' or menopause; . . . they are in a sense beyond time amd thus have a godlike status. . . . having known what it is to be sexually active women, they now share with men the knowledge that they can never give birth. Although now barren themselves, they are consummately skilled at bringing forth fruit in others, and they can remake others through an uncanny power of influence over their lives" (6–7).

6. Jalland and Hooper, *Women from Birth to Death*, passim. In the same volume is recorded an incident wherein a man told a young woman that "all women over fifty should be shot" (299).

7. J. C. Webster, *Puberty and the Change of Life. A Book for Women*, 1892, qtd. in Jalland and Hooper 296.

8. Mary Scharlieb, *The Seven Ages of Woman. A Consideration of the Successive Phases of Woman's Life*, 1915, qtd. in Jalland and Hooper 18.

9. Qtd. in Merryn Williams, *Women in the English Novel* 112.

10. Passages like this prompt Nancy Pell ("The Father's Daughter in *Daniel Deronda*") to think that *Daniel Deronda* signals "George Eliot's growing awareness of the necessity of addressing women's wrongs, though she is not yet an enthusiastic advocate of women's rights" (425).

11. Moll Flanders is the only exception I can think of, but since she doesn't seem to recognize that giving her children away to various takers may be questionable, it cannot be worth comparing the two here.

Fig. 1. Mrs. Bennet rebukes Elizabeth for refusing Mr. Collins. Illustration by Hugh Thomson for *Pride and Prejudice* (London: George Allen, 1894) 146. Reprinted by permission of The Beinecke Rare Book and Manuscript Library, Yale University.

Fig. 2. Lady Catherine: "I assure you, I feel it exceedingly." Illustration by
Charles E. Brock for *Pride and Prejudice* (London: MacMillan, 1895) 193.

Fig. 3. "'Hum'—said Mrs. Ferrars—'very pretty'—and without regarding them at all, returned them to her daughter." Illustration by C. E. Brock for *Sense and Sensibility* (New York and Philadelphia: Frank S. Holby, 1906) facing 98, vol. 2.

Fig. 4. "The Gentleman next door declares his passion for Mrs. Nickleby."
Illustration by Hablot K. Browne for *Nicholas Nickleby* (Phiz) (London:
Chapman and Hall, 1838-39) facing 402.

Fig. 5. Mrs. Tulliver appeals to the lawyer Wakem. Illustration by C. O. Murray for *The Mill on the Floss* (Boston: Dana Estes, 1898) facing 352, vol. 1.

Fig. 6. Mrs. Gibson and Molly: "The New Mamma." Illustration by George du Maurier for *Wives and Daughters* (London: Smith, Elder, 1866) 124, vol. 1. Reprinted by permission of The Beinecke Rare Book and Manuscript Library, Yale University.

Fig. 7. Rachel Esmond and Henry: "She smiled an almost wild smile, as she looked up at him." Illustration by Harry Furniss for *The History of Henry Esmond* (London: MacMillan, 1911) facing 179.

Fig. 8. Daniel Deronda meets his mother, the Princess Halm-Eberstein.
Illustration by F. W. Freer for *Daniel Deronda* (Boston: Dana Estes, 1898)
facing 108, vol. 3.

Chapter Four

"Love and Hate Lie Close Together": Transitional Mothers

The shift in characterization of mothers in the novel is obviously not something one can assign a precise date to. The change does not happen all at once, nor does it happen with every author in the same way all of the time, nor, for that matter, is it ever "completed." Hardy's mothers, for instance, range from the flawed vitality of one of the earliest transitional mothers, Mrs. Yeobright (*The Return of the Native*, 1878), to the mixed strengths and weaknesses of Susan Henchard (*The Mayor of Casterbridge*, 1886), to the stereotypical foolishness of Mrs. Durbeyfield in the fairly late *Tess of the D'Urbervilles* (1891). Thus, while intimations of the change are noticeable as early as the 1870s, mothers in the "old" style, like the fainthearted Mrs. Yule and the gold-digging Mrs. Reardon in Gissing's *New Grub Street* (1891), persist at least through the end of the century, if indeed they ever disappear entirely.[1] The possibility that an older, married woman might be given a leading role is apparently still somewhat foreign to most novelists, as the majority of heroines continue to be single and young; nonetheless, an increasing number of mothers at this time are featured in relatively commanding, relatively sympathetic roles, prefiguring the emergence in the modern novel of mothers as protagonists.

Obviously, any attempt to bracket the duration of the transitional period must be somewhat artificial, like using the dates of Victoria's reign to circumscribe the social, political, and artistic flavor of the nineteenth century. However, there is some useful logic in doing so, and it is with such logic that I place the transitional period for mothers from about 1876, the date of the publication of *Daniel Deronda*, to 1913, the date of Lawrence's *Sons and Lovers*. The fact that these dates correspond to an especially active phase of the women's movement in England, during which significant changes took place in women's social, legal, and economic status,[2] and the fact that the latter date coincides almost exactly with the beginning of World War I, when "the women at home [took] on traditionally male occupations and responsibilities" (Ruderman 17), is by no means accidental. The turn of the century is momentous in women's history, and novels written during this period reflect the changing status of women just as surely as do the British laws that guaranteed them greater equality. Indeed, said Henry James, the responsible novelist is obliged to respond to these changes: failure to do so would threaten the viability of the genre. In 1901 James wrote:

> [As] nothing is more salient in English life today, to fresh eyes, than the revolution taking place in the position and outlook of women—and taking place much more deeply in the quiet than even the noise on the surface demonstrates—so we may very well yet see the female elbow itself, kept in increasing activity by the play of the pen, smash with final resonance the window all this time most surreptitiously closed.[3]

Though hardly one of the leading proponents of women's rights, James was, as Merryn Williams notes, "well aware that women were living in a time of transition, and he did not want them to be slaves."[4] Indeed, most novelists of the period express at least qualified sympathy with the women's movement. In *A Drama in Muslin* George Moore writes,

> [T]he gates of the harem are being broken down, and the gloom of the female mind clears. . . . but beneath the great feminine tide there is an undercurrent of hatred and revolt. This is particularly observable in the leaders of the movement; women who . . . proclaim a higher mission for women than to be the mother of men. (195–96)

Similarly George Gissing writes in a letter to Eduard Bertz, "I am convinced there will be no social peace until women are intellectually trained very much as men are" (*Letters* 171). In his novel about the women's movement, *The Odd Women* (1893), the spinster-by-choice

Rhoda Nunn gently admonishes Monica Madden Widdowson for marrying purely out of fear of being an old maid: "Your mistake was in looking only at the weak women. You had other examples before you . . . who live bravely and work hard and are proud of their place in the world" (316). Presumably the effectiveness of the opening scene of *The Mayor of Casterbridge* derives from not only the moral implications of Henchard's selling his wife but also the late Victorians' heightened awareness of inequities in British law that still encouraged, if not actually allowed, such things to happen. Though neither usual nor legal, the practice of wife-selling occasionally took place among the lower classes as late as 1881, reflecting the tendency of some men to think of their wives as possessions, which indeed their inferior legal status implied they were.[5]

Though there is no way to prove that socio-economic reforms, whether consciously or unconsciously, affected the altered portrayal of mothers in the novel, there is every reason to assume that they did. Novelists like James make an explicit connection as regards women in general; it is but a short step of logic to assume that mothers should be one of the principal subjects of the change. For while the movement obviously sought alternative roles for women, and although the national birthrate fell drastically from 1870 onward,[6] it was never the intent of the early feminists, except perhaps the most radical ones, that those new roles should replace or otherwise deny the importance of the role as mother. According to Ann Dally, "the early feminists did not regard motherhood as a problem because to them it was no problem" (136). Rather, the emphasis was on "mothercraft": developing skills, interests, and understanding which elevate this most essential of responsibilities.[7] Josephine Butler argued that "women's powers of guidance, their spiritual wisdom and maternal qualities should be represented in Parliament" (qtd. in Lewis 95). Similarly, in 1894 Millicent Fawcett pressed for the vote on the grounds that she wanted "to see the womanly and domestic side of things weigh more and count for more in all public concerns." She assured the women she addressed that the suffragists did not want them to give up "one jot or tittle of your womanliness, your love for children, your care for the sick, your gentleness, your self-control, your obedience to conscience and duty." Rather, she said, these are the very qualities wanted in the political arena.[8] It is the combination of these traditionally maternal traits with traditionally "masculine" qualities such as aggressiveness and decision-making that distinguish mothers during and after the transitional stage.

Another possible external motive for the change in the treatment of mothers is the rise of psychoanalysis at the turn of the century and its emphasis on the role of the mother in personality development. The theories of Freud and his colleagues, widely discussed even by the lay public,[9] offered at least one explanation for the parent-child tensions which had increasingly occupied *fin-de-siècle* writers such as George Meredith and Samuel Butler. Though Lawrence, for instance, claimed to reject Freud's theory of incest-craving (instead affirming its opposite, incest-aversion), Judith Ruderman sees him as more closely aligned with the Freudians than he would admit:

> [H]e wrote his essays on psychology precisely in order to define scientifically the "kind of incest" that he wrote of incessantly in his letters, poetry, and narrative prose—a pre-oedipal, pre-genital desire to merge with the caretaker mother—and, by this definition, to provide ammunition for use in combating the "devouring mother" and her perversion of life. (24)

It is important to note that the growing interest in (or, in Lawrence's case, obsession with) motherhood and mothers is not exclusively sympathetic: if it were, we would have merely another form of idealization. Rather, what is increasingly probed by writers is the power, the ambiguity, and often the great difficulty of maternal relationships. In *The Education of the People*, Lawrence went so far as to say that "[t]here should be a league for the prevention of maternal love, as there is a society for the prevention of cruelty to animals" (*Phoenix* 621). What the representation of mothers has come to stress, then, is not her vacuity but her complexity.

Numerous features distinguish what I call a transitional mother from earlier mothers, but the chief is that she reflects, if imperfectly, the reconciliation of the Bad Mother with the Good Mother. No longer exclusively obstructive, her role now asserts her dual nature—great *and* terrible, loving *and* threatening. However, unlike Rachel Esmond, there is no vast schism between the two sides of her nature: her goodness is marred by her faults (whatever they are), and her faults are mitigated by her goodness. Her judgment is fallible, but not consistently so, and though consequently responsible for much that is amiss in her family, she is responsible for much that is positive and sustaining in it as well. In marked contrast to the typical earlier mothers, the transitional mother is typically intelligent, strong, and centrally important. In conversation, understanding, logic, and authority she can hold her own with almost anyone; she is widely respected, perhaps even a little feared. However, there is one area in which she usually falls short, and that is her humanity. The feature most often separating her from the fully-evolved twentieth-century mother is that her moral vision, one might say her sense of justice, is still imperfect. It is in this deficiency, I believe, that the dominance of the "Terrible Mother" is still most evident. What one tends to see in her, then, is a remarkable, compelling personality but one somehow lacking in compassion or other moral quality. She is not herself a heroine, though she is often as dramatically significant as any of the central characters.

It is interesting to note that children's fantasy fiction during this period produced similar transitional figures. According to Edith Honig, the fairy godmother is one such type: "with her magic, her maternity, and power, and her very positive image, the classical fairy godmother is a clear precursor of the magical woman" (116). Significantly, the fairy godmother is extremely popular with two late-century children's authors, Louisa Molesworth and George MacDonald. The witch Watho in MacDonald's "The Day Boy and the Night Girl," published in 1879, is a good-bad figure, "tall and graceful, with a white skin, red hair, and black eyes, which had a red fire in them." The tale begins:

> There once was a witch who desired to know everything. But the wiser a witch is, the harder she knocks her head against the wall when she comes to it. Her name was Watho, and she had a wolf in her mind. She cared for nothing in itself—only for knowing it. She was not naturally cruel, but the wolf had made her cruel. (177)

MacDonald's treatment of Watho is strangely sympathetic, or at least strangely objective, emphasizing her mystery and complexity above all: "She was straight and strong, but now and then would fall bent together, shudder, and sit for a moment with her head turned over her shoulder, as if the wolf had got out of her mind on to her back" (176). Says Honig:

> This witch is a complex and powerful woman, almost admirable for these qualities. She cannot be accused of succumbing to feminine physical vanity, like Snow White's stepmother. Hers is the sin of *hubris*, the placing of man's law over God's. Like Faust or Frankenstein, she is obsessed with the pursuit of knowledge for its own sake. Hers are not petty, "feminine" errors, but majestic flaws.
>
> Yet, even her cruelty is tempered with some maternal love. If she did not have maternal longings, her experiment would not have taken the form of raising children. She nurtures them carefully and comes to love them. Still she is capable of cruelty to them. MacDonald explains the confusion of Watho's feelings: "In the hearts of witches, love and hate lie close together, and often tumble over each other". . . (199).
>
> As a woman of great power who, though a witch, is not a completely negative stereotypical ugly old witch, Watho forms a bridge between two power women—the negative witch and the positive magical woman. (115–116)

I quote Honig at such length in order to demonstrate my continuing point that mothers in the novel have always had strong affinities with more patently archetypal genres such as fantasy and folklore. Of course, there is a distinction to be made between the anonymous folklore of oral tradition, and the carefully-scripted "folklore" of individual modern writers. One could even make a case that "The Day Boy and the Night Girl" does not belong in the same genre as the similar-sounding "East o' the Sun and West o' the Moon," based on the differences in their origins and their purposes. The anonymous fairy tales were never consciously didactic in purpose, or so we believe, while according to Jack Zipes, Victorian fairy tales were written with a deliberate political motive: to get readers, adult and child alike, to "take a noble and ethical stand against forces of intolerance and authoritarianism." MacDonald and others, Zipes says, sought to "use the fairy-tale form in innovative ways to raise social consciousness about the disparities among the different social classes and the problems faced by the oppressed due to the industrial revolution" (*Victorian Fairy Tales* xix). Nonetheless, their admitted polemicism aside, they conform to the more traditional, orally-transmitted fairy tales in their symbolic patterns of weaning, challenge, and patently archetypal images. They are, to borrow Adriaan de Witt's definition of folk tales, "down-to-earth accounts of life in its universal and psychological aspects."[10]

Thus, whether MacDonald's Watho is merely a conscious political statement about late Victorian socio-economic conditions[11] or whether she is also, on a level that is impossible to gauge, an unconscious expression of the composite mother archetype reasserting itself as a result of those same social conditions, is impossible to say. If the latter is true, it says a great deal about the subconscious motivations behind even the most conscious of artistic acts.

Another reason for suspecting the transitional mother (in all her forms) to be a further cognate of the archetypal family of the Great Mother is that, like the earlier mothers in the novel and like the mothers in fairy tales the transitional mother continues to be an obstruction to her child's happiness. The difference now is that she is also, in some complex way, vital to it. The son or daughter cannot afford, nor indeed desires, a complete rupture with her: he or she may wish to be free of some psychological burden that the mother represents, but the mother has so inextricably become part of the way he or she copes with life that severing that connection would be more traumatic than continuing it. Even those who were victimized by the witch Watho come to see that "even the wicked themselves may be a link to join together the good" (MacDonald 207).

The transitional mother is thus both the devouring and the nurturing mother, which earlier genres split into separate (and thus more easily dealt with) identities but which is now being reassembled into a single figure. Many examples are available, and I will discuss Mrs. Morel in *Sons and Lovers* and Mrs. Gereth in *The Spoils of Poynton* at greater length, but this brief passage from *The Return of the Native* epitomizes how a character (in this case Clym Yeobright) may be bound by conflicting ties to mother, self, and others—the implication here being that the claims of the mother are the strongest of the three:

Three antagonistic growths had to be kept alive: his mother's
trust in him, his plan for becoming a teacher, and Eustacia's
happiness. His fervid nature could not afford to relinquish one
of these, though two of the three were as many as he could
hope to preserve. Though his love was as chaste as that of
Petrarch for his Laura, it had made fetters of what previously
was only difficulty. A position which was not too simple when
he stood whole-hearted had become indescribably complicated
by the addition of Eustacia. Just when his mother was
beginning to tolerate one scheme he had introduced another
still bitterer than the first, and the combination was more than
she could bear. (*RN* 166)

Despite her power to give pain to Clym, Mrs. Yeobright is a primarily
sympathetic character, and one whom we are expected to admire as
well as criticize. A "well-known and respected widow," her "features
[are] of the type usually found where perspicacity is the chief quality
enthroned within" (*RN* 30). A bit of a snob, her reticence is somewhat
excused as "the consciousness of superior communicative power." Yet
her superior standing among the community of Egdon Heath is of less
consequence to her than the welfare of her niece and above all her son,
and she is generally astute in the advice she gives to both Thomasin and
Clym. It is when her advice is rejected that she shows how powerful—
and heartless—she can be. When Clym tells her he is old enough to
know what is best for him in marrying Eustacia Vye, she retorts, "Best?
Is it best for you to injure your prospects for such a voluptuous, idle
woman as that? Don't you see that by the very fact of your choosing
her you prove that you do not know what is best for you?" (*RN* 168).
As it turns out, Eustacia is *not* good for Clym, much less for his mother.
But the significant point here is not whether Mrs. Yeobright is right or
wrong but that she takes such advantage of her maternal force, which is
both positive and negative. Clym's devotion to her simultaneously
urges him toward and holds him back from self-fulfilment (fulfilment
being variously defined, of course). Thus it is no easy matter for him to
achieve the separation from her which is necessary for full
individuation. And therein lies the complexity of the turn-of-the-
century mother.

These fundamental changes in the treatment of mothers demonstrate the extent to which novelists now accept mothers and mothers' issues as the stuff of complex, provocative fiction. When Henry James overheard the anecdote which inspired *The Spoils of Poynton* (1897) he was immediately struck by the potential for a story in the controversy between an expropriated widow and her son. Yet whereas the mother in the original version, "obviously much coarser than Mrs. Gereth," says Edward Wagenknecht (95), tried to reclaim her property by having her son declared illegitimate, James tells his story from the mother's point of view, creating a conflict of considerably greater interest than merely deciding who gets to keep the keys to Poynton and stacking, at least initially, our prejudice in the mother's favor.

Mrs. Gereth has our support by the end of the first chapter: we admire her wit and urbanity ("[i]t was hard for her to believe that a woman could look presentable who had been kept awake for hours by the wallpaper in her room" [*SP* 5]) as well as her superior taste (her "passion for the exquisite" [*SP* 7]); we commend her instinctive affinity—her "tremendous fancy, as it came to be called" (*SP* 6)—for Fleda Vetch; we pity her unhappy position as a dispossessed widow about to be turned out of her beloved home. And we certainly condole with her as the future mother-in-law of Mona Brigstock, she of the big hands and big feet, who demands from behind her "motionless mask" that everything at Poynton be delivered to her intact, not for the sake of any aesthetic pleasure it will give but simply because, as she would say "in that voice like the squeeze of a doll's stomach: 'It goes with the house—it goes with the house'" (*SP* 14–15). Fortunately Mrs. Gereth has a well-developed sense of the absurd that scorns self-pity while compensating for her injuries somewhat by giving them a sort of theatrical extravagance. She tells Fleda, for instance, that rather than surrender her house quietly she prefers to be dragged out of it by constables—prompting the narrator to declare her "the heroine of Poynton" (*SP* 37). Clearly both the author and Fleda Vetch herself enjoy this flamboyant character, a cue which the reader is expected to follow, for this early attachment will help determine how we judge her actions later on, after she has plundered Poynton and deceived and insulted those who have been most loyal to her.

Coming as she does in the wake of several generations of silly, often tiresome mothers, to experience Mrs. Gereth's vigorous personality seems almost an unlooked-for privilege. "[M]asterful and clever, with a great bright spirit, she was one of those who impose themselves as an influence" (*SP* 10). Her influence is indeed strong, and James, with his typical adjectival excesses, seems to want the reader as well as Fleda to fall under Mrs. Gereth's spell: there is something almost exalting in his descriptions of her. Hers is a passion not of the flesh but of the spirit: "to be faithful to a trust and loyal to an idea" (*SP* 35). Her whole life had been no less than "an effort towards completeness and perfection," while her "exquisite old house" is said to be "supreme in every part: it was a provocation, an inspiration, a matchless canvas for the picture" (*SP* 11) and "she trod the place like a reigning queen" (*SP* 35). Her twenty-six year marriage had likewise been the best, characterized by "sympathy and generosity, . . . knowledge and love . . . perfect accord" (*SP* 11). As for the superb private collection of precious art objects which are the cause of the dispute, they show "the high pride of [Mrs. Gereth's] taste, a fine arrogance, a sense of style which, however amused and amusing, never compromised nor stooped" (*SP* 19).

No wonder that this "genuine English lady, fresh and fair," should be so "fascinating to poor Fleda, who hadn't had a penny in the world" (*SP* 12). Her magnificence is not the least insincere or contrived: she really is devoted to the abstract ideals of harmony and proportion. Unlike earlier mothers, she cares little about prestige, or at any rate she esteems only the kind that accompanies true refinement—the kind the Brigstocks, no matter how great their fortune, will never have. It is therefore understandably grievous to her that Owen, her "handsome, heavy" son, has chosen a Brigstock for his wife. But what is not pardonable, let her alarm for the fate of her treasures be ever so genuine, is that she has let the "things" become more important to her than her relationship to human beings, particularly her only son.

James is unambiguous as to what is "wrong" with Mrs. Gereth: "her ruling passion had in a sense despoiled her of her humanity" (*SP* 29)—her moral sensitiveness, says Wagenknecht, has not kept pace with her aestheticism (105). This is a long way to drop after having been exalted so high; but I think that by speaking so effusively before and so bluntly now, James means to emphasize that Mrs. Gereth made a deliberate choice to commit her life to aesthetic rather than human values—that is why she has been so extraordinarily successful in the former, and why she should not be pitied, certainly she should not be surprised, if she is disappointed in the latter. Fleda puzzles over the "strange relation between mother and son when there was no fundamental tenderness out of which a solution would irrepressibly spring." Is Owen responsible for it? but she quickly decides not "when she remembered that, so far as he was concerned, Mrs. Gereth would still have been welcome to have her seat by the Poynton fire" (*SP* 33–24). The fact is that Owen Gereth actually likes his mother, in his obtuse fashion. With more than enough provocation to wish her dead, he merely wishes that she would "come round" (*SP* 31)—his is not an aggressive temperament, and he is clearly miserable being in the midst of such hostilities. We do not see much of Owen and his mother together, but judging from his manner with other women, we can imagine that he has always been happy to be led by the nose by her.

So Owen is not the problem; Mrs. Gereth is. She really does not much like her son; during the fight over Poynton she doesn't "like him at all" (*SP* 39). Her feelings have to do, as everything about her does, with the fact that "things" are "the sum of the world" to her (*SP* 20), her "life," indeed her "religion" (*SP* 24). However, her unkindness toward Owen is not a case of simple neglect. It is a case of rejection: Mrs. Gereth, with her disgust for commonness and her passion for rarified beauty, rejected Owen on these grounds long ago. Nor is it exactly that he embarrasses her—she has too much pride to suffer that way—but rather that he is too much like the rest of the world outside Poynton, the blundering, coarse-grained world that makes his mother "wince" and turn away (something in the manner of another of James' amoral aesthetes, Gilbert Osmond, although her appreciation of art is real, Gilbert's that of a dilettante[12]). The qualities that Fleda loves in Owen—his innocence, his simplicity, his decency—mean nothing to her; "Mrs. Gereth had really no perception of anybody's nature—had only one question about persons: were they clever or stupid?" (*SP* 100). And since Owen is hardly clever, she treats him as rudely as if he had no more feelings than a stump: "try, for God's sake, to cultivate a glimmer of intelligence" (*SP* 110), she exasperatedly demands. The only nice thing she ever says about him, and it is not much, is that there is no harm in him; "he *is* a dear" (*SP* 91). She is more likely, especially when frustrated, to accuse him of being unkind, spineless, "a jackass" (*SP* 157).

There is indeed an element of frustrated anger in her rudeness to Owen, and in a passage that reveals far more about the mother than about the son, the narrator explains why:

> The great wrong Owen had done her was not his "taking up" with Mona—that was disgusting, but it was a detail, an accidental form; it was his failure from the first to understand what it was to have a mother at all, to appreciate the beauty and sanctity of the character. She was just his mother as his nose was just his nose, and he had never had the least imagination or tenderness or gallantry about her. One's mother, gracious heaven, if one were the kind of fine young man one ought to be, the only kind Mrs. Gereth cared for, was a subject for poetry, for idolatry. (*SP* 37)

This strikes me as a peculiar passage. What Mrs. Gereth is referring to here is the idealized mother stereotype, and considering how shabbily she has treated her son, it is queer that she feels entitled to better. But equally peculiar is that a woman who so appreciates rare, genuine beauty would place any value in the conventional emotions expressed in so conventional a medium as a poem extolling the sanctity of the mother. Perhaps the answer is not logical at all, merely human: precious art objects may be aesthetically rich, but they may also be emotionally sterile. Mrs. Gereth has invested a lifetime of devotion into her "things" and, quite understandably, would like to receive love of the same intensity in return; but they, being things, are incapable of feeling. Now that her husband, who apparently *had* worshiped her, is dead, she turns to her son for the feeling she believes should be forthcoming—but since she has put nothing into that vessel, there is nothing to take out.[13]

Ironically, this little bit of insight into Mrs. Gereth's selfish core allows us to feel more real pity for her than elsewhere, for we see now that some of her anger at Owen is a symptom of her unaccustomed loneliness and inconsequence. "She hated the effacement to which English usage reduced the widowed mother . . . contrasted it with the beautiful homage paid in other countries to women in that position, women no better than herself, whom she had seen acclaimed and enthroned, whom she had known and envied" (*SP* 37). I have said before that Mrs. Gereth is not very moving as a figure of compassion, having made all her own decisions, and being, on the whole, satisfied with them; but there are occasional moments when, taking the toll of those decisions, she shows how much it affects her, and then we *are* moved, because, as James saw that we would be, we were on her side at the beginning and are willing to be on her side now.

Still it is not an easy matter to settle on the "correct" interpretation of her. That is one reason the story has Fleda Vetch—to provide the correct moral pitch. She is as sensitive to fine things and fine feelings as Mrs. Gereth, but in contrast to her, Fleda knows people "by direct inspiration" (*SP* 100). She is capable of a greater devotion than ever her companion felt for Poynton, because she feels it for another human being, Owen Gereth: "I love him so that I'd die for him—I love him so that it's horrible" (*SP* 155). Why so humane a woman as Fleda should continue to stay with Mrs. Gereth may seem odd, but it is only partly a puzzle. The narrator acknowledges that Fleda is "in her small way a spirit of the same family as Mrs. Gereth" (*SP* 10)—but that means simply that she too is conscious of being superior. The truth is that Fleda has been somewhat duped. Granted that her deep sympathy for the fine things at Poynton is sincere, even perhaps a little self-serving; nonetheless Mrs. Gereth herself admits that she "pounced on [Fleda] and caught [her] up" (*SP* 159). Once Fleda realizes the limitations of Mrs. Gereth's regard for her (that of "a good agent" [*SP* 28]) she begins uncomfortably to draw away, to develop "reserves and conditions" (*SP* 144). It is a measure of Fleda's honor, not her opportunism, that she stands by Mrs. Gereth, because her freedom to desert has been effectively canceled by "the intense pressure of her confidence" (*SP* 144). However, in spite of her continued loyalty to Mrs. Gereth, Fleda, with her "intenser consciousness" (*SP* 9), can see clearly the rents in that lady's integrity. The sight makes her own scrupulous soul recoil by degrees, so that by the end of the novel her relation with the ousted mistress of Poynton is based "almost wholly on breaches and omissions" (*SP* 183).

The gradual signs of wear that Fleda detects in Mrs. Gereth's character seem to have physical parallels that give one the sense almost of witchcraft: when she is first introduced to her Mrs. Gereth is "fresh and fair, young in the fifties" (*SP* 12); but after the spoliation of Poynton Fleda finds her "cloaked and perceptibly bowed, [leaning] on her heavily and [giving] her an odd, unwonted sense of age and cunning" (*SP* 85)—one is reminded of Spenser's Duessa. Some of the language seems chosen to reinforce the suggestion that Mrs. Gereth is a "sorceress," a "wizard," a "conjurer": she worries that Owen will marry "in spite of all her spells" (*SP* 6); she boasts of the "almost infernal cunning" which had allowed her to fill Poynton with riches on very little money (*SP* 12); she looms "gaunt and unnatural" anywhere save in the "thick, coloured air" of Poynton; "then she vanishe[s] as if she had suddenly sunk into a quicksand" (*SP* 105).

Since this is not one of James' ghost stories, Mrs. Gereth's apparent lack of substance is moral, not corporeal. The allusions are entirely figurative and perhaps not even deliberate; nonetheless, their effect is to recall some of the associations of the hag-witches of fairy tale—transformations of the bad mother, according to psychologists[14]—namely their ability to lure young victims into their power by tempting them with sweets or coins or even with kindness. It seems to me that Mrs. Gereth has behaved in such a way to Fleda, "possessing and absorbing her so utterly" (*SP* 103) that Fleda is, for all intents and purposes, unable to break away; then turning the girl to her own use—in this case, to seduce Owen away from Mona Brigstock. In this effort, and incidentally in the fact that Fleda's own mother is dead, there are faint echoes of a Mother Midnight: "[Fleda] had the sense not only of being advertised and offered, but of being counselled and enlightened in ways that she scarely understood—arts obscure even to a poor girl who had had, in good society and motherless poverty, to look straight at realities" (*SP* 101).

To speak of Mrs. Gereth, who shrinks from anything remotely vulgar, in the vocabulary of procuring or witchcraft may seem excessive, but it is meant merely to demonstrate once again that archetypal images from our past may influence present perceptions and reappear in modern settings, especially when that setting includes a "bad" mother. In fact, the images need not come from so far back, either. Ellen Douglass Leyburn, for instance, sees Mrs. Gereth as playing one of James' comic "fatal fools," who are apt "to be all the cause of . . . trouble."[15] That James should cast so shrewd a woman as a fool tends to undercut that shrewdness; it is especially ironic, considering Mrs. Gereth's hatred of the Brigstocks, that it should be Mona playing opposite her. Leyburn concedes, of course, that Mrs. Gereth is the infinitely more interesting and complex fool, and James treats her with as much sympathy as mockery (78). But after all it is Mona who gains her point, if not ultimately the spoils, which are destroyed in the fire; while Mrs. Gereth comes away with nothing at all—unless it is the satisfaction, which must be a sorry recompense indeed, that no one will enjoy the treasures of Poynton. Thus Mrs. Gereth, though her part as a bad mother is not played in the traditional manner in that it is displaced to a great extent by her depth as a character, still fits into some of the traditional costumes of the role.

Gertrude Morel, on the other hand, does not readily conform to *any* of the traditional types—or perhaps it is more accurate to say that she is an extreme expression of them. For Mrs. Morel does not merely reflect the archetypal mother simultaneously nurturing and devouring her offspring, she personifies it—and *Sons and Lovers* personifies the child's archetypal struggle for individuation. The initial oneness and harmony of the child with its mother is so profound in this story that we first "meet" Paul, in a sense, while he is still *in utero*: standing in the moonlight in her garden, Mrs. Morel loses herself in a sort of swoon, "[e]xcept for a slight feeling of sickness, and her consciousness in the child" (*SL* 24). When the baby comes, "[s]he held it close to her face and breast. With all her force, with all her soul she would make up to it for having brought it into the world unloved. She would love it all the more now it was here; carry it in her love"; and yet she fears it, too, with a sort of foreboding: "Did it know all about her? When it lay under her heart, had it been listening then?" (*SL* 37). But the boy Paul does not consciously reproach her, at least not for many years: "The two shared lives" (*SL* 114). It is not until he realizes that he cannot love other women that he tries, too late, to separate from her: "I shall never meet the right woman while you live" (*SL* 351), he tells her, and therefore he must take the symbolic, desperate step of murdering her: "I s'll give her morphia," he says grimly, and "[y]et he loved her more than his own life" (*SL* 394, 393). The novel ends with Paul refusing to follow her into the grave, walking "quickly" towards the "humming, glowing" town (*SL* 420).[16]

That Lawrence saw this novel as an allegory of some primordial truth about human relations is suggested by the quasi-prophetic style of his proposed foreword to *Sons and Lovers*, composed in tendentious imitation of Genesis: "*We* are the Word."

> But if the man does not come home to a woman, leaving her to take account of him, but is a stranger to her . . . she shall turn to her son, and say, "Be you my Go-Between."
> But the man who is the go-between from Woman to Production is the lover of that woman. And if that Woman be his mother, then is he her lover in part only; he carries for her, but is never received into her for his confirmation and renewal, and so wastes himself away in the flesh. The old son-lover was Oedipus. The name of the new one is legion.[17]

There is no doubt the novel owes much of its authenticity to the fact that Lawrence had so much at stake in it: "one sheds one's sicknesses in books—repeats and presents again one's emotions, to be master of them."[18] We know enough about Lawrence's childhood and can deduce even more from some of his writings besides *Sons and Lovers*, such as *Fantasia of the Unconscious* and *Psychoanalysis and the Unconscious* as well as *The Virgin and the Gypsy*, to know that he drew upon his personal experiences of women, especially his mother, Lydia Beardsall Lawrence, in developing his rather hysterical views about mothers.[19] But the often paranoid quality of these writings suggests that they owe at least as much to Lawrence's imagination as to his actual experiences. In *The Education of the People*, a work composed between 1818 and 1820, ostensibly to express concern about the inadequate educational system in England, he writes:

> [W]ith the cunning of seven legions of devils and the persistency of hell's most hellish fiend, the cooing, clapping, devilish modern mother traduces the child into the personal mode of consciousness. She succeeds, and starts this hateful "personal" love between herself and her excited child, and the unspoken but unfathomable hatred between the violated infant and her own assaulting soul, which together make the bane of human life, and give rise to all the neurosis and neuritis and nervous troubles we are all afflicted with. (*Phoenix* 625)

Yet Lawrence did not (and for this we may be thankful) allow *Sons and Lovers* to degenerate into hysterical misogyny; somehow his artistry managed to keep control of what was clearly a deeply personal and frequently painful topic. "I *have* patiently and laboriously constructed that novel," he wrote to Garnett (*Letters* 78; 14 Nov 1912). Lerner says of *Sons and Lovers* that Lawrence seems to write "better, not worse, for incompletely detaching himself from an autobiographical situation"—it saves him from the "didactic passion" that later led him astray as an artist (*Truthtellers* 214, 229–30). In any event, Lawrence's deep personal involvement with Paul and Gertrude Morel allows us a remarkably clear view into the "raw" psychology of the neurotic mother-child relation and the individuation process which it makes at once imperative and impossible.

> [Paul] felt he had ... to defend himself against her; he felt condemned by her. Then sometimes he hated her, and pulled at her bondage. His life wanted to free itself of her. It was like a circle where life turned back on itself, and got no farther. She bore him, loved him, kept him, and his love turned back into her, so that he could not be free to go forward with his own life, really love another woman. At this period, unknowingly, he resisted his mother's influence. He did not tell her things; there was a distance between them. (*SL* 345)

Eliseo Vivas has said that Lawrence only partly knew what he was presenting us with. "Neither through irony nor by any other means does he give us an indication that he sees through Gertrude Morel and her children. He is utterly lucid about the miner's faults. But about Paul's and his mother's false values he is blind" (182). This may be overtly true about the manner of the presentation, but I doubt it accurately reflects the extent of Lawrence's own awareness nor his artistic intention. Indeed, when Lawrence summarized his new novel in a letter to Garnett, it is the mother, not the father, who is depicted as the source of the conflict. The father is mentioned only twice, as being rejected first by his wife, then by his children.

> She has had a passion for her husband, so the children are born of passion, and have heaps of vitality. But as her sons grow up she selects them as lovers—first the eldest, then the second. These sons are *urged* into life by their reciprocal love of their mother—urged on and on. But when they come to manhood,

they can't love, because their mother is the strongest power in their lives, and holds them. . . . all the sons hate and are jealous of the father. (*Letters* 78; 14 Nov 1912)

Therefore I think there *is* a subtle irony in Paul Morel's seemingly blind partisanship for his mother, and the passages in which Paul expresses his awareness of her emotional tyranny are provided to make sure we are aware of it. "It was as if the pivot and pole of his life, from which he could not escape, was his mother" (*SL* 222). Surely we are not meant to blame the father entirely in the scene in which Morel and Paul exchange blows, because Morel is justly, if futilely, provoked by his son's intimacy with his wife. Morel has come home, drunk, to find Paul giving his mother an emotional goodnight kiss. "At your mischief again?" (*SL* 213), he says, a comment Lawrence describes as "venomous," but as Sheila MacLeod points out, "we can take it as we may" (32). The miner then helps himself to the pork-pie Mrs. Morel bought specially for Paul, according to her custom, and when Paul objects, Morel challenges his son to a fight. This over, Morel stumbles off to bed, possibly aware that he has now been vanquished utterly— "[h]is last fight was fought in that home" (*SL* 214)—and Paul goes to cry over his mother. "Sleep with Annie, mother, not with him," he pleads, though she will not agree. In bed himself, Paul is "in a fury of misery. And yet, somewhere in his soul, he was at peace because he still loved his mother best" (*SL* 215).

This scene, told from Paul's limited point of view, captures perfectly the slightly sexual indignation of the lover-child against the intruding husband—we will see very much the same thing in *To the Lighthouse* when James Ramsay yearns to kill his father with a poker for threatening his exclusive possession of his mother. But this is no reason to think that when Lawrence wrote the novel his thoughts and feelings had achieved no distance whatsoever from those of the immature son-lover. Rather, what is so convincing about the work is that he has subjected, if only slightly, the undiscriminating perspective of the participant to the critical perspective of the observer. Thus it seems to me that Lawrence holds all three parties responsible in the scene just recalled, but the mother above all. Certainly Morel is repugnant, coming home drunk, pugnacious, surly, "toppling in his balance." But after all, what had been going on between Paul and his mother before Morel arrives is not so blameless, either. Mrs. Morel has been extracting from Paul his confession and repentence regarding Miriam.

> "No, mother—I really *don't* love her. I talk to her, but I want to come home to you."
>
> He had taken off his collar and tie, and rose, bare-throated, to go to bed. As he stooped to kiss his mother, she threw her arms around his neck, hid her face on his shoulder, and cried, in a whimpering voice, so unlike her own that he writhed in agony:
>
> "I can't bear it. I could let another woman—but not her. She'd leave me no room, not a bit of room—"
>
> And immediately he hated Miriam bitterly.
>
> "And I've never—you know, Paul—I've never had a husband—not really—"
>
> He stroked his mother's hair, and his mouth was on her throat.
>
> "And she exults so in taking you from me—she's not like ordinary girls."
>
> "Well, I don't love her, mother," he murmured, bowing his head and hiding his eyes on her shoulder in misery. His mother kissed him a long, fervent kiss.
>
> "My boy!" she said, in a voice trembling with passionate love. (*SL* 213)

Sheila MacLeod says that Mrs. Morel's manipulation of Paul here is altogether conscious and deliberate: "Every mother, Mrs. Morel included, knows better than to be able *knowingly* to confuse and distress her children. Once she has taken her son into a loverlike embrace and he has responded in passionate kind, she is prepared to be generous. 'Perhaps I'm selfish,' she concedes. 'If you want her, take her, my boy'" (31). Although Mrs. Morel is surely in emotional pain herself, I agree with MacLeod that there are ample clues in the text that she is aware of her power and willing to use it: "She would fight to keep Paul" (*SL* 222). "Life was so rich for her. Paul wanted her, and so did Arthur" (*SL* 246). When Paul ceases to meet Miriam on Thursdays,

"Mrs. Morel sniffed with satisfaction" (*SL* 172) even though she knows even then "how he was suffering for want of a woman" (*SL* 280). When at length she realizes that "he had made up his mind" and that "nothing on earth would alter him" from leaving Miriam, she begins "to give up at last" (*SL* 280). As Lawrence wrote to Garnett, her death comes when she "realizes what is the matter" (*Letters* 79; 14 Nov 1912).

If Paul/D. H. Lawrence seems to be unfairly hard on Walter Morel/Arthur Lawrence, this is hardly a flaw in the artistry of the novel and certainly not in its psychology. Indeed, says Lerner, we should be grateful that Lawrence never rewrote the book to be more sympathetic to his father and less to his mother, as in later life he said he perhaps should. "For it cannot be coincidence that Morel, the most successful of Lawrence's surly sexed and vital men, is the one against whom he bears a grudge" (*Truthtellers* 213). Likewise, Mrs. Morel is successful because the author's feelings toward her are equally irrational, even if understandably so. The fact is, if Mrs. Morel were less sympathetic, Paul's anguish would be ungrounded—he would have only normal difficulty separating from her. But the tendency of the mother to devour is not so much a straightforward function of her badness as it is a perversion of her power, which derives in large part from her goodness. And Mrs. Morel is not only an extraordinarily powerful woman but even, especially during the early years when her children's lifelong attachments to her are being formed, a basically good one. "The companionship between mother and sons is described, at first, in completely wholesome terms," says Mark Spilka. "It is not her interference which destroys her sons, but the strength and peculiar nature of her love" (74, 76).

When we first meet her, Mrs. Morel is negotiating in her brusque but good-natured way about who may go to the wakes, a sort of local carnival: "Well, and you shall go, whining, wizzening little stick!" (*SL* 3) she says to Annie. Though she does not like the wakes herself, she goes because they wish her to, William, the oldest, "tipful of excitement now she had come." He leads her to the peep-show, where "she explained the pictures, in a sort of story, to which he listened as if spellbound" (*SL* 4). Surely there is no cause to see these homely, actively loving scenes as ambiguous or "blind." Nor do we have any reason to doubt the authority of the scene in which Mrs. Morel, locked out of the house by Morel, forgets her predicament when she sees a bed of "tall white lilies . . . reeling in the moonlight. . . . [S]he drank a deep draught of the scent. It almost made her dizzy." Later, back inside, "she smiled faintly to see her face all smeared with the yellow dust of lilies" (*SL* 24, 26). According to Spilka, in *Sons and Lovers* the inward state of the major characters is symbolized by their relation with flowers: Mrs. Morel's affinity with lilies suggests her strong life-force and that of the unborn Paul, who will inherit it; "the dust becomes a kiss of benediction for them both, the confirmation of their vitality" (11, 44). There is a strong suggestion of the procreative, nurturing element of the mother goddess here; it is one of the benefits she confers upon those she loves. "From his mother [Paul] drew the life-warmth, the strength to produce. . . . 'I can do my best things when you sit there in your rocking-chair, mother,' he said. 'I'm sure!' she exclaimed, sniffing with mock skepticism. But she felt it was so, and her heart quivered with brightness" (*SL* 158).

If Gertrude Morel's position in the household is that of the ruling matriarch, we can hardly hold it against her. She cannot help being "the strongest force in the field—and easily the most vital woman in the novel" (Spilka 74). This vitality is not, at least at first, a flaw in her. "She had a curious, receptive mind which found much pleasure and amusement in listening to other folk. . . . She loved ideas, and was considered very intellectual. What she liked most of all was an argument on religion or philosophy or politics with some educated man" (*SL* 9). Such independence of thought and spirit show that she is indeed an unusual woman, taking after her father, "an engineer—a large, handsome, haughty man, proud of his fair skin and blue eyes, but more proud still of his integrity" (*SL* 7). It is likely that if poor Walter Morel had been more the equal of this ambitious, proud woman, their union might have proceeded differently, but, says the narrator with a trace of condemning irony directed more against her than him, though "she strove to make him moral, religious" (*SL* 14), "[t]he pity was, she was too much his opposite."

> She could not be content with the little he might be; she would have him the much that he ought to be. So, in seeking to make him nobler than he could be, she destroyed him. She injured and hurt and scarred herself, but she lost none of her worth. She also had the children. (*SL* 16)

A woman with such strength and pride is hardly going to take her disappointments lying down, and Gertrude Morel begins to manifest the terrible side of her archetypal nature, becoming a Clytemnestra-like avenging goddess: wronged by her husband and seeing him wrong her children ("I could kill you!" she screams when Morel cuts the baby William's hair [*SL* 15]), she subconsciously retaliates by demanding more and more of her children's love, appropriating to herself the love they had once felt for their father. She thinks of their devotion to her as "compensation" for her suffering (*SL* 82), their achievements as personal fulfilment: "Not for nothing had been her struggle" (*SL* 183). And it is indeed a struggle: those critics, like Vivas, who seem to think Walter Morel more sinned against than sinning have never lived with an alcoholic in their own families. If we can trust the narrator, Mrs. Morel had been happy for nine months after her marriage, despite "flashes of fear" at his ignorance (*SL* 11), until she discovered Morel had lied to her about their finances. "She said very little to her husband, but her manner had changed towards him. Something in her proud, honourable soul had crystallised out hard as rock" (*SL* 13). And this unwonted coolness apparently intimidates her husband who, feeling guilty and inadequate, chooses to avoid her by drinking and fighting. In such households it is natural that the children should side with the mother against the father. "Paul never forgot coming home from the Band of Hope one Monday evening and finding his mother with her eye swollen and discoloured, his father standing on the hearth-rug, feet astride, his head down, and William, just home from work, glaring at his father" (*SL* 58).

"To be sure," says Spilka, "there is a dual responsibility here, since Mrs. Morel has actually driven him to destroy himself. But the fact remains that Lawrence holds his men accountable, in the end, for their own integrity of being" (75). Thus Mrs. Morel's most culpable wrong lies not so much in rejecting her husband as in replacing him first with William, then with Paul. Though it is true that she does so in response to Morel's degradation—"[she] loved [William] passionately [since he] came just when her own bitterness of disillusion was hardest to bear" (*SL* 14)—and true that her capacity for nurturance is great, and true that her children seek her out for it; nonetheless she is deeply to blame for encouraging their self-destructive love. Thus Gertrude Morel is very much what Paul/Lawrence perceives her to be: a woman in whom the life force is strong but the urge toward dissolution even stronger.

As I have said earlier, the ultimate power of the archetypal mother goddess depends on the balanced fusion of her two antagonistic personalities, great and terrible, nurturing and devouring. This power makes her as strong as any male, if not stronger. Up until the transitional period mothers in the novel have been either one or the other, and therefore their "power" has been limited (the idealized mother is ineffectual, the bad mother is overthrown). Mrs. Gereth, though a transitional mother, also is overthrown because she, like the bad mothers before her, does not have the nurturing force which would balance the devouring force. Mrs. Morel possesses both but allows the latter to pervert the former in a conflict which destroys not only her but many of those under her power. We will see that in the fully-synthesized mothers in the final chapter, the antagonistic impulses manage somehow to live side by side productively and fairly peaceably.

Notes

1. The twentieth century has its share of silly and selfish mothers, though as I will show in the last chapter, their dramatic purpose is different from what it had been in the earlier periods.

2. Especially important was the drop in the birth rate throughout this period, accompanied by increasing use of birth control. Freed from the pressure of always having children, women were now more likely to have careers. For instance, in England in 1882 only 26 women were registered as physicians; by 1900 the number had increased to 258—still a fraction of the total but progress nonetheless. The industrializing nineteenth century found women useful as office staff or sales clerks, but the more enterprising ones made their way closer to the top. Women by the turn of the century were not only admitted to study in universities but to lecture in them as well; the Education Act passed in 1870 required adequate primary education for girls as well as boys, followed in 1902 by an act requiring secondary education. Also important: the Married Women's Property Act passed in 1870, while the first law giving working class wives the right to sue for separation came in 1878, the second in 1886. The Women's Cooperative Guild, founded in 1884, though allowing only

a minor role in central decision-making bodies, still gave its members a sense of self-worth and purpose. Labor organizations such as the Women's Labor League lobbied to improve working women's wages and working conditions. Of course, improvements were often inadequate or half-hearted. For instance, the National Health Insurance Act of 1911 protected insured workers, male and female, but not their dependents, who were mainly women and children; and the 1889 findings of two biologists, Geddes and Thompson, stressed that women's attributes were equal to men's—but different, best suited by physiology to motherhood and domestic duties. See especially Bauer and Ritt, *Free and Ennobled*; Jane Lewis, *Women in England 1870–1950: Sexual Divisions and Social Change*; and Peter Gay, *The Bourgeois Experience: Victoria to Freud*, especially vol. I, *Education of the Senses*.

3. "The Future of the Novel," in *The Universal Anthology* xxiii-xxiv; rpt. in Veeder and Griffin, eds., *The Art of Criticism: Henry James on the Theory and the Practice of Fiction* 250.

4. *Women in the English Novel* 176. Williams adds that James also "wanted [women] to retain the traditional virtues—to be cultivated, refined, and unwilling to demand their rights. Isabel, Claire, and Fleda Vetch would be unwomanly if they fought for their happiness as Basil [Ransom] unashamedly does" (176).

5. Bauer and Ritt, *Free and Ennobled* 166. There is a scattering of such incidents on record, the prices charged ranging from a few shillings to an ox to a quart of beer. Although as John R. Gillis says in *For Better, For Worse: British Marriages, 1600 to the Present*, wife sales were "the eighteenth and nineteenth centuries' most visible form of self-divorce" (211), making the practice an economic or class issue as well as a women's issue, the fact remains that the tradition probably grew out of the old rules of betrothal that allowed men—not women—to buy themselves out of a premarital contract. In other words, it was predicated on the view that women are negotiable quantities; indeed, one man sold his wife by the pound!

6. See Jane Lewis, *Women in England* 3–7. Legitimate live births per 1000 married women aged 15–44 fell from 295 in the 1870s to 222 by 1901 to only 111 by the 1930s.

7. See, for instance, Lewis, *Women in England*, Jalland and Hooper, *Women from Birth to Death*, and Dally, *Inventing Motherhood*.

8. Quoted in Lewis 95. Notice that this is not a demand for careers: J. A. Banks says that there "was no question . . . at that time, of the feminists working to make Victorian marriage so much of a partnership that the wife could become a breadwinner . . . along the lines of, say, the twentieth-century 'dual career' professional and quasi-professional families" (*Victorian Values* 36–37).

9. Following the public's initial hostility toward Freud, psychoanalytic theories regarding the role of the unconscious and the role of sexuality in determining personality and human relations evidently grew to be well known if not well understood. "Psychoanalytic terms or perversions of them became catch-phrases, every man his neighbour's analyst became a—largely middle-class—vogue," while by the 1920s "special societies and discussion clubs" for the informal study of psychoanalysis were formed (Juliet Mitchell, *Psychoanalysis and Feminism* 295–97).

10. "Mothers and Stepmothers in Fairy Tales and Myths" 315–16. Similarly, Bengt Holbek believes that although the same archetypes are expressed everywhere and across time, "their concrete appearances may be individually determined" (*Interpretations of Fairy Tales* 295).

11. It is hardly likely that political reforms alone can account for the transition, since none of the transitional mothers in any genre are exclusively or even primarily didactic in function or tone.

12. Wagenknecht agrees with Edwin Bowden (*The Themes of Henry James*) that Mrs. Gereth is no such monster as Osmond appears in *The Portrait of a Lady*; however, he disagrees with Bowden's claim that her love of the objects grants her a measure of redemption (*Eve and Henry James* 104–05). I agree with Wagenknecht on both points.

13. As I have already said, mothers reap what they sow throughout the history of the novel, but it is not until the transitional period that their children begin to confront them with the fact. Owen Gereth is perhaps too dense to make the connection or at any rate too mild-mannered to make it to his mother's face, but Clym Yeobright does so in *The Return of the Native*, during the bitter exchange about Eustacia Vye. When Mrs. Yeobright tearfully protests, "You are unnatural, Clym, and I did not expect it," Clym replies, "Very likely. . . . You did not know the measure you were going to mete me, and therefore did not know the measure that would be returned to you again" (*RN* 168).

14. See my first chapter, or, for instance, Paulo de Carvalho-Neto, *Folklore and Psychoanalysis*, or Adriaan de Witt, "Mothers and Stepmothers in Fairy Tales and Myths."

15. *Strange Alloy: The Relation of Comedy to Tragedy in the Fiction of Henry James* 75. Leyburn quotes here from James' *The Art of the Novel* 67.

16. Harry Moore, in *The Life and Works of D. H. Lawrence*, notes that "quickly" means alive in this context (105).

17. Lawrence felt a strong need to write this foreword but said he would "die of shame" if it were printed (letter to Edward Garnett, 1 Feb 1913, *Letters* 104).

18. Letter to A. D. McLeod, 27 Oct 1913, *Letters* 152.

19. The autobiographical nature of Lawrence's fixation with mothers is of course well established. See, for instance, John Middleton Murry, *Son of Woman: The Story of D. H. Lawrence*; Harry T. Moore, *The Priest of Love: A Life of D. H. Lawrence*; Daniel A. Weiss, *Oedipus in Nottingham: D. H. Lawrence*; and Ruderman, *D. H. Lawrence and the Devouring Mother*.

Chapter Five

"The Fruits of Ambivalence": Mothers in the Twentieth Century

When Paul Morel walks away from his mother's grave at the conclusion of *Sons and Lovers*, he is finally enacting the separation from his mother that had not been possible while she lived. He walks toward the town "quickly"—as if in her dying, the mother has given life back to the son. Although later novelists will rarely concede that so difficult a maternal relationship can have so clear cut a resolution, Lawrence's novel is undeniably prophetic in other ways. In the years and the novels since *Sons and Lovers*, the problematic yet vitalizing relationship with the mother has become one of this century's most absorbing themes; indeed, some critics consider it to be *the* central issue confronted by a number of women writers. "Many autobiographical or confessional novels trace the coming to adulthood, that is, to individual identity, of a daughter who must define herself in terms of her mother," writes Judith Kegan Gardiner (147). In her study of Virginia Woolf, Ellen Bayuk Rosenman says, "I consider the mother-daughter relationship the central problem of female experience" (ix). Adrienne Rich, using a term coined by the poet Lynn Sukenick, sees "matrophobia" (the fear not of one's mother or of motherhood but of *becoming* one's mother) in writers from Woolf to Kate Chopin to Doris Lessing to Sylvia Plath to Margaret Atwood to Tillie Olsen. "Thousands of daughters see their mothers as having taught a compromise and self-hatred they are struggling to win free of, the one through whom the restrictions and degradations of a female existence were perforce transmitted" (235). But the maternal theme is of interest not only to women. James Joyce explores the mother's influence through Stephen Daedalus; Evelyn Waugh examines the negative force of mothers like Lady Marchmain (*Brideshead Revisited*) and Brenda Last (*A Handful of Dust*); and several of E. M. Forster's plots reflect his awareness of the power of the mother and, depending on how she uses this power, the need of others either to assimilate or escape from it. Mrs. Wilcox's ability to "connect" is the redeeming value of *Howards End*, for instance, while in *Where Angels Fear to Tread* characters wisely resist the "malign matriarchy" of Mrs. Herriton. Forster's interest in matriarchy, says Christopher Gillie, is only partly accounted for by the fact that he spent his solitary childhood in the care of strongly maternal women.

> The theme of matriarchy is not merely an idiosyncrasy of Forster's, arising from the eccentricity of his own experience. One of the qualities by which we recognise major artists is their capacity to universalise what is at first merely personal to them, and through the image of the matriarch he taps one of the deep themes of European culture, whether we think of the malign Clytemnestra or Mary the Mother of God. (106)

As Gillie implies, and as I have been demonstrating throughout this study, the centrality of the mother has never been far from human consciousness nor its artistic expressions. However, until this century the novel has repressed her influence. As Gillie goes on to note, "Our civilisation in the last two hundred years has obscured the importance of the great mother figure. . . . Forster is one of the few writers of this century to have given it close attention" (106-07). To this last I will only add that Forster is not one of the "few" but merely one of the first.

A great deal of the fiction of the twentieth century (on both sides of the Atlantic) has confirmed the importance of the Great Mother figure—has recreated a modern version of the maternal archetype as schematised by Neumann and others: the ultimate commixture of negative and positive powers. As I have discussed elsewhere, patriarchal cultures have tended to divide the archetype into its two opposing aspects, one wholly destructive, the other wholly benevolent; numerous cultural and mimetic forms reinforce this division. The effect—and presumably the subconscious intent—is to undermine the potency of the quintessential woman and so maintain the dominance of the patriarchy. One can see how this strategy has succeeded heretofore in Western literature, the novel included. Mothers of idealized wisdom, courage, and compassion are trivialized, dead, or dying; mothers of exaggerated aggressiveness, greed, and rancor are vanquished. The result has been that the enormous potential power—spiritual, emotional, rational, creative, physical, and political—of the fully-integrated mother has been discredited or ignored.

The twentieth-century fictional mother, at her most positive, may be seen as a reaffirmation of this androgynous power.[1] However, one need only recall Paul Morel's anguish or reread psychoanalytic theory to know that this power is as likely to be viewed as destructive and overwhelming as much as benevolent and creative. As Nancy Chodorow and numerous others have shown, the mother is an inescapably ambiguous figure. Children wish to remain one with their mother and expect that she will never have different interests from them, yet they define development in terms of growing away from her. "In the face of their dependence, lack of certainty of her emotional permanence, fear of merging, and overwhelming love and attachment, a mother looms large and powerful," says Chodorow (82). As we have seen, much older cultures than ours created myths and folklore to articulate this emotional ambivalence; and if my theory is correct, two hundred years of the novel have likewise dealt with the problem by segregating the maternal personality into two relatively innocuous camps. However, these subconscious impulses have not faded in the present century. On the contrary, certain forms of popular culture, particularly advertising and commercial television, continue to promote maternal stereotypes. For instance, the grandmother in advertising is invariably depicted as the soul of domestic comfort, dusting flour from her hands, and delighted to see (and spend money on) her grandchildren. How this cozy image would be blasted by May Quest, mother and grandmother in Doris Lessing's *Children of Violence* series, who, critically watching her son and daughter-in-law add to their large family and large farm, mutters at last, "Well, if they want to kill themselves in the process I suppose it's their affair" (*The Four-Gated City* 243). And yet Mrs. Quest is not simply an ill-tempered old lady. Martha's relationship to her is beyond easy definition; Mrs. Quest is part of the "terrible dark blind pit" that Martha feels she must fight her way out of (*FGC* 68). Adrienne Rich says that in such novels the "mother stands for the victim in ourselves, the unfree woman, the martyr" (236). As Doris Lessing has said elsewhere, "We use our parents like recurring dreams, to be entered into when needed; they are always there for love or for hate" (*A Small Personal Voice* 83). And as Ellen Rosenman writes about Virginia Woolf's mother-daughter relationships, "the daughter must define herself both with and against the mother to achieve selfhood" (ix).

The "fruits of this ambivalence," as Rosenman calls it, can be seen across the whole expanse of twentieth-century fiction, yet the attempt to come to terms with it is a much more harrowing ordeal for some than for others. Jean Rhys' work, for instance, is "located around" dead mothers, dying mothers, stepmothers, absent mothers, and surrogate mothers, says Deborah Kloepfer; it is preoccupied with abortions and infant death. "Although Rhys insists that she thinks about her mother less and less, she encodes her more and more into her texts; [there is in all her work] a hearkening for the mother's voice, a search for the mother's body."[2] In *Wide Sargasso Sea* the heroine, Antoinette Mason, tells of loving and hating her mother on their lonely estate in the West Indies: "Once I would have gone back quietly to watch her asleep on the blue sofa—once I made excuses to be near her when she brushed her hair, a soft black cloak to cover me, hide me, keep me safe. But not any longer. Not any more" (468). As it did for Lawrence, the task of confronting the mother in one's fiction is bound to have a strongly personal, frequently painful dimension. In "A Sketch of the Past" Virginia Woolf said that in recreating Julia Stephen (who died when Woolf was thirteen) as Mrs. Ramsay in *To the Lighthouse*, she did for herself "what psycho-analysts do for their patients" (*Moments of Being* 81). Thus many of the maternal portraits of this century are marked by a mixture of the feelings psychoanalysts note in their real-life clients: guilt, hostility, confusion, yearning, loss, rejection. In "The Oxen of the Sun," a chapter full of birthing references, Stephen Daedalus recalls the period of brief but perfect union with his mother: "Before born babe bliss had. Within womb won he worship." But then came the inevitable disillusionment, and he accuses his mother's ghost. "But thou hast suckled me with a bitter milk: my moon and my sun thou hast quenched forever. And thou hast left me alone for ever in the dark ways of my bitterness: and with a kiss of ashes hast thou kissed my mouth"

(*Ulysses* 384, 393). This insistent mingling of images of life and death, of nurture and decay, even of sexual desire and revulsion, are at the very heart of the Great Mother imago and consequently at the heart of the new maternal archetype of the twentieth century.

For this is what May Daedalus, May Quest, Mrs. Ramsay *et al.* represent: a new archetype, a version of the mother that recalls the simultaneously devouring and life-giving force of the Great Mother goddess, only with the limitations of human, not supernatural abilities. Annis Pratt sees the progression from stereotypes to archetypes as a significant one:

> Stereotypes differ from archetypes, I feel, in representing clusters of symbols that have become rigid and hence restrictive to full personal development. Archetypes, conversely, are fluid and dynamic, empowering women's personalities to grow and develop. . . . [A]rchetypes are both projective and "repetitious," futuristic and rooted in women's history. (132)

Although much of today's fiction expresses tremendous anger at the mother, occasionally casting her as obtuse, selfish, narrow-minded, and domineering, there is almost always a sense, as there rarely is in the novels of the past two centuries, that her role and character have been complicated, rather than simplified, by her being a mother. The conflicting emotional implications of that role, whether they are being considered from another's point of view or from the mother's own, tend to make her more, not less, problematic, and more, not less, sympathetic.

For in spite of the anger and resentment that apparently drive many of these writers, they often depict their fictional mothers as sympathetic, even admirable figures, especially when they have ceased to accuse and try rather to understand. "Easier by far to hate and reject a mother outright," says Adrienne Rich, "than to see beyond her to the forces acting upon her" (235). Not surprisingly, some of the most memorable maternal portraits of this century are those which explore these forces which "act upon" mothers. In 1978 Judith Gardiner saw signs that "the bitter hostility shown by our twentieth-century fictional daughters" was finally passing (160). If the heroines of Margaret

Drabble's novels seem to be more generous in their judgments of their mothers, perhaps it is because they, mothers themselves, have perceived how easily the prosaic demands of motherhood may constrict one's freedom. Frances Wingate in *The Realms of Gold*, though still critical of her mother, nonetheless watches her "with onslaughts of fear, of pity, and of love. . . ." For she remembers a time when, "in seeking to avoid her mother's ghost, she had behaved exactly like her mother" (87, 84-85). It is interesting to note that when Doris Lessing moves the point of view of her protagonist from that of Martha Quest the daughter to that of Kate Brown the mother, the resentment (and our sympathy) move accordingly. Here is Martha Quest:

> When her mother had gone, Martha cupped her hands protestingly over her stomach, and murmured to the creature within it that nothing would deform it, freedom would be its gift. She, Martha, the free spirit, would protect the creature from her, Martha, the maternal force; the maternal Martha, that enemy, would not be allowed to enter the picture. (*A Proper Marriage* 111)

And here is Kate Brown:

> The climactic moment of three years ago had been when Tim, then a tumultuous sixteen, had turned on her at the supper table and screamed that she was suffocating him. This had been wrenched from his guts, it was easy to see that. . . . She saw herself at one end of the table, tender and swollen like a goose's fattening liver with the frightful pressure of four battling and expanding egos that were all in one way or another in conflict or confluence with herself, a focus, a balancing point. (*Summer Before the Dark* 98-99)

Perhaps as novelists exorcise the mother demons that plague them (as Lessing does in the Martha Quest novels), or perhaps it is merely as they themselves grow older, they begin to identify more readily with the generation of their mothers. Kate Brown's maternal crisis is brought on by her approaching middle age and the feeling that she is obsolete; this also happens to Susan Rawlings in Lessing's short story "To Room Nineteen." Yet at thirty-nine the still-vital Martha Quest idealizes the way in which *she* will age, in deliberate contrast to her mother. In the appendix of *The Four-Gated City*, Martha predicts her death in a letter written in 1997 from an island community established to escape a nuclear holocaust. She describes her productive life there, caring for children orphaned by the war. As Claire Sprague points out in *Rereading Doris Lessing*, "In a community brought together by the right shared ideology, aging seems to present no dangers" (116). Yet Martha is anxious for the children in her care: "I think of these people, babies in appearance, out in the world and—I can't bear it. They tell us not to be afraid" (*FGC* 608). It seems to be Lessing's somewhat ironic intent that Martha, though a clairvoyant, should seem a bit naive and therefore unable or unwilling to appreciate the fact that her mother has left her certain invaluable legacies. What we see here is a significant difference from novels of a century or two ago. Even though the maternal figure is perceived by Martha as the "enemy," the narrator remains somewhat detached and therefore able to see, as Sprague defines it, "the complex circularity of daughters fighting mothers and then becoming mothers themselves" (110).

As a result of the modern novel's emphasis on the ambiguity, complexity, and eternality of the mother, it has been obliged to reject or at least reconsider the former traditions that split the mother into separate and subordinate natures. This is why, when modern novelists incorporate fairy tales or fairy tale paradigms into their mother portraits, they often seem to do so deliberately, conspicuously, and to a degree ironically. Their intent is not to deny the historical and psychological authenticity of folktales; on the contrary, they perhaps even more than their eighteenth- and nineteenth-century predecessors are keenly aware of the complex psychological forces implicit in archetypal literature and of their continued impact on "modern" civilizations. Unlike earlier novelists, however, whose uncritical use of fairy tale paradigms may be interpreted today as a tacit endorsement of the patriarchal social structure, when twentieth-century novelists call attention to fairy tales, they often do so in order to question their assumptions and to suggest an alternative mythology. In this respect they may be seen as refining what George MacDonald and the other Victorian writers of children's fiction were attempting to do in rewriting fairy tales.

On this subject of the need for and the possibilities of a new archetypal literature, Karen E. Rowe argues that a balance must be struck "between romantic fantasies and contemporary realities":

> While feminist political movements of the last century may seem to signal women's liberation from traditional roles, too often the underlying truth is that . . . the female psyche has not matured with sufficient strength to sustain a radical assault on the patriarchal culture. Despite an apparent susceptibility to change, modern culture remains itself stubbornly antithetical to ideals of female and male equality. . . . Whether expressed in pornographic, domestic, or gothic fictions or enacted in the daily relations of men and women, fairy tale visions of romance also continue to perpetuate cultural ideals which subordinate women. As a major form of communal or "folk" lore, they preserve rather than challenge the patriarchy. (222-23)

Far from dismissing their significance, Rowe sees fairy tales and the standards they advocate as responsible for much of the confusion, guilt, and anger historically suffered by women. "[A]s long as modern women continue to tailor their aspirations and capabilities to conform with romantic paradigms, they will live with deceptions, disillusionments, and/or ambivalences." The solution, she suggests, is "to cultivate a newly fertile ground of psychic and cultural experience from which will grow fairy tales for human beings in the future."

This, I think, is what Doris Lessing tries to accomplish in *The Summer Before the Dark*, through Kate Brown's recurring dream of the seal. This dream is strongly archetypal—"more and more, [its flavor is] that of another time; myth, or an old tale" (*SBD* 114). Like a twentieth-century version of the "big dreams" described by Adriaan de Witt, this one seems of such impact to Kate that she feels "compelled" to tell it to Maureen, "beginning like a fairy story or fable" (*SBD* 234). Likewise, the scenes and images of her dream are strangely primitive and Teutonic, the landscape of the Brothers Grimm. She dreams of walking "in a country where pine trees and spruce stood around her in thick clean snow"; she enters a village "built all of wood" and is picked out of the crowd to dance with the handsome young king (*SBD* 159-60).

But here the traditional fairy tale takes a detour: the King, suddenly and without explanation, begins to dance with a younger partner. "Kate was running away, in a desolation of grief. The people of the village came after her, shouting: she had become an enemy, because she had been discarded" (*SBD* 160). Kate's dream not only reveals her long-repressed hurt over her own husband's chronic infidelity; on a deeper level it expresses the timeless frustration of all women who are rejected because they are old or ugly. As Marcia Lieberman notes, "The beauty contest is a constant and primary device" in fairy tales; "the focus [is] on beauty as a girl's most valuable asset, perhaps her only asset" (187-88). However, unlike the traditional fairy tale where "being ill-favored is corollary to being ill-natured" (196), Lessing's "tale" rejects the superficial and often persecutory standards by which a patriarchal culture rewards or punishes its women.

By having Mrs. Ramsay read "The Fisherman and His Wife" to her youngest, James, Virginia Woolf is likewise renouncing the standards implicit in the fairy tale. The image of mother and son trying to enjoy the story in spite of Mr. Ramsay's disconsolate pacing up and down just outside their window forms a leitmotif for interpreting Mrs. Ramsay's role in the novel. Mrs. Ramsay herself thinks of the story as "the bass gently accompanying a tune" (*TL* 87). However, in this classic Grimm tale about the errors of female dominance, the relationship of the fisherman to his wife is less a mirror than an inversion of the relationship between Mrs. Ramsay and her husband. While Ilsabil complains about the inconveniences of their home—"it's dreadful to have to live all one's life in this hut that is so small and dirty; you ought to have wished for a cottage" (*Green Fairy Book* 344)—Mrs. Ramsay considers the ramshackle state of their Hebrides home with cheerful resignation.

[She] saw the room, saw the chairs, thought them fearfully shabby. Their entrails, as Andrew said the other day, were all over the floor; but then what was the point, she asked, of buying good chairs to let them spoil up here all through the winter . . . ? Never mind, the rent was precisely twopence halfpenny; the children loved it; it did her husband good to be three thousand, or if she must be accurate, three hundred miles from his libraries . . . ; and there was room for visitors. Mats,

camp beds, crazy ghosts of chairs and tables whose London
life of service was done—they did well enough here. (*TL* 43)

However, much as we prefer Mrs. Ramsay to her counterpart in the
folktale—Ilsabil typically gets her husband's attention by digging her
elbows into his side—Woolf wishes us to notice a crucial similarity
between the two women. Both have tremendous power. But in only one
is that power an affirmation. Mrs. Ramsay's power, as I discuss at
length below, is a function of her ultimate (good-bad) nature; it is what
makes people both afraid of and in love with her. The constant
reference to her knitting, for instance, is a subtle reminder not only of
the procreative power of the female but the incontestable will of the
Fates themselves: "Flashing her needles, confident, upright, she created
drawing-room and kitchen. . . . She laughed, she knitted" (*TL* 59).The
force of Mrs. Ramsay is instinctive, the power of the superior nature,
and she accepts it almost in spite of herself: "she did not like, even for a
second, to feel finer than her husband" (*TL* 61). In Ilsabil, on the other
hand, power is a perversion of the negative side of the disjointed Great
Mother, the power of brute and ignorant will, seized by her in defiance
of natural and moral law (as attested by the increasingly violent
changes in the weather). The fact that the fisherman allows himself, if
protestingly, to be ordered around by his wife is intended not as an
indictment of male weakness but of female hubris: the implication is
that, until such a woman is overcome, as she inevitably will be
according to the formula, no virtue is equal to her vice. By making Mrs.
Ramsay both powerful *and* virtuous, Woolf has written the new
archetype into the old tale.

The mothers on whom this discussion now focuses—Forster's Mrs.
Moore in *A Passage to India* (1924), as well as Mrs. Ramsay (1927)
and Kate Brown (1973)—are all examples of the integrated mother in
whom the archetypal powers of the Good Mother—love, procreation,
intuition, harmony, nurturance, charity—stand up powerfully alongside
those of the Terrible Mother—anger, judgment, vengefulness, rapacity,
domination, annihilation. The negative qualities give force and
stringency to the positive; the positive give moderation and humanity to
the negative. Love, for instance, softens judgment; judgment in turn
gives value to love. These mothers may be seen as retaining the
compassion while rejecting the pathos and timidity of mothers like Mrs.

Copperfield; likewise they retain the authority but eliminate the brutality and caprice of mothers like Catherine de Bourgh. The result is mothers who inspire deference equally with affection.[3] Nor is this tribute paid only by their children; invariably they inspire a larger community of both men and women. For they all have an uncanny influence that extends beyond their immediate families: their personalities have the force of a spell. Lily Briscoe says as much about Mrs. Ramsay: "There was something frightening about her. She was irresistible. . . . She put a spell on them all" (*TL* 152). This power, even though it is wielded over people who are not their own children, is related indisputably to the fact that they are mothers, for having children is "utterly transformative" of the psyche (Whittier 202).

These new archetypal mothers share a certain mystical quality which it is not quite accurate to label religious, nor yet pagan; nonetheless, there is no question they are spiritually more attuned than most of their associates. Occasionally their spirituality has an explicitly Christian or monotheistic flavor—an example is Mrs. Moore's hesitant reminder to her xenophobic son Ronny Heaslop, City Magistrate of Chandrapore, that "God has put us on earth to love our neighbors and to show it, and He is omnipresent, even in India, to see how we are succeeding" (*PI* 51); yet she gradually abandons her rather dogmatic religiosity in favor of a more Eastern mysticism. Forster emphasizes this explicitly in the final section "Temple" when the Hindu Godbole recalls "a wasp seen he forgot where," but he "loved the wasp equally" (*PI* 286)—just as Mrs. Moore had done earlier in the novel, when she murmured "Pretty dear" to a wasp which any other Englishwoman would have swatted as a pest (*PI* 35).

In some ways the spirituality of these mothers is depicted as predominantly pagan or secular. For instance, Mrs. Ramsay moves "like some queen" among her people, accepting "their devotion and their prostration before her" (*TL* 124); and they all have a keen affinity to flowers and nature: Mrs. Wilcox with her wisp of hay is an incarnation of the goddess Ceres (*HW* 22, 74), and Mrs. Ramsay reflects how, "if one was alone, one leant to inanimate things; trees, streams, flowers; felt they expressed one, felt they became one; felt they knew one, in a sense were one" (*TL* 97). Yet this mingling of images from Western, Eastern, and pagan religions merely reinforces the archetypal nature of the mother character, for (religious orthodoxy aside) the maternal archetype has its origins in precisely the same place as religion, that is, in the collective human psyche. Inasmuch as anthropologists tell us that the mother goddess archetype evolved out of prehistoric matriarchies which existed much earlier than doctrinal patriarchal religions, it is to be expected that the pervasive spirituality of the archetype should be expressly *un*systematic. (This absence of a system is reflected in Forster's humanistic creed, Woolf's belief in androgyny, and Lessing's Sufism.[4]) Yet it is inevitable that over the centuries the maternal archetype should have assimilated the more sympathetic rituals, images, and doctrines of Christian orthodoxy (such as the sanctity of the mother with her child or the New Testament precept of unconditional love). However, though it undoubtedly was enlarged by patriarchal forms, the archetype was never *replaced* by them.

One of these forms, the concept of the tripartite godhead, seems to be reflected in the new archetypal mother, only transformed into a matriarchal Trinity. Thus she appears variously as an aloof, impersonal figure sitting in judgment on the world; a holy spirit ennobling and inspiriting the world; and above all, an incarnate Christ living in, loving, teaching, and ultimately redeeming the world. Together these roles emphasize the profound, almost allegorical role of the mother goddess to restore meaning and harmony to a world which, as James McConkey says, "has become alien to man; the God, the order, the unity, which had been perceived through that earth must perforce be discovered again" (85).

Images of the mother as a detached, often disgusted or ironic deity occur fairly frequently in these novels (although her compassionate involvement *with* humanity is ultimately more central to her identity). Nonetheless, such echoes remind us that she is clearly different from others, related to them in a way that, for all that it is intensely and genuinely intimate yet has an element of impersonal and dispassionate removal at the same time. All three of these mothers are spoken of as being at times inscrutable, stand-offish, anti-social. Even though Margaret Schlegel learns from Ruth Wilcox "to be humble and kind, to go straight ahead, to love people rather than pity them, to remember the submerged" (*HW* 73), still Mrs. Wilcox seems to her "out of focus" and "nearer the line that divides daily life from a life that may be of greater importance" (*HW* 76); Margaret's last view of her is as a "lonely figure" disappearing into a building (*HW* 85). Likewise, even when Kate Brown is absorbed into the demands of her family and community, still she customarily detaches herself in order to contemplate others from afar—"To sit here quietly, as invisible as she could make herself—it was like the theatre" (*SBD* 46). She even regards herself in this same, dissociated way, almost as if she were studying a stranger: "A woman dressed suitably for a family afternoon walked back across the lawn . . ."; "A woman stood on her back step, arm folded, waiting" (*SBD* 8, 1). Kate, torn between her maternal and non-maternal identities, relies on these third person observations as the most objective way to evaluate her life and options; ironically, by splitting off from her physical self, she manages to save her metaphysical self from disintegration.

Mrs. Ramsay, likewise the most communal of women, also detaches frequently from the group, "drifting into that strange no-man's land where to follow people is impossible and yet their going inflicts such a chill on those who watch them that they always try at least to follow them with their eyes as one follows a fading ship" (*TL* 127). Yet these momentary abstractions are not meant to be offensive: she simply cannot take anyone with her, any more than a clairvoyant can be accompanied in her visions. These are the essential breathing spaces in which Mrs. Ramsay searches out and acknowledges her feelings, her insights, her fears.

> She could be by herself, by herself. And that was what now she often felt the need of—to think; well, not even to think. To be silent; to be alone. All the being and the doing, expansive, glittering, vocal, evaporated; and one shrunk, with a sense of solemnity, to being oneself, a wedge-shaped core of darkness, something invisible to others. (*TL* 95)

Sometimes the private thoughts are disturbing, disgruntled: "she must admit that she felt this thing that she called life terrible, hostile, and quick to pounce" (*TL* 93). But just as often they are tranquil, fragmented, glowing with impressionistic affection: "She hovered like a hawk suspended; like a flag floated in an element of joy which filled every nerve of her body fully and sweetly" (*TL* 157). There is nothing selfish in these brief absences to check on the state of her soul; they are,

I think, what allow her to minister so well to others when she rejoins them.

Mrs. Moore, on the other hand, becomes more and more like a disgusted deity, pulling away from humankind because the "twilight of the double vision" (*PI* 207) has proven too disillusioning for this elderly woman: "she didn't want to write to her children, didn't want to communicate with anyone, not even with God" (*PI* 150). There had been a time, when she first got to India, that she had felt capable of striving toward the "dignified and simple" goal of being one with the universe, but no more: "there was always some little duty to be performed first, . . . and while she was pottering about, the Marabar struck its gong" (*PI* 208). Her response, when Aziz is made to stand trial for a rape he did not commit, is not one of sympathy but profound impatience that sounds like querulousness. "Oh, why can't I walk away and be gone? . . . And all the time this to do and that to do . . . and everything sympathy and confusion and bearing another's burdens. Why can't this be done and that be done . . . and they be done and I at peace?" (*PI* 201). Yet clearly it is her penetrating vision, not any mere pettiness, that so disturbs her soul. Richard Martin says that "Mrs. Moore's 'double vision' enables her to see evil and good equally. . . . This double vision connects her inextricably with Godbole in his vision of the universal responsibility for good and evil" (172). Lionel Trilling echoes this when he says that despite the "sullen disillusionment" in which she dies, Mrs. Moore "had been right when she said to Ronny that there are many different kinds of failure, some of which succeed" (90).

Mrs. Moore is by no means the only mother who loses patience. They all occasionally bristle in resentment against the demands and expectations of motherhood: it is one of the reassuringly human things about them. Theirs is not the beatific renunciation of a saint nor the complacent acceptance of self-abnegation. Even though these are all unusually strong, vibrant women, with healthy minds and strong egos, the notion that marriage and children should cure mothers of every vestige of self-centeredness is a fraud perpetuated by patriarchal interests. Mrs. Ramsay thinks wearily that while others have romantic love, all she has is "this—an infinitely long table and plates and knives" (*TL* 125). And Kate Brown worries that she has been turned into an "obsessed maniac" by the "long, grinding process of always, always being at other people's beck and call, always having to give out attention to detail, minuscule wants, demands, needs, events, crises" (*SBD* 106). However, having weighed the attractions of remaining on the level of pure self against those of moving to the more rigorous level of community, they all (even Mrs. Moore, whose apostasy is only temporary) find the latter ultimately more worthwhile. That is why Mrs. Ramsay so quickly gives herself "the little shake that one gives a watch that has stopped" (*TL* 126) and why Kate Brown returns to her family when her dream voyage into the "darkness" ends. It is also why Mrs. Moore's "passive cynicism . . . gives way to a new stirring of life" as she sails out of India (Gillie 155). Her commitment to the human community is most compellingly reaffirmed when Ralph, her son from her second marriage, brings about the important reconciliation between Aziz and Fielding.

Merely human disillusionment cannot destroy the redemptive force of this new archetypal mother. Though occasionally alarmed by all that is demanded of them, they respond to these demands almost as if to a destiny being fulfilled. In this they are like reluctant messiahs. Kate's dream of saving the seal, Mrs. Ramsay's hopefulness about the lighthouse, Mrs. Moore's accidental meeting in the mosque with Aziz, in which she instinctively reveals her sympathy and natural piety ("you know what others feel," the Moslem says gratefully [*PI* 23]), all these small acts of grace later take on the inevitableness of prophecy. During the climactic moments in Aziz' trial on charges of raping Adela Quested, Mrs. Moore's name becomes the battle cry of thousands of persecuted Indians: "Esmiss Esmoor, Esmiss Esmoor. . . ." And much as it annoys her son the City Magistrate to hear his mother "travestied into . . . a Hindu goddess," it is clearly this invocation of Mrs. Moore's deep-sighted soul that saves Aziz, for it provokes Adela to see the events at the Marabar clearly for the first time: "Dr. Aziz never followed me into the cave" (*PI* 225, 229). Even though Forster ultimately rejects the possibility of reconciling East and West, presumably he is not a nihilist, because in spite of the fact that Mrs. Moore herself finally despairs of ever being "one with the universe," she is still meant to be seen as a force for inspiriting that hope in others. That is why, even as her body is being lowered into the Indian Ocean, her spirit continues to empower good over evil. It acts like a talisman to exonerate Aziz; it is present in Ralph Moore's visit to the embittered

Aziz, who softens at last for he "knew with his heart that this was Mrs. Moore's son" (*PI* 313); and it even endures in the marriage of the empiricist Fielding to Mrs. Moore's daughter Stella. Fielding is a "blank, frank atheist" for whom intuitive reasoning is a form of "misunderstanding"; nonetheless, he is forced to concede the power of Mrs. Moore:

> [I]t struck him that people are not really dead until they are felt to be dead. As long as there is some misunderstanding about them, they possess a sort of immortality. . . . He had tried to kill Mrs. Moore this evening, on the roof of the Nawab Bahadur's house; but she still eluded him, and the atmosphere remained tranquil. (*PI* 255)

Like Mrs. Wilcox and Mrs. Ramsay, Mrs. Moore's death occurs while the novel is still in progress, and it is not until later that people begin to apprehend the full significance of her life; the parallels with a resurrected spirit seem particularly intentional here.[5] Similarly Mrs. Wilcox, another of Forster's "elemental characters,"[6] dies within the first quarter of *Howards End*, but her spirit—the one that loved both the past and the present—lives indelibly in the future through her house. But in no one is the metaphor of resurrection more complicatedly at work than in Mrs. Ramsay. Though her death is announced so nonchalantly that it is actually parenthesized—"Mrs. Ramsay having died rather suddenly the night before" (*TL* 194)—it nevertheless serves as the fulcrum of this unusual novel. Mrs. Ramsay is responsible for the restoration of life on two levels: the obvious one, the acknowledged one by which her spirit impels Mr. Ramsay, James, and Cam finally to make it to the lighthouse and Lily to complete her vision; but also the deeper one, the one by which her dying allows those left behind to wean themselves of her intense hold.

There are some obvious echoes here of the final scene of *Sons and Lovers*, but they are faint. For there is an essential difference between the freedom conferred by Gertrude Morel's death and the freedom that comes with Mrs. Ramsay's. Paul Morel has to put his mother behind him in order to move forward, but in *To the Lighthouse*, none of the characters, including Lily Briscoe/Virginia Woolf, needs to renounce or deny Mrs. Ramsay's positive force in order to come to terms with her negative one. Jane Lilienfeld is correct, I think, when she says that a main objective of the novel is to bring Lily Briscoe to the point where she

> accepts and acknowledges her hostility to Mrs. Ramsay's beliefs and machinations. Recognizing her love for Mrs. Ramsay, Lily moves beyond it to a love and respect for herself dependent on that love and integrated with her mature assessment of Mrs. Ramsay.
>
> It is Virginia Woolf's genius to have re-created the process that a woman who wishes not to be the archetypal wife and mother must go through in order to separate herself from her almost overwhelming urge to fuse herself with such a mother. (347)

For that devouring aspect of Mrs. Ramsay is inextricably tied to the positive one: as Herbert Marder points out, the ideal domestic harmony which Mrs. Ramsay preserves at great cost to herself (several critics suggest it is this effort which kills her[7]) "can be maintained only by means of a subtle pressure, unrelenting, and almost despotic" (46). Without such effective power for harmony and proportion, Mrs. Ramsay would be no threat—but she would likewise be no inspiration. Lily Briscoe, recognizing in Mrs. Ramsay that which she herself is struggling to acquire—that is, the principle of generativity—finds it "impossible not to be drawn to this admirable woman of strength, resolution, beauty, gaiety," says Lilienfeld (347). Lily can barely resist the impulse to "fling herself" at Mrs. Ramsay's knee and say to her, "I'm in love with you" or "I'm in love with this all," meaning the whole prolific picture of children, hedges, house (*TL* 32). Nonetheless, Lily's single-minded creativity as an artist is stifled by Mrs. Ramsay's ambiguous force, and her death does not immediately propel her to great feats of artistry (Transue 82). Rather, when Mrs. Ramsay dies, all vitality seems to die with her. Indeed, things fall apart simply because she is not there to hold them together. "[D]irectly she went [from the dining room] a sort of disintegration set in" (*TL* 168). After her unexpected death, the Hebrides house is shut up, Prue Ramsay dies in childbirth, war starts, Andrew Ramsay is killed, the house begins to decay. Thus the descent into hell. But then peace comes, and life, impelled by the enduring spirit of the matriarch, returns to the island house. After ten years of nearly ruinous grief, Lily too returns, and manages at last to re-imagine the mother. She does so not, as Joan Lidoff says, as "merged identity," but as "both connection and separateness" (47) and is able to complete her vision. "But what a power [is] in the human soul!" Lily thinks with gratitude and some awe:

> The great revelation had never come. The great revelation perhaps never did come. Instead there were little daily miracles, illuminations, matches struck unexpectedly in the dark; here was one. This, that, and the other; herself and Charles Tansley and the breaking wave; Mrs. Ramsay bringing them together; Mrs. Ramsay saying, "Life stand still here"; Mrs. Ramsay making of the moment something permanent . . . this was in the nature of a revelation. In the midst of chaos there was shape; this eternal passing and flowing (she looked at the clouds going and the leaves shaking) was struck into stability. Life stand still here, Mrs. Ramsay said. "Mrs. Ramsay! Mrs. Ramsay!" she repeated. She owed it all to her. (*TL* 240-41)

It is as if Mrs. Ramsay has again given the little shake which sets "the old familiar pulse beating," renewing a cycle that had only temporarily stopped.

If there is something Christlike in the redemptive power of these mothers, so is there also in their rather humbly human forms. Unlike Margaret Drabble's glamorous heroines (this one a famous anthropologist, that one a successful psychotherapist), these mothers do not look like the traditional sort of modern female power-broker. Mrs. Moore, for instance, is an elderly, increasingly ill-tempered widow with a red face and white hair (*PI* 20); and Mrs. Ramsay, though married to a famous scholar, is neither rich nor celebrated nor even particularly clever: "A square root? What was that?" (*TL* 159). She is, admittedly, beautiful; that does set her apart, possibly above, somehow. But she is not vain about her beauty, and as it is usually spoken of by others in almost reverential (certainly not erotic, nor even very specific) terms, the impression is that her looks (like Mrs. Moore's voice, which deceives Aziz into thinking she is young) are a reflection of her heart. "She had been admired. She had been loved. She had entered rooms where mourners sat. Tears had flown in her presence" (*TL* 65). Her beauty, then, though important, is secondary. It is "the quivering thing, the living thing" one must remember: a woman knitting a brown sock, or "[running] across the lawn in goloshes to snatch a child from mischief" (*TL* 47), or dishing a roast from an earthenware pot and handing it around the table. "Mrs. Ramsay as wife, mother, hostess," says Herbert Marder, "is the androgynous artist in life": she "creates the family and at the same time embodies a spiritual principle" (39, 128). Hers are the everyday, human rhythms of the mother in her home, but in the smallest detail of them is such a power for acceptance or rejection that I think they are why the archetype is so compelling, and so enduring.

Kate Brown's case is a little different, a bit more problematic, but it finally affirms the same things. To look at Kate, to read her resumé, one might expect heroic things more than from the others, for she speaks several languages, is married to an internationally-recognized neurologist, translates novels, dresses with style, and can turn her sexuality on as with a "thermostat" (*SBD* 41). But these are not the qualities by which Kate has been used to identify herself; for twenty-odd years of marriage she has been defined by what others expect to see. For them, and therefore for her, she is a housewife, wife, and mother, saying the expected things, adopting the expected hairdo. "She did not allow her appearance to bloom, because she had observed early in the children's adolescence how much they disliked her giving rein to her own nature" (*SBD* 9); and "no young person likes to see dear mother all glossy and gleaming and silky" (*SBD* 37). Kate's realization that she has been killing her spirit by degrees is not altogether pleasant for her; it is the thing that prompts her dream-journey to discover whether or not she has been genuinely happy in this constricted life. But this is not a story about how a middle-aged woman walks out on house and family and takes up singing with a rock-and-roll band. Kate's determined protection of the seal, even the maternal role she reluctantly but eventually assumes with Maureen, symbolize Kate's deep-seated instinct to nurture and protect others. On the other hand, the degeneration of her conventional beauty, seen particularly in the horrific condition of her hair, symbolizes her need to nurture and

protect her own growth. On the day the serial dream ends and the seal
has been restored to the sea, Kate too goes back to her family, one
condition excepted: that from now on she will wear her hair any way
she likes.

> Her experiences of the last months, her discoveries, her self-
> definition; what she had hoped were now strengths, were
> concentrated here—that she would walk into her home with
> her hair undressed, with her hair tied straight back for utility;
> rough and streaky, and the widening grey band showing like a
> statement of intent. It was as if the rest of her—body, feet,
> even face, which was aging but amenable—belonged to
> everyone else. But her hair—no! No one was going to lay
> hands on that. (*SBD* 273)

This implicit debate over self-assertion versus self-effacement—as
if it has to be one or the other—is not new in fiction; it is what the
Princess was struggling with in *Daniel Deronda*, and in a certain way it
even characterizes mothers like Moll Flanders, Mrs. Pardiggle, Mrs.
Jellyby, Mrs. Gibson, and the other mothers who insist on following
paths other than those prescribed for them by the rest of society. Yet the
issue has never really been whether this option is an absolute good and
the other option an absolute evil; it has been, and still is, a matter of
debate primarily because of fluctuating social prejudices. In the
nineteenth century, social opinion valued enterprise but was
uncomfortable with self-assertion in women and so gave it the name of
contumacy; in this last quarter of the twentieth century it values
adaptability but frowns on self-effacement and so gives it the name of
subjugation. Kate Brown's neighbor Mary Finchley epitomizes the
prevailing ideology which asks (rhetorically), "Why should we scale
ourselves down, children shouldn't be allowed to be tyrants" (*SBD* 9).
As I have noted elsewhere, other contemporary novelists, even
occasionally Lessing herself, seem to imply that the really self-fulfilled
mother is one who would hardly be recognized as a mother were it not
for the occasional diaper or school book glimpsed among the scattered
trophies of careers and love affairs. These heroines are angry with their
own mothers for (as it seems to them) submitting passively to
patriarchal falsehoods and oppressions and bringing up their daughters

to do the same. Yet even Lessing has found that perfect freedom is not necessarily the answer to the mother's dilemma, for Kate's decision to return home is a deliberate one.

It may indeed be a common dilemma, this question of how far it is possible to be free when one is a mother, but these three mothers seem to embody a response which has a sort of natural logic: that is, they do not seem to see their alternatives in terms of power/nonpower or free/nonfree. For the fact is, they have all been transformed by their experience of motherhood into the most powerful members of their respective communities: here the ancient myth of *mutterrecht* brushes up closely against the new archetype. At fifty years old and with eight children, Mrs. Ramsay is nevertheless "formidable to behold" (*TL* 14); no one in her circle is her equal. Only Fielding among the English, and only Professor Godbole among the Indians, are equal to Mrs. Moore, the one for his integrity and the other for his depth; and not one of Kate Brown's friends is not shallow, self-centered, or small-minded. Of course I am talking about the power of character, not the power of the corporate boardroom or the legislative chamber, although presumably theirs could be adapted to political, strategic, academic or other uses. (Indeed, Mrs. Wilcox had once declared, "I am sure that if the mothers of various nations could meet, there would be no more wars" [*HW* 90]). The power of these mothers is compounded, rather, of all the human skills required of them as mothers, and the most refined of these is insight. In general all these mothers rely less on their intellect than on their intuition, by which I mean they do not pause, consider, weigh advantages against disadvantages; instead they know or learn a thing without conscious reasoning. This is what Doris Lessing would call the Sufi's sixth sense and which others understand as a form of prescience, but it is "merely another sensory power of the fully 'awake' being," says Seligman (193). At times the new archetypal mother pointedly rejects prudence as inferior to instinct as when Mrs. Moore grows quickly intimate with Dr. Aziz during their first meeting. Ronny scolds his mother for talking to an Indian alone in a dark mosque: according to him, "whether the native swaggers or cringes," he is always trying "to score" (*PI* 33).

In the light of her son's comment she reconsidered the scene at the mosque, to see whose impression was correct. Yes, it could be worked into quite an unpleasant scene. The doctor had begun by bullying her, . . . had been unreliable, inquisitive, vain. Yes, it was all true, but how false as a summary of the man; the essential life of him had been slain. (*PI* 34)

Later, of course, her instinct knows so absolutely that Aziz is innocent of the charges brought by Adela that she does not even bother to go to his trial. Mrs. Moore seems to have a preternatural ability to discern truth and falsity, an almost psychic insight into motives and feelings, and an unalarmed acceptance that reality may exist on multiple planes. This is why Peter Burra calls her one of Forster's "elemental" characters, "one who sees straight through perplexities and complications, who is utterly percipient of the reality behind appearances" (29).

The words preternatural and psychic are figurative but deliberate, intended to suggest that these mothers possess a transcendent understanding of things that are invisible or opaque to people of average sensitivity. This quality is not restricted only to mothers in the novel, of course; indeed, Peter Burra sounds a little surprised "to find vested in middle-aged women the elemental quality which is more obviously associated with the athletic" in Forster (29); still, seeing mothers with this quality makes one think of the "wise women who know herbs" who, in less tolerant times, were persecuted as witches. This quality is particularly apparent in Mrs. Moore, perhaps because she is in a setting which (according to Forster) does not hold superstition inferior to fact, and Mrs. Moore's own visionary gifts seem heightened in consequence. When she learns that Ronny and Adela had an accident in the Nawab Bahadur's car, she shivers, "'A ghost!' But the idea of a ghost scarcely passed her lips" (*PI* 97). The literal likelihood of a ghost is not what matters, but that Mrs. Moore somehow picked up on the Nawab's own fears: nine years before, the Chandrapore official had run over a drunken man whose ghost, he is convinced, has been waiting for him ever since. It is this instinctive communion with the beliefs and spirit of India that make Indians love and respect Mrs. Moore, while her fellow Englishmen (all but Fielding and occasionally Adela) distrust her. In this novel, to be hated by a British imperialist is to have the author's stamp of approval: therefore Mrs. Moore's instincts are the correct, true, worthy ones, while Adela's assertion and Ronny's concurrence that the car was hit by a hyena show the limitations of their vision and the shallowness of their souls.

Mrs. Moore is the most avowedly Christian of the mothers I am discussing, but this incident about the ghost is strongly unorthodox. This and numerous other incidents suggest that her deeply-engrained Protestantism is being absorbed into an older, larger form of spiritual expression. "[God] had been constantly in her thoughts since she entered India, though oddly enough he satisfied her less. She must needs pronounce his name frequently, as the greatest she knew, yet she had never found it less efficacious" (*PI* 52). Presumably this dissatisfaction has to do with the limitations of Christianity as an anthropocentric religion, the preferred religion of the Turtons and the Burtons; part of her instinct seems to be that the God she has been worshipping all these years does not stand up to the manipulations of those like her son Ronny who "approved of religion as long as it endorsed the National Anthem, but [who] objected when it attempted to influence his life" (*PI* 52). Mrs. Moore is more Eastern in her sympathy with all innocent life: yet really the source of her vision defies sectarian labeling.

Still less can one label as strictly religious the instinct for truth that characterizes either Mrs. Ramsay or Kate Brown. Kate never speaks in deliberately Judeo-Christian language, and Mrs. Ramsay does only once, when she inadvertently says "We are in the hands of the Lord." The depth of soul, or wisdom, or whatever it is that distinguishes these mothers is not dependent on any prescribed system of beliefs, because as Mrs. Ramsay suspects, those very systems are liable to be ridden with error.

> [I]nstantly she was annoyed with herself for saying that. Who had said it? Not she; she had been trapped into saying something she did not mean. . . . [I]t seemed to her like her own eyes [were] meeting her own eyes, searching as she alone could search into her mind and her heart, purifying out of existence that lie, any lie. . . . How could any Lord have made this world? (*TL* 97)

Like Mrs. Moore to the charge that Aziz is a rapist, Mrs. Ramsay responds with instinctive disbelief to the claim that a benevolent deity knowingly created a malevolent world. "There was no treachery too base for the world to commit; she knew that. No happiness lasted; she knew that." This "thing that she called life" she feels to be "terrible, hostile, and quick to pounce on you if you gave it a chance" (*TL* 92). Nonetheless Mrs. Ramsay seems to know happiness better than any one on her island—"she had known happiness, exquisite happiness, intense happiness." And the reason she can be happy, I think, is that she does not confuse or deny or make excessive demands of the truth. "Her simplicity fathomed what clever people falsified. Her singleness of mind made her drop plumb like a stone, alight exact as a bird, gave her, naturally, this swoop and fall of the spirit upon truth" (*TL* 46).

Because of this precision Mrs. Ramsay sees, usually quite accurately, into the hearts of others no less than into her own. When the frustrated intellectual Tansley overreacts to William Bankes' criticism of the Waverley novels, it is all, she thinks, "because Prue will not be nice to him" (*TL* 159); she sees her husband smiling into a book and knows at once that "[he is] acting it—perhaps he [is] thinking himself the person in the book" (*TL* 176). Words are rarely necessary. Throughout the evening meal she seems to take part in two conversations, one in regular speech but the other, the one the reader is privy to, entirely psychic. She knows that the criticism about Scott is making her husband depressed about his own uncertain immortality; she understands his scowls to mean that Augustus Carmichael had asked for another bowl of soup; she infers from a flirtatious remark to Mr. Ramsay that Minta Doyle is engaged to Paul Rayley, and secretly rejoices.

But a further truth is, as Virginia Woolf knows, and as Lily gradually comes to acknowledge, that Mrs. Ramsay's perceptions are liable to distortion by what Rosenman calls "her allegiance to heterosexuality" (95). This allegiance is so absolute that, in spite of "her instinct for truth" (*TL* 62), she is frequently dishonest with her husband rather than risk undermining the patriarchal foundations of their marriage. She accepts it as both her portion *and* her power that she must protect and bolster the male ego: "she had the whole of the other sex under her protection" (*TL* 13). But this allegiance also leads her into other errors. The worst, from where Lily stands, lies in not perceiving (or refusing to admit) that the married life may not be equally fulfilling for all women. In fact, in her half-sprightly, half-malicious insistence to Lily and Minta that "they all must marry" (*TL* 77), Mrs. Ramsay shows that though her intuition is certainly acute in other ways, it is not above the errors and smallness of prejudice, mild though it may be. Thus she decides that Lily must marry William Bankes (though to no avail, since Lily and William are beyond that reach of her power); but she does bring about a match between Paul Rayley and Minta Doyle. "[S]omehow . . . she was the person that made him do it. She had made him think he could do anything" (*TL* 118-19). Her power is not, however, strong enough to make a good marriage of what proves to be a poor one. For that matter, her own marriage to a rather immature, self-absorbed husband is hardly ideal. And yet it is impossible to feel that her influence is seditious, for her mistakes are ultimately what enable Lily Briscoe to break free of her power. At the close of the novel Lily is able to see Mrs. Ramsay, "shorn of clouds of emotion" (Lilienfeld 367), as a person equal to herself in meaning. "She would feel a little triumphant, telling Mrs. Ramsay that the marriage had not been a success. . . . It has all gone against your wishes. They're happy like that; I'm happy like this. Life has changed completely" (*TL* 260). Moreover, even in Mrs. Ramsay's imperceptiveness there is candour: "she was driven on, too quickly she knew, almost as if it were an escape for her too, to say that people must marry; people must have children. . . . Was she wrong in this. . . . Was she not forgetting again how strongly she influenced people?" (*TL* 92-93).

For in spite of appearing at times rather glib about her effect on others, Mrs. Ramsay is deeply conscious of her power, which seems to her at times that almost of a goddess, presiding over the proceedings of mortals:

> [A] curious sense [rose] in her, at once freakish and tender, of celebrating a festival, as if two emotions were called up in her, one profound—for what could be more serious than the love of man for woman, what more commanding, more impressive, bearing in its bosom the seeds of death; at the same time these lovers, these people entering into illusion glittering eyed, must be danced round with mockery, decorated with garlands. (*TL* 151)

There is this price to be paid for the kind of acute sensitivity of mothers like Mrs. Ramsay, Mrs. Moore, and Kate Brown: a certain loneliness, the isolation that comes from knowing too much, or seeing too clearly. The burden occasionally makes Mrs. Ramsay ironic, as here; or sad, as when, walking out of the dining room on Minta's arm, she realizes that the scene "was vanishing even as she looked" (*TL* 167); or even terrified, as when, singing nursery songs to her children, she suddenly becomes aware of "a ghostly roll of drums," a warning to her "whose day had slipped past in one quick doing after another that it was all ephemeral as a rainbow" (*TL* 28).

For Kate Brown the disturbing insights have to do with living among an over-intellectualized society whose prescribed values, from wife-swapping to socialism, while she cannot say precisely what it is she does not like about them, nonetheless make her uneasy. Her husband has had affairs throughout their marriage, and she has fought earnestly not to be jealous, yet the first time she tries to be unfaithful herself she can think only of the children. She remembers a visit with Mary Finchley, the neighborhood iconoclast, in which they started laughing uncontrollably at such social-science jargon as "nuclear family unit" and "parent-child confrontation," until finally they were shrieking at "family," and "home" and "mother" and "father" (*SBD* 167-68). But at this point Kate had begun to feel uncomfortable: something about these things—family, home, children—she feels to be, if not exactly sacrosanct, then at least sources of structure, points of reference, in a world that seems constantly to be tending toward chaos. As for politics, "[m]ore and more the political attitudes seemed like the behaviour of marionettes, or little clockwork figures wound up and continuing to display their little gestures while they were being knocked about and around and blown in all directions in a typhoon" (*SBD* 219).

Until the summer of her journey Kate's secure position in her family provided stability where social or political customs could not, but this year, with everyone gone for three months,

> her days were emptier than they had been for years—she was conscious of her emotional apparatus working away in a vacuum: the objects of her emotions were all elsewhere, they were not present to react with or against her. What was the

sense of loving, hating, wanting, resenting, needing, rejecting—and sometimes all in the space of an hour—when she was here, by herself, free; it was like talking to yourself, it was insane. (*SBD* 38)

She has a guilty sense that she has allowed herself to be a doormat for her husband and children and seizes the chance of three months on her own to chase down her own personality—or in the imagery of her dream, to carry the seal to a place where it can thrive. And after nearly dying herself, after the feverish illness which, paradoxically, clears her system, she succeeds: "She was no longer anxious about the seal, that it might be dead or dying: she knew that it was full of life, and, like her, of hope" (*SBD* 269). Once her dream ends, she feels she can return home. However, in Lessing "chaos is not temporary; order is not restored by marriage or even by a death" (Friedman 455). There is no reason to suppose that Kate has reclaimed her former security nor that she will slip back into former patterns, either personal or political; the structure of the book returns to normalcy but the tone does not. Kate's work with Global Foods, "in which international organizations feed not the hungry but one another" (Sprague and Tiger 13), has intensified rather than calmed her political fears. But for Lessing the individual life can be a significant response to the larger patterns of history. The image of herself in her heightened role of protector and nurturer has become her counterpoint to the disintegration of society.

Like Mrs. Ramsay's "swoop and fall of the spirit upon truth," these new archetypal mothers somehow seem to have an almost infallible instinct for what is right—an internal judicial system that manages somehow to discount the distorted values, prejudices, and hypocrisies that influence or interfere with inferior judgments. Obviously they differ vastly in this regard from the typical nineteenth-century fictional mother, whose judgment is reliable only in being invariably flawed. In fact, the difference between the mothers of these two periods can hardly be one merely of technique but virtually of medium: the new archetype is made of finer cloth altogether, with more texture, more richness, more substance. A mother knitting a stocking in Virginia Woolf, for instance, holds far more literary promise than a similar image in Elizabeth Gaskell.

However, the richness of the new archetype depends equally on the fact that a mother knitting represents one of the most fundamental, primordial impulses in the universe: the creative feminine. No other single quality so emphatically identifies the new archetypal mother as her association with images of fertility, children, nurturance, family, nature, the earth, the womb. These are the images that—crude, voluptuous, mysterious, serene—decorated the artifacts of the earliest matriarchal/agricultural societies, until the succeeding patriarchies circumscribed them into non-threatening idealizations such as the madonna and child. According to Susan Gubar, women writers as dissimilar as George Eliot, Rossetti, and HD have been largely responsible for sanctifying the female through symbols of female divinity, myths of female origin, metaphors of feminine creativity, and rituals of female power. Their task has been to "celebrate uniquely female powers of creativity without perpetuating destructive female socialization," and by the turn of the century, "[t]he substitution of the female divinity for the male god, the womb for the penis, as the model of creativity was pronounced" ("'The Blank Page' and Female Creativity" 92).

The elemental, mysterious, even primordial beauty and power of procreation may be what, more than anything else, the twentieth-century novel has reclaimed for its mothers. In Margaret Atwood's *Surfacing* the heroine, who has had one abortion, has a vision of reclaiming that lost child:

> I can feel my lost child surfacing within me, forgiving me, rising from the lake where it has been prisoned for so long, its eyes and teeth phosphorescent; the two halves clasp, interlocking like fingers, it buds, it sends out fronds. This time I will do it myself, squatting, on old newspapers in a corner alone; or on leaves, dry leaves, a heap of them, that's cleaner. The baby will slip out easily as an egg, a kitten, and I'll lick it off and bite the cord, the blood returning to the ground where it belongs; the moon will be full, pulling. (191)

The modern novel's celebration of fecundity and childbearing is at the heart of the new evaluation of mothering in the novel. This is in stark contrast to the Victorian fear and avoidance of these processes—one thinks of Queen Victoria's repugnance at feeling like "a cow or a dog" during childbirth. Katherine Moore in *Victorian Wives* notes that during the earlier period "sex for 'ladies' was completely taboo, not only any enjoyment, but even any knowledge or recognition of it, and so, because of its undeniable connection with childbirth, any mention of this in public . . . was considered improper" (xiv-xv). In the modern novel the mother's creativity is implicit not only in having sex and babies but in molding and nurturing human relationships in general. At international conferences Kate Brown becomes the "group mother": strangers bask in "the atmosphere of loving sympathy which was the oil of her function in her home" (*SBD* 44). Even in her subconscious her maternal identity is predominant. Barbara Lefcowitz notes that the seal Kate encounters in her dream is a foetal metaphor: "the relative lack of mobility . . . slippery skin, its smooth, almost featureless face, and its small flippers are especially suggestive of a human foetus in the early stages of development" (110). This seal represents Kate's abandoned private self, but in nurturing it she repeats the motions that have become instinctive from years of raising and nursing her other children: she guides it, feeds it, warms it, splashes salt water on its parched hide, even chews medicinal plants into a poultice for its wounds. Her struggles with the seal are thus ancient, primitive, instinctive, reminding one of National Geographic specials about sea animals struggling ashore to give birth, then back to the sea for protection and nourishment. "The seal was heavy, and slippery. It was hard to keep it in her arms. She was staggering among the sharp rocks. Where was the water, where was the sea?" (*SBD* 47). But she struggles on with her burden until at last "she was breathing in salty sea air." The water is "blue deepening on blue. On the rocks seals lay basking" (*SBD* 241).

Even more than Kate, Mrs. Ramsay is the embodiment of the fecund mother. There "throb[s] through her . . . the rapture of successful creation" (*TL* 61). This impulse is manifested as much in the brown wool stocking or the boeuf en daube as it is in her eight children, and she regards them all, the least to the greatest, as fitting tributes to her love and care as well as to their own beauty. Mr. Bankes pronounces the dinner "a triumph," and she feels "all his reverence" with great pleasure (*TL* 151). Like the earth mother she is, Mrs. Ramsay does not seem to have a rigid sense of ownership: everyone under her roof is equally under her protection and care—especially the men, whom she pities "always as if they lacked something—women never" (*TL* 129). They have an "attitude towards herself which no woman could fail to feel or to find agreeable, something trustful, childlike, reverential" (*TL* 13).

But for all that Mrs. Ramsay accepts their reverence "like a Queen," as though it is her due, this matriarch does not use love as a tool, withholding it as punishment or bestowing it as a reward. It is simply the medium by which she lives, and by which she assumes others live. She takes an elemental joy in all natural things: the pair of rooks whose shapes she knows by heart and to whom she has given names; the sea rolling in "waves of pure lemon." She takes Lily under her maternal wing, as she takes the shy Paul Rayley. This is what she does so well and so instinctively, this nurturing: soothing egos, making others feel secure and loved and important. She praises her husband's books, she lets Lily put her head on her knee; she even makes friends of Charles Tansley, whom nobody else likes and who had "snubbed her little boy" (*TL* 28). Herbert Marder says she "not only creates life by giving birth to sons and daughters, she creates meaning by giving harmonious form to their lives in common" (39).

Nonetheless, she saves her best for her own. As truly as she knows other sources of joy, Mrs. Ramsay is sure there is no greater happiness than children. "[A]n unmarried woman has missed the best of life" (*TL* 77), she tells Lily with the confidence of a mother of eight. "She would have liked always to have had a baby. She was happiest carrying one in her arms" (*TL* 90). Her children are her companions, her soul-mates; by modern child psychologists' standards she would undoubtedly be considered an excellent mother.

> If they could be taught to wipe their feet and not bring the beach in with them—that would be something. Crabs, she had to allow, if Andrew really wished to dissect them, or if Jasper believed that one could make soup from seaweed, one could not prevent it; or Rose's objects—shells, reeds, stones; for they were gifted, her children, but all in quite different ways. (*TL* 44)

She has a child's delight in the things that delight them, and they include her as another playmate. "[S]he said she was ready now, and they would go down, and Jasper, because he was the gentleman, should give her his arm, and Rose, as she was the lady, should carry her handkerchief" (*TL* 123). Partly because she does appreciate the way things look to her children and partly because she sees them that way herself, she is their shield against the bleaker imaginations of adults. When first her husband, then Mr. Tansley interrupt the fairy tale she and James are reading in order to assure the child that he cannot possibly go to the lighthouse in the morning, she is furious. She reassures James that the wind may yet change, but to herself she thinks, "[H]e will remember that all his life" (*TL* 95).

> To pursue truth with such astonishing lack of consideration for other people's feelings, to rend the thin veils of civilisation so wantonly, so brutally, was to her so horrible an outrage of human decency that, without replying, dazed and blinded, she bent her head as if to let the pelt of jagged hail, the drench of dirty water, bespatter her unrebuked. (*TL* 51)

Obviously there is in her outrage the sense of an injury against herself no less than against her son. Though she knows truth instinctively, she also knows there are other kinds of truth than mere sallow fact. These assaults of heartless logic seem to her "the fatal sterility of the male plung[ing] itself, like a beak of brass, barren and bare," into hers and James' peace, "this delicious fecundity, this fountain and spray of life" (*TL* 58).

Thus Mrs. Ramsay's devotion to her children has in it an element of self-defense: her children are her shield as much as she is theirs, her guarantee of innocence and permanence against the final rending of the thin veils of civilization, the falling of the island into the sea. "[S]he never wanted James to grow a day older! or Cam either. These two she would have liked to keep for ever just as they were, demons of wickedness, angels of delight, never to see them grow up into long-legged monsters. Nothing made up for the loss" (*TL* 89). Her love for her children is so intense that it cannot be totally happy—that is one of those saddening truths that "her instinct for truth" cannot avoid.

A Passage to India, though to first appearances even less hopeful about birth and creation than *To the Lighthouse*, is nonetheless very much about the cycles of history and the possibilities of new life. The opening pages of the middle section ("Caves") comprise one long metaphor of the continuity of creation.

> In the days of the prehistoric ocean the southern part of the [Indian] peninsula already existed, and the high places of Dravidia have been land since land began, and have seen on the one side the sinking of a continent that joined them to Africa, and on the other the upheaval of the Himalayas from a sea. They are older than anything in the world. . . .
>
> Yet even they are altering. As Himalayan India rose, this India, the primal, has been depressed, and is slowly re-entering the curve of the earth. It may be that in aeons to come an ocean will flow here too, and cover the sun-born rocks with slime. (*PI* 123)

Inside one of the Marabar caves, this macrocosmic view of history continues on a smaller scale: the cave becomes a primeval womb, the reflections of a match light the first conception, birth, and death: "the two flames approach and strive to unite . . . the radiance increases, the flames touch one another, kiss, expire" (*PI* 125). The eternal cycles of life constitute the pervasive metaphor of this novel, and Mrs. Moore is the agent by which they are focused in the present.

What the story despairs of then is not life in general but of life for Anglo-India (or indeed any system based on oppression). The final scene, in which Fielding the Englishman and Aziz the Moslem are forced by their cultures to separate even though they love each other as individuals, states clearly that the union attempted by the characters in the novel had failed. It is a dreary conclusion, and Mrs. Moore's leavetaking of Chandrapore had also been miserable.

But Mrs. Moore is not a failed character; on the contrary she is largely responsible for the possibilities of new life the novel agrees to. For though her soul had suffered an almost fatal blow, two factors rescue it. One is simply that once out of Chandrapore her battered spirit begins to revive: "I have not seen the right places," she thinks as her train passes through Bombay, Asirgarh, the Vindyas. "She watched the indestructible life of man and his changing faces, and the houses he has built for himself and God, and they appeared to her not in terms of her own trouble but as things to see." They make her think anew of the variety and mystery and beauty that entranced her when she first arrived in Chandrapore, before the blunderings of selfish Englishmen and women ruined her visit and her peace of mind. As her boat sails the palm trees seem to laugh at her, "So you thought an echo was India; you took the Marabar caves as final?" (*PI* 209-10).

The other factor that keeps Mrs. Moore's soul vital are her children from her second marriage, Stella and Ralph. Though the three are never seen together it is clear that her love for them is the sustaining force in her life: if the English in India represent the evil of the world to her, Stella and Ralph embody that which is true and good. In fact she is so disturbed by the world of officially-sanctioned persecution—a world which includes Ronny, the only product of her first marrige—that she tries to keep that world physically separate from the purer atmosphere of Stella and Ralph. Though she knows instinctively that she can tell Aziz about Ralph and Stella during their first meeting in the mosque, yet "[s]he will never talk about them to [Adela]" (*PI* 143)—even though Miss Quested may soon be her daughter-in-law. Indeed Mrs. Moore does not like Ronny himself to get too close: "Mrs. Moore had tended to keep the products of her two marriages apart" (*PI* 266).

It is important to her to maintain that segregation because Ralph and Stella are her spiritual true north: whenever she feels her belief in the sanctity of life threatened, she instinctively turns to them. The moment she escapes from the cave she goes to her writing pad and begins, "Dear Stella, Dear Ralph." It has become to her a matter of the utmost urgency that she return to them at once, before her faith in existence slips away entirely. She seems to associate the salvation of the world by the baby Jesus with the salvation of her own soul by these two children, but her faith in all of them is wavering. "Unto us a Son is born, unto us a Child is given," she quotes mechanically, "and am I good and is he bad and are we saved? . . . I used to be good with the children growing up, also I meet this young man in his mosque. . . . Good, happy, small people. They do not exist, they were a dream" (*PI* 205).

Before the Marabar Mrs. Moore had been able to accept the strong whispers of death that accompany life, even to rejoice in them as necessary aspects of the same process. Like the Oriental Aziz says she is, she is not unsettled by contradictions. Contemplating the Ganges with its crocodiles and corpses floating in its life-giving waters, she

sighs, "What a terrible river! what a wonderful river!" (*PI* 32). Like the
Hindu Godbole she reverences all life as well as inanimate nature:

> She watched the moon, whose radiance stained with primrose
> the purple of the surrounding sky. In England the moon had
> seemed dead and alien; here she was caught in the shawl of
> night together with earth and all the other stars. A sudden
> sense of unity, of kinship with the heavenly bodies, passed
> into the old woman and out, like water through a tank, leaving
> a strange freshness behind. (*PI* 29-30)

But the echo in the cave had distorted the whispers into chaos: "the
echo began in some indescribable way to undermine her hold on life.
Coming at a moment when she chanced to be fatigued, it had managed
to murmur, 'Pathos, piety, courage—they exist, but are identical, and so
is filth. Everything exists, nothing has value'" (*PI* 149). But her journey
back to Stella and Ralph had already begun to restore her equilibrium.
Like Mrs. Ramsay, her children's names are the mantra that gives her
strength. And even though she dies before she sees them, the
affirmative power of her life has already set new life in motion:
Fielding and Stella have a child, and Aziz repeats to Ralph the precise
words he had used when he first met Mrs. Moore in the Mosque: "You
are an Oriental" (*PI* 311). As E. K. Brown says in "Rhythm in *A
Passage to India*," every important movement in this novel is rhythmic:
"It may be said of Ralph that he is what his mother is so far as she
eternally matters" (95). And as Glenn Pederson observes, "the final
movement onto and eventually into the water symbolizes a great
baptism into rebirth. . . . we remember that Mrs. Moore's body had
been committed to the depths of the sea; now the spirit she symbolizes
is also upon the water, incarnate in Ralph" (245). Indeed, it is on or
through water (which represents, as Karen Horney says, the primal
element "woman" [134]) that all three mothers effect rebirth: Kate
returns her seal to the womblike protection of the northern sea; and
James, Cam, and Mr. Ramsay all must cross the water to achieve the
reconciliation represented by the lighthouse. To Lily Briscoe, "[t]he sea
was more important now than the shore" (*TL* 284).

  If the creative impulse is dominant in the new archetypal mother,
where then lies her destructiveness, her "terrible" aspect? It is

impossible to separate them entirely. The mother, embodying generation, also embodies degeneration. Embodying protection and nurturance, she also embodies insecurity and devouring. When Susan in Woolf's *The Waves* compares herself to Demeter—"I shall lie like a field bearing crops in rotation; in the summer heat will dance over me; in the winter I shall be cracked with cold" (94)—she is calling upon one of the oldest metaphors of maternal ambiguity. This ambiguity exists throughout the three texts I have been discussing, for when mothers withhold or are perceived to withhold their nurturance and protection, they appear terrible. What Lily Briscoe perceives as Mrs. Ramsay's frightening irresistibleness is part of her terrible side: Lily pictures Mrs. Ramsay, laughing, leading her victims to an altar, and the word conveys sacrifice as well as marriage—the sense that Mrs. Ramsay enjoys manipulating people, which indeed she does. The "terrible" side of Mrs. Moore is most pronounced when her spirit begins to surrender: her usually reassuring nature seems to disappear and she becomes spiteful and mean, irritably assuring Adela, who has appealed to her for comfort, that the echo in her head will most likely never go away. And even before Kate Brown has left for the summer she is frightening in her unwonted hostilities against her family.

But their terribleness has to do above all with associations of death. The potential for death is strong in all three novels (though as I have pointed out earlier, so is the promise of resurrection). Kate's seal is on the brink of death every night she reenters her dream; if she did not take on its burden it would assuredly die. Joan Lidoff says that Mrs. Ramsay's alliance is with death (47). When Paul Morel rages at his mother for getting old he is in fact confronting the Terrible Mother in her most horrifying aspect. So, too, is the Wilcox family when it reacts not with grief but with a sense of betrayal at Mrs. Wilcox's sudden death. And so, too, is Lily's anger at Mrs. Ramsay: "Giving, giving, giving, she had died—and had left all this. Really, she was angry with Mrs. Ramsay. . . . Here was Lily, at forty-four, wasting her time, unable to do a thing, standing there, playing at painting, playing at the one thing one did not play at, and it was all Mrs. Ramsay's fault" (*TL* 223-24). The mother is so identical with the creative principle that her death may seem in fact a perversion of the natural order. But of course it is merely an affirmation of it. Mrs. Moore, for instance, dies just at the time when India endures a sort of seasonal immolation. Fish burrow into the mud, life retreats from "the source of life, the treacherous sun" (*PI* 211). The mother, most elemental of figures, the embodiment of physicality, can reproduce life but cannot immortalize it. And yet all forms of life, from the most primitive to the most advanced, do resume in due course. Even Mrs. Moore returns, symbolically, in the form of her children and grandchildren: her son renews the former kinship with Aziz.

The boar's skull nailed to the wall of the nursery in *To the Lighthouse*, concealed but not eliminated by Mrs. Ramsay's green shawl, epitomizes both the extent of and limitations of the mother's power. Because she is "of the whole group the one most aware of and attracted by the all-pervading darkness that lies behind the veils of life," says Lee Whitehead (407), Mrs. Ramsay alone can reassure Cam and James who are terrified of this monstrosity in their room.

> [N]ot seeing anything that would do, she quickly took her own shawl off and wound it round the skull, round and round and round, and then she came back to Cam and laid her head almost flat on the pillow beside Cam's and said how lovely it looked now; how the fairies would love it; it was like a bird's nest; it was like a beautiful mountain such as she had seen abroad, with valleys and flowers and bells ringing and birds singing and little goats and antelopes. (*TL* 172)

Mrs. Ramsay is always aware that she, and every one of those she loves, will die. It is not morbidness in her, just a consciousness of history making at every moment, the eventual "destruction of the island and its engulfment in the sea" (*TL* 28). She wishes to withhold this consciousness from her children as long as possible; that is why, rather than insist that "it's only an old pig," she creates fantasies to help them through their youth.

Surely this is one of the most poignant scenes of mother love ever written, the more so for being so understated. Whitehead says that "Mrs. Ramsay is continually pulling veils over disconcerting reality not for her own sake but for others" (401). The fact that she does not try to deny or ignore the reality but does try, within her limited power, to deflect some of its pain, suggests how fully the new archetypal mother lives in the world.

Conclusion

This study of mothers in the English novel is a study, first and foremost, of the development of the genre. My concern has been to show how novelists are part of a centuries-old tradition that has seen mothers as primarily comic types, interfering, bungling, bossing women who are ultimately forced to yield to a greater authority based on a higher morality. The English novelist reworked this tradition into the newer tradition of realism, but for the first two centuries of the novel the mother remained a peculiarly transitional figure: a sort of female minotaur, half-farcical, half-believable. The idealized mother is the flip side of this tradition, established by cultural and psychological imperatives but basically irrelevant to the plot that is based on conflict and so present in the action only as a sort of token, a forgotten standard-bearer. Thus for many years, just about the only good mothers in fiction were the dead ones. However, by the late nineteenth century, this could no longer be said. For a variety of reasons, the role of the mother began at about this time to be allotted more sense, more humanity, and more power, with the result in the twentieth century that there are characters now whose status as a mother reflects on her as a virtue, not a curse.

The treatment of the mother in fiction tends to parallel the treatment of the mother in society, and so it would be absurd to say that as society got better so did the fiction. Dickens' novels are no less masterpieces because they have a Mrs. Pardiggle in them, nor is Austen's artistry any less consummate because she created Mrs. Bennet. Nonetheless, if there has been a somewhat teleological drift throughout this study, I am not sure I wish altogether to disclaim it. For if there is to be such a thing as continuing growth and development in the novel, if the genre is to take seriously its role as not only documentor but shaper of human possibilities, then I believe the revisioning of mothers has been an inevitable part of that process.

Notes

1. I use this term as Virginia Woolf uses it, meaning a reconciliation of the masculine, critical side of the mind with the feminine, intuitive side. "If one is a man, still the woman part of the brain must have effect; and a woman also must have intercourse with the man in her. Coleridge perhaps meant this when he said that a great mind is androgynous. It is when this fusion takes place that the mind is fully fertilized and uses all its faculties. Perhaps a mind that is purely masculine cannot create, any more than a mind that is purely feminine" (*A Room of One's Own* 171).

2. "*Voyage in the Dark*: Jean Rhys's Masquerade for the Mother" 447. See also Ronnie Scharfman, "Mirroring and Mothering in Simone Schawz-Bart's *Pluie et Vent Sur Télumée Miracle* and Jean Rhys' *Wide Sargasso Sea*."

3. It is probably more a reflection of the threatening ambiguity of the integrated mother than any flaw in her characterization that has led several critics vehemently to deny the life-giving aspect of all three of these mothers. Glenn Pederson, for instance, sees Mrs. Ramsay as a veritable witch, insisting that she is "the negative force" which prevents the integration of her family, that she refuses to subordinate her individuality to community, that her relationship with James is blatantly incestuous, etc. ("Vision in *To the Lighthouse*"). More moderate critics acknowledge simply that Mrs. Ramsay's life-giving gifts are inextricably bound to her life-denying qualities. Similarly, most critics have dismissed Edwin Nierenberg's thesis in "The Withered Priestess: Mrs. Moore's Incomplete Passage to India" that Mrs. Moore's "considerable failure to help others and herself toward an understanding of love" is an error of "the uninformed heart" (198). However, in an even less defensible article Peer Hultberg claims that Mrs. Moore is, like Mrs. Wilcox before her, treacherous and deceptive, and her mythical influence after her death is not real but a result of the characters' "defensive maneuver of splitting" ("The Faithless Mother: An Aspect of the Novels of E. M. Forster" 248-49). And finally, while most critics have recognized the significance of Kate Brown's journey, yet some feminist critics have felt betrayed by her return to home and family in middle-class London, as if the nurturant side of the mother is by definition a weakness; for instance, see Elayne Antler Rapping, "Unfree Women: Feminism in Doris Lessing's Novels."

4. E. M. Forster discovered at Cambridge "a concept of the Good as that which is centered in personal relations and aesthetic satisfaction"

(Richard Martin, *The Love that Failed: Ideal and Reality in the Writings of E. M. Forster* 13). Lessing's interest in Sufism is similarly non-doctrinal: often called Islamic mysticism, Sufism lacks a rigid hierarchy. "The Sufi way or path leads to a direct perception of reality without need of the mediation of the logical mind" (Dee Seligman, "The Sufi Quest" 191.) Similarly, Virginia Woolf's spiritual vision is embodied in her theory of androgyny.

5. Benita Parry echoes F. R. Leavis in feeling that Mrs. Moore's transformation is "too easy": "Forster asks us to suspend disbelief in the operation of mysteries without quite trusting in them himself" ("Passage to More than India" 173). But E. K. Brown sees Mrs. Moore's role as a redemptive character consistent with the cyclical structure of the whole novel: "unable to save herself, she did miraculous things for others" (*Rhythm in the Novel* 156).

6. "Elemental characters" is Peter Burra's term ("The Novels of E. M. Forster" 29). E. K. Brown calls them "contemplative characters."

7. For instance, see Rosenman 96ff and Lilienfeld 358.

Bibliography

Primary Sources

Atwood, Margaret. *Surfacing*. New York: Fawcett Crest-Simon & Schuster, 1972.

Austen, Jane. *Jane Austen's Letters to Her Sister Cassandra and Others*. Ed. R. W. Chapman. London: Oxford UP, 1932.

———. *The Novels of Jane Austen*. Ed. R. W. Chapman. 6 vols. London: Oxford UP, 1923.

Bronte, Charlotte. *Jane Eyre*. New York: Signet, 1960.

Burney, Fanny. *Evelina*. New York: Norton, 1965.

Butler, Samuel. *The Way of All Flesh*. Harmondsworth: Penguin, 1966.

Dickens, Charles. *Bleak House*. New York: Bantam, 1983.

———. *David Copperfield*. New York: Signet, 1962.

———. *Dombey and Son*. Ed. Alan Horsman. Oxford: Oxford UP, 1982.

———. *Nicholas Nickleby*. Ed. Michael Slater. Harmondsworth: Penguin, 1978.

———. *Our Mutual Friend*. New York: Signet, 1964.

Dickens, Sir Henry F. *Memories of My Father*. [New York]: Duffield, 1929.

Drabble, Margaret. *The Realms of Gold*. New York: Ivy-Ballantine, 1975.

Ellis, Sarah. *The Wives of England, Their Relative Duties, Domestic Influence, and Social Obligations*. New York: Edward Walker, 1850.

Eliot, George. *Adam Bede*. New York: Signet, 1961, 1981.

———. *Daniel Deronda*. Ed. Graham Handley. Oxford: Oxford UP, 1984.

———. *The Mill on the Floss*. Ed. A. S. Byatt. Harmondsworth: Penguin, 1979.

Engels, Frederick. *The Origin of the Family, Private Property, and the State*. 1877. Rpt. New York: Pathfinder, 1972.

Forster, E. M. *Howards End*. New York: Vintage-Random, 1921.

———. *A Passage to India*. New York: Harvest-Harcourt Brace Jovanovich, 1952.

Freud, Sigmund. *New Introductory Lectures on Psychoanalysis*. Trans. and ed. James Strachey. New York: Norton, 1965.

Gaskell, Elizabeth. *Mary Barton*. Ed. Stephen Gill. Harmondsworth: Penguin, 1970.

———. *North and South*. Vol. 8 of *The Works of Mrs. Gaskell*. London: Smith Elder, 1906.

———. *Wives and Daughters*. Ed. Frank Glover Smith. Harmondsworth: Penguin, 1969.

Gissing, George. *The Letters of George Gissing to Eduard Bertz*. Ed. Arthur C. Young. London: Constable, 1961.

———. *The Odd Women*. New York: Norton, 1977.

Green Fairy Book. 1892. Ed. Andrew Lang. Rpt. New York: Dover, 1965.

Grimm, Jakob, and Wilhelm Grimm. *Grimms' Tales for Young and Old*. 1819. Trans. Ralph Manheim. New York: Anchor-Doubleday, 1977.

Hardy, Thomas. *The Return of the Native*. Ed. A. Walton Litz. Boston: Riverside-Houghton Mifflin, 1967.

James, Henry. "The Future of the Novel." 1899. In *The Universal Anthology*. Vol. 28. Ed. Richard Garnett. New York: Merrill & Baker, 1901. xiii-xxiv. Rpt. in *The Art of Criticism: Henry James on the Theory and the Practice of Fiction*. Ed. William Veeder and Susan M. Griffin. Chicago: U of Chicago P, 1986. 242–56.

————. *The Spoils of Poynton*. Harmondsworth: Penguin, 1963.

Joyce, James. *Ulysses*. New York: Vintage-Random, 1961.

Jung, C[arl] G[ustave]. *The Collected Works of C. G. Jung*. Trans. R. F. C. Hull. 20 vols. Bollingen Series 20. New York: Pantheon-Random, 1959.

————. *Memories, Dreams, Reflections*. Recorded and ed. Aniela Jaffé. Trans. Richard and Clare Winston. New York: Pantheon-Random, 1963.

Lawrence, D. H. *The Letters of D. H. Lawrence*. Ed. Aldous Huxley. New York: Viking, 1932.

————. *Phoenix: The Posthumous Papers of D. H. Lawrence*. Ed. Edward D. McDonald. London: Heinemann, 1936.

————. *Sons and Lovers*. Harmondsworth: Penguin, 1913.

Lessing, Doris. *The Four-Gated City*. New York: Knopf, 1969.

————. *A Proper Marriage*. New York: Simon & Schuster, 1964.

————. *A Small Personal Voice: Essays, Reviews, Interviews*. Ed. Paul Schleuter. New York: Knopf, 1974.

————. *The Summer Before the Dark*. New York: Bantam, 1973.

MacDonald, George. "The Day Boy and the Night Girl." 1879. Zipes, *Victorian Fairy Tales* 175–208.

Mill, John Stuart. *The Subjection of Women*. 1869. Rpt. Cambridge, MA: M.I.T. Press, 1970.

Moore, George. *A Drama In Muslin*. Gerrards Cross, Bucks.: Colin Smythe, 1981.

Oliphant, Mrs. [Margaret]. *Hester*. New York: Virago-Penguin, 1984.

Radcliffe, Ann. *The Mysteries of Udolpho*. Ed. Bonamy Dobrée. Oxford: Oxford UP, 1970.

Rhys, Jean. *Wide Sargasso Sea. The Complete Novels*. New York: Norton, 1985. 463–574.

Richardson, Samuel. *Clarissa*. Ed. John Angus Burrell. New York: Modern-Random, 1950.

"Rights and Conditions of Women." *Edinburgh Review* 73 (April, 1841): 189–209.

Ruskin, John. *Sesame and Lilies*. New York: Metropolitan, [1865].

Thackeray, William M. *The History of Henry Esmond, Esq., Colonel in the Service of Her Majesty Queen Anne*. London: Macmillan, 1911.

———. *Vanity Fair*. Ed. J. L. M. Stewart. Harmondsworth: Penguin, 1968.

Trollope, Anthony. *Barchester Towers*. Ed. Robin Gilmour. Harmondsworth: Penguin, 1983.

Wollstonecraft, Mary. *A Vindication of the Rights of Woman*. 1792. Ed. Carol H. Poston. New York: Norton, 1975.

Woolf, Virginia. *Moments of Being: Unpublished Autobiographical Writings of Virginia Woolf*. Ed. Jeanne Schulkind. New York: Harcourt Brace Jovanovich, 1976.

———. *A Room of One's Own*. 1929. New York: Harcourt, Brace & World, 1957.

———. *To the Lighthouse*. New York: Harvest-Harcourt Brace Jovanovich, 1955.

———. *Virginia Woolf: Selections from her Essays*. Ed. Walter James. London: Chatto & Windus, 1966.

———. *The Waves*. London: Hogarth, 1955.

Secondary Sources

Adrian, Arthur A. *Dickens and the Parent-Child Relationship*. Athens, OH: Ohio UP, 1984.

Armstrong, Nancy. *Desire and Domestic Fiction: A Political History of the Novel*. Oxford: Oxford UP, 1987.

Auerbach, Erich. *Mimesis: The Representation of Reality in Western Literature*. Trans. Willard R. Trask. Princeton, NJ: Princeton UP, 1953.

Axton, William. "*Dombey and Son*: From Stereotype to Archetype." *ELH* 31 (1964): 301–17.

Bachofen, J. J. *Myth, Religion, and Mother Right: Selected Writings.* 1926. Trans. Ralph Manheim. Rpt. Princeton, NJ: Princeton UP, 1954.

Bamber, Linda. *Comic Women, Tragic Men: A Study of Gender and Genre in Shakespeare*. Stanford: Stanford UP, 1982.

Banks, J. A. *Victorian Values: Secularism and the Size of Families.* London: Routledge & Kegan Paul, 1981.

Bannan, Helen M. "Spider Woman's Web: Mothers and Daughters in Southwestern Native American Literature." Davidson and Broner 268– 79.

Basch, Francoise. *Relative Creatures: Victorian Women in Society and the Novel.* New York: Schocken, 1974.

Bauer, Carol, and Lawrence Ritt, eds. *Free and Ennobled: Source Readings in the Development of Victorian Feminism*. Oxford: Pergamon, 1979.

Bazargan, Susan. "Oxen of the Sun: Maternity, Language, and History." *James Joyce Quarterly* 22 (1985): 271–80.

Bell, Vereen. "Parents and Children in *Great Expectations*." *Victorian Newsletter* 27 (1965): 21–24.

Berger, John. *Ways of Seeing*. Harmondsworth: Penguin, 1972.

Berger, Morroe. *Real and Imagined Worlds: The Novel and Social Science*. Cambridge: Harvard UP, 1977.

Bettelheim. Bruno. *Symbolic Wounds: Puberty Rites and the Envious Male*. New York: Collier, 1954.

———. *The Uses of Enchantment: The Meanings and Importance of Fairy Tales*. New York: Knopf, 1976.

Birkhäuser-Oeri, Sibylle. *The Mother: Archetypal Image in Fairy Tales.* Ed. Marie-Louise von Franz. Trans. Michael Mitchell. Toronto: Inner City, 1988.

Blotner, Joseph L. "Mythic Patterns in *To the Lighthouse.*" *PMLA* 71 (1956): 547–62.

Bowden, Edwin. *The Themes of Henry James.* New Haven: Yale UP, 1956.

Bradbrook, Frank W. *Jane Austen and Her Predecessors.* Cambridge: Cambridge UP, 1967.

Bradbury, Malcolm, ed. *Forster: A Collection of Critical Essays.* Englewood Cliffs, NJ: Prentice-Hall, 1966.

———, ed. *Forster's* A Passage to India: *A Casebook.* London: Macmillan, 1978.

Briffault, Robert. *The Mothers: A Study of the Origins of Sentiments and Institutions.* New York: Macmillan, 1927.

Briggs, Katherine M., and Ruth L. Tongue, eds. *Folktales of England.* Chicago: U of Chicago P, 1965.

Brown, E. K. *Rhythm in the Novel.* Toronto: U of Toronto P, 1950. Rpt. as "Rhythm in E. M. Forster's *A Passage to India.*" Bradbury, *Critical Essays* 144–59.

Brown, Lloyd W. "The Business of Marrying and Mothering." McMaster, *Achievement* 27–43.

Bullough, Vern. *The Subordinate Sex: A History of Attitudes toward Women.* Urbana: U of Illinois P, 1973.

Burra, Peter. "The Novels of E. M. Forster." *The Nineteenth Century and After* 116 (1934): 581–94. Rpt. in Bradbury, *Critical Essays* 21–33.

Canarella, Eva. *Pandora's Daughters: The Role and Status of Women in Greek and Roman Antiquity.* Trans. Maureen B. Fant. Baltimore: Johns Hopkins UP, 1987.

Chance, Jane. *Woman as Hero in Old English Literature.* Syracuse, NY: Syracuse UP, 1986.

Chesler, Phyllis. *Women and Madness*. Garden City, NY: Doubleday, 1972.

Childers, J. Wesley. *Tales from Spanish Picaresque Novels: A Motif-Index*. Albany: State U of New York P, 1977.

Chodorow, Nancy. *The Reproduction of Mothering: Psychoanalysis and the Sociology of Gender*. Berkeley: U of California P, 1978.

Clark, Robert. "Riddling the Family Firm: The Sexual Economy of *Dombey and Son*." *ELH* 51 (1984): 69–84.

Clarke, Micael. "Thackeray's *Barry Lyndon*: An Irony Against Misogynists." *Texas Studies in Language and Literature* 29 (1987): 261–77.

Colby, Vineta. *Yesterday's Woman: Domestic Realism in the English Novel*. Princeton: Princeton UP, 1974.

Coveney, Peter. *Poor Monkey: The Child in Literature*. London: Rockliff, 1957.

Dally, Ann. *Inventing Motherhood: The Consequences of an Ideal*. New York: Schocken, 1983.

Daly, Mary. *Beyond God the Father, Toward a Philosophy of Women's Liberation*. Boston: Beacon, 1973.

Damico, Helen. *Beowulf's Wealhtheow and the Valkyrie Tradition*. Madison: U of Wisconsin P, 1984.

Dasent, George Webbe. *Popular Tales from the Norse*. London: George Routledge & Sons, n.d.

Davidson, Cathy, and E. M. Broner, eds. *The Lost Tradition: Mothers and Daughters in Literature*. New York: Frederick Ungar, 1980.

Davies, Rosemary Reeves. "The Mother as Destroyer: Psychic Division in the Writings of D. H. Lawrence." *D. H. Lawrence Review* 13 (1980): 220–38.

Davis, Earle. *The Flint and the Flame*. London: Victor Gollancz, 1964.

de Beauvoir, Simone. *The Second Sex*. Trans. and ed. H. M. Parshley. New York: Knopf, 1971.

de Carvalho-Neto, Paulo. *Folklore and Psychoanalysis.* Trans. Jacques M. P. Wilson. Coral Gables: U of Miami P, 1968.

Deegan, Dorothy Yost. *The Stereotype of the Single Woman in American Novels.* New York: King's Crown, 1951.

de Witt, Adriaan. "Mothers and Stepmothers in Fairy Tales and Myths." *Journal of Evolutionary Psychology* 6 (1985): 315–28.

Dinnerstein, Dorothy. *The Mermaid and the Minotaur: Sexual Arrangements and Human Malaise.* New York: Harper & Row, 1963.

Donovan, Frank. *Never on a Broomstick.* New York: Bell, 1971.

Drabble, Margaret. Introduction. *Lady Susan/The Watsons/Sanditon.* By Jane Austen. Harmondsworth: Penguin, 1974. 7–31.

Dundes, Alan. *Cinderella: A Folklore Casebook.* New York: Garland, 1982.

Duthie, Enid L. *The Themes of Elizabeth Gaskell.* Totowa, NJ: Rowman & Littlefield, 1980.

Ehrlich, J. W. *Ehrlich's Blackstone.* San Carlos, CA: Nourse, 1959.

Erickson, Robert A. *Mother Midnight: Birth, Sex, and Fate in Eighteenth-Century Fiction (Defoe, Richardson, and Sterne).* New York: AMS, 1986.

Ermarth, Elizabeth. "Maggie Tulliver's Long Suicide." *Studies in English Literature* 14 (1974): 587–602.

———. *Realism and Consensus in the English Novel.* Princeton, NJ: Princeton UP, 1983.

Ferguson, Margaret W., Maureen Quilligan, and Nancy J. Vickers, eds. *Rewriting the Renaissance: The Discourse of Sexual Difference in Early Modern Europe.* Chicago: U of Chicago P, 1986.

Fildes, Valerie. *Women as Mothers in Pre-Industrial England: Essays in Memory of Dorothy McLaren.* London: Routledge, 1990.

Friedman, Ellen G. "Doris Lessing: Fusion and Transcendence of the Female and the 'Great Tradition.'" *Centennial Review* 30 (1986): 452–70.

Gardiner, Judith Kegan. "A Wake for Mother: The Maternal Deathbed in Women's Fiction." *Feminist Studies* 4 (1978): 146–65.

Gay, Peter. *Education of the Senses.* New York: Oxford UP, 1984. Vol. I of *The Bourgeois Experience: Victoria to Freud.* 2 vols. 1984–86.

Gilbert, Sandra M. "Horror's Twin: Mary Shelley's Monstrous Eve." *Feminist Studies* 4 (1978): 48–73.

Gilbert, Sandra, and Susan Gubar. *The Madwoman in the Attic: The Woman Writer and the Nineteenth Century Literary Imagination.* New Haven: Yale UP, 1979.

Gillie, Christopher. *A Preface to Forster.* New York: Longman, 1983.

Gillis, John R. *For Better, For Worse: British Marriages, 1600 to the Present.* New York: Oxford UP, 1985.

Gubar, Susan. "'The Blank Page' and Female Creativity." *Writing and Sexual Difference.* Ed. Elizabeth Abel. Chicago: U of Chicago P, 1982. 73–94.

Halperin, John. *Egoism and Self Discovery in the Victorian Novel: Studies in the Ordeal of Knowledge in the Nineteenth Century.* New York: Franklin, 1974.

———. *The Life of Jane Austen.* Baltimore: Johns Hopkins UP, 1984.

Harding, D. W. "Character and Caricature in Jane Austen." *Critical Essays on Jane Austen.* Ed. B. C. Southam. London: Routledge & Kegan Paul, 1968. 83–105.

Hardy, Barbara. "The Complexity of Dickens." Slater, *Dickens 1970* 29–51.

Heineman, Helen. *Restless Angels: The Friendship of Six Victorian Women.* Athens: Ohio UP, 1983.

Hellerstein, Erna Olafson, Leslie Parker Hume, and Karen M. Offen, eds. *Victorian Women: A Documentary Account of Women's Lives in Nineteenth-Century England, France, and the United States.* Stanford: Stanford UP, 1981.

Helterman, Jeffrey. "*Beowulf*: The Archeytpe Enters History." *ELH* 80 (1969): 1–20.

Hemlow, Joyce. "Fanny Burney and the Courtesy Books." *PMLA* 65 (1950): 732–61.

Hillman, James. *The Myth of Analysis: Three Essays in Archetypal Psychology.* New York: Harper Colophon, 1972.

Hirsch, Marianne. *The Mother/Daughter Plot: Narrative, Psychoanalysis, Feminism.* Bloomington: Indiana UP, 1989.

Hirvonen, Kaarle. *Matriarchal Survivals and Certain Trends in Homer's Female Characters.* Helsinki: Suomalainen Tiedeakatemia, 1968.

Holbek, Bengt. *Interpretations of Fairy Tales: Danish Folklore in a European Perspective.* FF Communications No. 239. Helsinki: Suomalainen Tiedeakatemia, 1982.

Holloway, John. "Dickens and the Symbol." Slater, *Dickens 1970* 53–74.

Honan, Park. *Jane Austen: Her Life.* New York: St. Martin's Press, 1987.

Honig, Edith Lazaros. *Breaking the Angelic Image: Woman Power in Victorian Children's Fantasy.* Contributions in Women's Studies 97. New York: Greenwood, 1988.

Horney, Karen. *Feminine Psychology.* Ed. Harold Kelman. New York: Norton, 1967.

Hoy, Cyrus. "Forster's Metaphysical Novel." *PMLA* 75 (1960): 126–36.

Huff, Cynthia. *British Women's Diaries: A Descriptive Bibliography of Selected Nineteenth-Century Women's Manuscript Diaries.* New York: AMS, 1985.

Hultberg, Peer. "The Faithless Mother: An Aspect of the Novels of E. M. Forster." *Narcissism and the Text: Studies in Literature and the Psychology of Self.* New York: New York UP, 1986. 233–54.

Hyde, William J. "George Eliot and the Climate of Realism." *PMLA* 72 (1957): 153–58. Rpt. in *A Century of George Eliot Criticism*, ed. Gordon S. Haight. London: Methuen, 1965. 294–98.

Jalland, Pat. *Women, Marriage, and Politics, 1860–1914*. Oxford: Clarendon, 1986.

Jalland, Pat, and John Hooper, eds. *Women from Birth to Death: The Female Life Cycle in Britain 1830–1914*. Atlantic Highlands, NJ: Humanities Press International, 1986.

Jeffreys, Sheila. *The Spinster and Her Enemies: Feminism and Sexuality 1880–1930*. London: Pandora, 1985.

Jenkins, Cecil. "Realism and the Novel Form." *The Monster and the Mirror: Studies in Nineteenth-Century Realism*. Ed. D. A. Williams. Oxford: U of Hull, 1978. 1–16.

Kahn, Coppelia. "The Absent Mother in King Lear." Ferguson, Quilligan, and Vickers 33–49.

Kerenyi, C. *Eleusis: Archetypal Image of Mother and Daughter*. Trans. Ralph Manheim. Bollingen Series 65. New York: Pantheon, 1967.

Kessler, Evelyn S. *Women: An Anthropological View*. New York: Holt, Rinehart and Winston, 1976.

Kirkham, Margaret. *Jane Austen: Feminism and Fiction*. Totowa, NJ: Barnes & Noble, 1983.

Kloepfer, Deborah Kelly. "*Voyage in the Dark*: Jean Rhys's Masquerade for the Mother." *Contemporary Literature* 26 (1985): 443–59.

Krohn, Kaarle. *Folklore Methodology*. 1926. Trans. Roger L. Welsch. Austin: U of Texas P, 1971.

Kucich, John. *Excess and Restraint in the Novels of Charles Dickens*. Athens: U of Georgia P, 1981.

Lane, Margaret. "Dickens on the Hearth." Slater, *Dickens 1970* 153–71.

Lansbury, Coral. *Elizabeth Gaskell: The Novel of Social Crisis*. London: Paul Elek, 1975.

Lauber, John. "Jane Austen's Fools." *Studies in English Literature* 14 (1974): 511–24.

Lauter, Estella, and Carol Rupprecht, eds. Introduction. *Feminist Archetypal Theory: Interdisciplinary Re-Visions of Jungian Thought.* Knoxville: U of Tennessee P, 1985. 3–22.

Lauter, Estella. "Visual Images by Women." Lauter and Rupprecht 46–92.

Leavis, F. R. "Sociology and Literature." *The Common Pursuit.* London: Chatto & Windus, 1952. 195–203.

Lefcowitz, Barbara F. "Dream and Action in Lessing's *The Summer Before the Dark.*" *Critique* 17 (1975): 107–19.

Leiberman, Marcia. "'Someday My Prince Will Come': Female Acculturation through the Fairy Tale." *College English* 34 (1972): 383–95. Rpt. in Zipes, *Don't Bet on the Prince* 185–200.

Lerner, Laurence. *Love and Marriage: Literature and its Social Context.* New York: St. Martin's, 1979.

———. *The Truthtellers: Jane Austen, George Eliot, D. H. Lawrence.* New York: Schocken, 1967.

Levine, George. *The Realistic Imagination: English Fiction from Frankenstein to Lady Chatterly.* Chicago: U of Chicago P, 1981.

Lewis, Jane. *Women in England 1870–1950: Sexual Divisions and Social Change.* Bloomington: Indiana UP, 1984.

Lewis, Judith Schneid. *In the Family Way: Childbearing in the British Aristocracy, 1760–1860.* New Brunswick, NJ: Rutgers UP, 1986.

Leyburn, Ellen Douglass. *Strange Alloy: The Relation of Comedy to Tragedy in the Fiction of Henry James.* Chapel Hill: U of North Carolina P, 1968.

Lidoff, Joan. "Virginia Woolf's Feminine Sentence: The Mother-Daughter World of *To the Lighthouse.*" *Literature and Psychology* 32 (1986): 43–59.

Lilienfeld, Jane. "'The Deceptiveness of Beauty': Mother Love and Mother Hate in *To the Lighthouse.*" *Twentieth Century Literature* 23 (1977): 345–76.

Litz, A. Walton. "'A Developement of Self': Character and Personality in Jane Austen's Fiction." MacMaster, *Achievement* 64–78.

MacDonald, Susan Peck. "Jane Austen and the Tradition of the Absent Mother." Davidson and Broner 58–69.

MacLeod, Sheila. *Lawrence's Men and Women.* London: Heinemann, 1985.

Marder, Herbert. *Feminism and Art: A Study of Virginia Woolf.* Chicago: U of Chicago P, 1968.

Martin, Richard. *The Love that Failed: Ideal and Reality in the Writings of E. M. Forster.* Paris: Mouton, 1974.

McConkey, James. *The Novels of E. M. Forster.* Ithaca: Cornell UP, 1957.

McMaster, Juliet, ed. *Jane Austen's Achievement.* London: Macmillan, 1976.

———. *Thackeray: The Major Novels.* Toronto: U of Toronto P, 1971.

Mews, Hazel. *Frail Vessels: Woman's Role in Women's Novels from Fanny Burney to George Eliot.* London: Athlone, 1969.

Miller, Jean Baker. *Psychoanalysis and Women: Contributions to New Theory and Therapy.* New York: Brunner/Mazel, 1973.

Mitchell, Juliet. *Psychoanalysis and Feminism: Freud, Reich, Laing and Women.* New York: Vintage, 1975.

Moore, Harry [T.]. *The Life and Works of D. H. Lawrence.* New York: Twayne, 1951.

———. *The Priest of Love: A Life of D. H. Lawrence.* New York: Farrar, Straus, & Giroux, 1974.

Moore, Katherine. *Victorian Wives.* New York: St. Martin's, 1974.

Morgan, Susan. *In the Meantime: Character and Perception in Jane Austen's Fiction.* Chicago: U of Chicago P, 1980.

Murry, John Middleton. *Son of Woman: The Story of D. H. Lawrence.* New York: Jonathan Cape & Harrison Smith, 1931.

Nardin, Jane. "Children and their Families in Jane Austen's Novels." *Jane Austen: New Perspectives.* Ed. Janet Todd. Women and Literature New Series 3. New York: Holmes & Meier, 1983. 73–87.

Neumann, Erich. *Art and the Creative Unconscious.* Trans. Ralph Manheim. Princeton, NJ: Princeton UP, 1974.

———. *The Great Mother: An Analysis of the Archetype.* Trans. Ralph Manheim. Bollingen Series 47. Princeton: Princeton UP, 1955.

———. *The Origins and History of Consciousness.* Trans. R. F. C. Hull. Bollingen Series 42. New York: Pantheon, 1954.

Nierenberg, Edwin. "The Withered Princess: Mrs. Moore's Incomplete Passage to India." *Modern Language Quarterly* 25 (1964): 198–204.

Obed, Brenda. "The Maternal Ghost in Joyce." *Modern Language Studies* 15 (1985): 40–47.

Ochshorn, Judith. "Mothers and Daughters in Ancient Near Eastern Literature." Davidson and Broner 5–15.

Paris, Bernard J. "The Inner Conflicts of Maggie Tulliver: A Horneyan Analysis." *Centennial Review* 13 (1969): 166–99.

Parry, Benita. "Passage to More than India." Bradbury, *Critical Essays* 160–74.

Pederson, Glenn. "Forster's Symbolic Form." *Kenyon Review* 21 (1959): 231–49.

———. "Vision in *To the Lighthouse.*" *PMLA* 73 (1958): 585–600.

Pell, Nancy. "The Father's Daughter in *Daniel Deronda.*" *Nineteenth-Century Fiction* 36 (1982): 424–51.

Perera, Sylvia Brinton. *Descent to the Goddess: A Way of Initiation for Women.* Toronto: Inner City, 1981.

Pomeroy, Sarah B. *Goddesses, Whores, Wives, and Slaves: Women in Classical Antiquity.* New York: Schocken, 1975.

Pratt, Annis, *et al. Archetypal Patterns in Women's Fiction.* Bloomington: Indiana UP, 1981.

Propp, Vladimir. *Morphology of the Folktale.* 1927. Trans. Laurence Scott. Ed. Svatava Pirkova-Jakobson. Bibliographical and Special Series 9. Philadelphia: American Folklore Society, 1958.

Puhvel, Martin. "The Might of Grendel's Mother." *Folklore* 80 (1969): 81–88.

Rabuzzi, Kathryn Allen. *Motherself: A Mythic Analysis of Motherhood.* Bloomington: Indiana UP, 1988.

Rapping, Elayne Antler. "Unfree Women: Feminism in Doris Lessing's Novels." *Women's Studies* 3 (1975): 28–44.

Rich, Adrienne. *Of Woman Born: Motherhood as Experience and Institution.* New York: Norton, 1986.

Rosenman, Ellen Bayuk. *The Invisible Presence: Virginia Woolf and the Mother-Daughter Relationship.* Baton Rouge: Lousiana State UP, 1986.

Rowe, Karen E. "Feminism and Fairy Tales." *Women's Studies* 6 (1979): 237–57. Rpt. in Zipes, *Don't Bet on the Prince* 209–26.

Ruderman, Judith. *D. H. Lawrence and the Devouring Mother: The Search for a Patriarchal Ideal of Leadership.* Durham, NC: Duke UP, 1984.

Rycroft, Charles. *Imagination and Reality.* London: Hogarth Press and the Institute of Psychoanalysis, 1968.

Schapiro, Barbara A. *The Romantic Mother: Narcissistic Patterns in Romantic Poetry.* Baltimore: Johns Hopkins UP, 1983.

Scharfman, Ronnie. "Mirroring and Mothering in Simone Schawz-Bart's *Pluie et Vent Sur Télumée Miracle* and Jean Rhys' *Wide Sargasso Sea.*" *Yale French Studies* 62 (1981): 88–106.

Schorer, Mark. "Pride Unprejudiced." *Kenyon Review* 18 (1956): 72–91

Seligman, Dee. "The Sufi Quest." *World Literature Written in English* 12 (1973): 190–206.

Showalter, Elaine. *A Literature of Their Own.* Princeton: Princeton UP, 1977.

————. "Towards a Feminist Poetics." *Women Writing and Writing About Women*. Ed. Mary Jacobus. New York: Croom Helm, 1979. 22–41.

Sjoo, Monica, and Barbara Mor. *The Great Cosmic Mother: Rediscovering the Religion of the Earth*. San Francisco: Harper & Row, 1987.

Slater, Michael, ed. *Dickens 1970: Centenary Essays*. New York: Stein & Day, 1970.

————. Introduction. *Nicholas Nickleby*. By Charles Dickens. Harmondsworth: Penguin, 1978. 13–31.

Smith, LeRoy W. *Jane Austen and the Drama of Woman*. New York: St. Martin's, 1983.

Spilka, Mark. *The Love Ethic of D. H. Lawrence*. Bloomington: Indiana UP, 1955.

Sprague, Claire. *Rereading Doris Lessing: Narrative Patterns of Doubling and Redoubling*. Chapel Hill: U of North Carolina P, 1987.

Sprague, Claire, and Virginia Tiger, eds. *Critical Essays on Doris Lessing*. Boston: G. K. Hall, 1986.

Stiller, Nikki. *Eve's Orphans: Mothers and Daughters in Medieval English Literature*. Contributions in Women's Studies 16. Westport CT: Greenwood, 1980.

Stone, Harry. "The Novel as Fairy Tale: Dickens' *Dombey and Son*." *English Studies* 47 (1966): 1–27.

Stone, Lawrence. *The Family, Sex and Marriage in England, 1500–1800*. New York: Harper & Row, 1977.

Stoneman, Patsy. *Elizabeth Gaskell*. Key Women Writers Series. Bloomington: Indiana UP, 1987.

Sudrann, Jean. "Hearth and Horizon: Changing Concepts of the 'Domestic' Life of the Heroine." *Massachusetts Review* 14 (1973): 235–56.

Todd, Janet, ed. *Gender and Literary Voice*. New York: Holmes and Meier, 1980.

Transue, Pamela J. *Virginia Woolf and the Politics of Style*. Albany: State U of New York P, 1986.

Trilling, Lionel. "*A Passage to India*." Bradbury, *Casebook* 77–92.

Trumbach, Randolph E. *The Rise of the Egalitarian Family: Aristocratic Kinship and Domestic Relations*. New York: Academic, 1978.

Veszy-Wagner, Lilla. "Little Red Riding Hood's on the Couch." *The Psychoanalytic Forum* 1 (1966): 400–15.

Vivas, Eliseo. *D. H. Lawrence: The Failure and the Triumph of Art*. Evanston: Northwestern UP, 1960.

von Franz, Marie-Louise. *Problems of the Feminine in Fairy Tales*. New York: Spring, 1972.

Wagenknecht, Edward. *Eve and Henry James: Portraits of Women and Girls in His Fiction*. Norman: U of Oklahoma P, 1978.

Watt, Ian. "Jane Austen and the Traditions of Comic Aggression." *Persuasions: Journal of the Jane Austen Society of North America* 3 (1981). Rpt. in *Jane Austen: Modern Critical Views*. Ed. Harold Bloom. New York: Chelsea House, 1986. 191–201.

———. *The Rise of the Novel: Studies in Defoe, Richardson and Fielding*. Berkeley: U of California P, 1957.

Weiss, Daniel A. *Oedipus in Nottingham: D. H. Lawrence*. Seattle: U of Washington P, 1962.

Welldon, Estela V. *Mother, Madonna, Whore: The Idealization and Denigration of Motherhood*. London: Free Association, 1988.

Whitehead, Lee M. "The Shawl and the Skull: Virginia Woolf's Magic Mountain." *Modern Fiction Studies* 18 (1972): 401–15.

Whittier, Gayle. "Mistresses and Madonnas in the Novels of Margaret Drabble." Todd 197–213.

Williams, Ioan. *The Realist Novel in England: A Study in Development*.

London: Macmillan, 1974.

Williams, Merryn. *Women in the English Novel, 1800–1900.* New York: St. Martin's, 1984.

Williamsen-Ceron, Amy. "The Comic Functions of Two Mothers: Belisa and Angela." *Bulletin of the Comediantes* 36 (1984): 167–74.

Wilson, Angus. "Dickens on Children and Childhood." Slater, *Dickens 1970* 195–207.

Wilt, Judith. "The Laughter of Maidens, the Cackle of Matriarchs: Notes on the Collision between Comedy and Feminism." Todd 173–96.

Zipes, Jack. *Don't Bet on the Prince: Contemporary Feminist Fairy Tales in North America and England.* New York: Methuen, 1986.

———, ed. *Victorian Fairy Tales: The Revolt of the Fairies and Elves.* New York: Routledge, 1987.

Index